SIMPLE
fortunetelling
with tarot cards

To Write to the Author

If you wish to contact the author or would like more information about this book, please write to the author in care of Llewellyn Worldwide and we will forward your request. Both the author and publisher appreciate hearing from you and learning of your enjoyment of this book and how it has helped you. Llewellyn Worldwide cannot guarantee that every letter written to the author can be answered, but all will be forwarded. Please write to:

Corrine Kenner
℅ Llewellyn Worldwide
2143 Wooddale Drive, Dept. 978-0-7387-0964-2
Woodbury, Minnesota 55125-2989, U.S.A.

Please enclose a self-addressed stamped envelope for reply, or $1.00 to cover costs. If outside U.S.A., enclose international postal reply coupon.

Many of Llewellyn's authors have websites with additional information and resources. For more information, please visit our website at http://www.llewellyn.com

SIMPLE

fortunetelling

with tarot cards

Corrine Kenner

Llewellyn Publications
Woodbury, Minnesota

First Edition
First Printing, 2007

Book design by Steffani Sawyer
Cover design by Ellen Dahl
Editing by Rhiannon Ross
Universal tarot cards on cover and interior from Universal tarot, by Roberto De Angelis, reprinted by permission from Lo Scarabeo.
The Llewellyn Tarot © 2006 Anna-Marie Ferguson
Liber T Tarot by Roberto Negrini, reprinted by permission from Lo Scarabeo.
Art on pages 17, 31 © 2007 Art Explosion

Llewellyn is a registered trademark of Llewellyn Worldwide, Ltd.

Library of Congress Cataloging-in-Publication Data
Kenner, Corrine, 1964–
  Simple fortunetelling with tarot cards : Corrine Kenner's complete
guide / by Corrine Kenner.—1st ed.
      p. cm.
  Includes bibliographical references and index.
  ISBN-13: 978-0-7387-0964-2
  1. Tarot. I. Title.
  BF1879.T2K457 2007
  133.3'2424—dc22
                         2007024776

Llewellyn Worldwide does not participate in, endorse, or have any authority or responsibility concerning private business transactions between our authors and the public.
  All mail addressed to the author is forwarded but the publisher cannot, unless specifically instructed by the author, give out an address or phone number.
  Any Internet references contained in this work are current at publication time, but the publisher cannot guarantee that a specific location will continue to be maintained. Please refer to the publisher's website for links to authors' websites and other sources.

Llewellyn Publications
A Division of Llewellyn Worldwide, Ltd.
2143 Wooddale Drive, Dept. 978-0-7387-0964-2
Woodbury, Minnesota 55125-2989, U.S.A.
www.llewellyn.com

Printed in the United States of America

Also by Corrine Kenner

Crystals for Beginners

The Epicurean Tarot

The Ma'at Tarot Workbook

Strange But True

Tall Dark Stranger: Tarot for Love and Romance

Tarot Journaling

Forthcoming Books

The Book of Shadows Tarot

To future readers

Contents

How to Use This Guide

If you've never read tarot cards before, this guide will help you choose a tarot deck, learn the basics of tarot reading, and consult the cards for key information about the past, present, and future.

This guide will also show you how—and why—tarot cards work. It's designed to serve as a basic, step-by-step introduction to reading tarot cards for yourself, your family, and your friends.

Here's what you'll find in the following pages:

- You'll discover how the structure of the tarot deck can help you learn to read the cards—quickly and easily.

- You'll learn how to phrase your questions to get clear answers.

- You'll learn some basic spreads and techniques that will help you find the answers to the questions you ask.

- You'll learn how to interpret the symbols and images you see in the cards.

- You'll learn what to do when the cards turn up reversed in a reading, or the messages seem contradictory and confusing.

- You'll also learn how to combine the use of tarot cards with your own common sense to make predictions—and how to improve your accuracy with practice and time.

- Most importantly, you'll learn how to read the cards ethically and responsibly.

The decks in this book

Inside this book, you'll see illustrations of every card in a standard seventy-eight-card deck, from three popular tarot decks: the Universal Tarot by Roberto De Angelis, the Llewellyn Tarot by Anna-Marie Ferguson, and the Liber T Tarot by Roberto Negrini.

The odds are good that if you own just one tarot deck, it will probably be the Rider-Waite, which is very similar to the Universal Tarot. In fact, the two decks are actually based on the same instructions from designer Arthur Edward Waite; the Universal Tarot is simply a newer, fresher design. In this book, the Universal Tarot is referred to as the Waite design.

When the Waite deck was first published in 1909, Waite was a leading member of a secret society called the Order of the Golden Dawn. He hired a fellow member of the order, Pamela Colman Smith, to execute his designs. She was a freelance artist for magazines, and a set designer for theaters and drama companies.

Together, Waite and Smith broke new ground. Before they created their deck, most artists simply used a repeating motif of wands, cups, swords, and pentacles on minor arcana cards. Waite and Smith, however, incorporated scenes and illustrations on every single card.

In the years since their work was first published by the Rider publishing company, the Rider-Waite-Smith deck has come to serve as the de facto standard for millions of tarot readers. It has also inspired hundreds of derivative decks.

One of those derivative decks, The Llewellyn Tarot, is featured in this guide. By comparing and contrasting the Llewellyn deck with the Waite cards, you can discover how easy it is to expand your view of the cards and read any Rider-Waite-Smith derivative.

The Llewellyn Tarot was introduced in 2006, to critical acclaim and praise from tarot readers around the world. Its creator, Anna-Marie Ferguson, is an expert on the history, legends, and mythic figures of the Arthurian world. Her illustrations, which are based specifically on Welsh myth and legend, lend a new dimension of interpretation and meaning to the cards.

The third deck in this book is the Liber T, based on the design of Aleister Crowley, with background imagery derived from the rituals of the Golden Dawn. Crowley's tarot cards—which he called the Thoth Tarot, in honor of the ancient Egyptian god of wisdom—are dark and mysterious. Tarot readers all over the world rely on them for no-holds-barred readings and fortune telling.

Like Waite, Crowley was a member of the Golden Dawn. Like Waite, too, he hired an artist to execute his design—in this case, a woman named Lady Frieda Harris. Crowley and Harris finished their work in 1943, but neither lived to see the cards' popularity. In fact, the Thoth Tarot wasn't even published until 1969. Since then, however, it has become one of the most influential decks in the art and study of tarot.

How to choose a tarot deck

While this book is illustrated with the Universal Waite, Llewellyn, and Liber T cards, you can use it in conjunction with any standard tarot deck. Just make sure the deck you choose is an actual tarot deck, and not simply an oracle deck.

A true tarot deck has seventy-eight cards, divided into two parts: a major arcana and a minor arcana.

The major arcana should have twenty-two cards: the Fool, the Magician, the High Priestess, the Empress, the Emperor, the Hierophant, the Lovers, the Chariot, Strength, the

Hermit, the Wheel of Fortune, Justice, the Hanged Man, Death, Temperance, the Devil, the Tower, the Star, the Moon, the Sun, Judgment, and the World. While the names of some cards can vary from deck to deck, the titles should be close enough that you're still able to tell which cards correspond to their counterparts in any other standard deck.

Likewise, the minor arcana cards in the deck you choose should be divided into four suits: wands, cups, swords, and pentacles, or their equivalents. Each of the four suits should have ten numbered cards, along with four court cards: a page, knight, queen, and king.

If you're relatively new to the cards, try to find a deck that has scenes and people on all of the minor arcana cards—like the Universal Tarot and the Llewellyn decks. The wide range of individual illustrations will give you more symbols and images to work with during a reading.

If you're already familiar with the cards, however—or if you would like to rely more on psychic impressions for your readings—the Liber T deck could appeal to you, because its minor arcana cards are based on simple motifs. You could also look for historical reproductions of French or Italian decks, which usually feature similar motifs and designs on the minor arcana cards.

As you search for a deck, be sure to look at sample cards in stores, or find card images on the internet. Look for cards that appeal to you on many levels. You should be able to recognize most of the images and symbols on the cards. The characters on the cards should seem approachable, and you should be able to imagine yourself walking around inside the illustrations, in the buildings and landscapes pictured on each card. If the sample cards you look at leave you completely stumped or unimpressed, keep shopping until you find a deck that you can call your own.

The card-by-card reference guide

Because this book has illustrations, you can read through it even if you don't have a tarot deck by your side. You'll get more out of it, however, if you have a set of tarot cards close at hand. As you read, look carefully at the images of each card. You might even want to use a handheld magnifying glass for a closer look.

Be sure to read through the detailed descriptions in this book. They're designed to help you spot the primary, most important symbols on each card—along with a range of meanings and suggested interpretations. You can use the suggestions whenever the cards come up in your readings, at least until you get a feel for interpreting the cards on your own.

Remember, however, that the suggested interpretations for each card are just that—suggestions. Once you read tarot cards for a while, you may find that the symbols in your deck speak to you in their own way. Your personal interpretations, even if they seem unorthodox to others, are as valid as mainstream meanings.

Throughout this guide, you'll also discover a wide range of facts about each card that you can use for future reference. For example:

- You'll learn the secret, esoteric names of all the tarot cards, used mostly by philosophers and scholars. Because the titles are so poetic, you'll get a hint of the depth of power and mystery associated with each card.

- You'll also find keywords gleaned from contemporary tarot readers and writers, as well as Waite, Crowley, and two of their predecessors: Jean-Baptiste Alliette, who wrote the first book on tarot fortune telling in 1785; and S. L. MacGregor Mathers, who introduced tarot divination to England in 1888. Because their work is dated now, some of the keywords may seem to contradict each other. Just use the keywords that apply to your question or situation.

- As you read, you'll discover some of the legends, myths, and stories associated with the cards, which you can weave into your own readings and discussion of the cards.

- You'll also find a numerical assessment of each card, for insight and additional information about its place in your readings.

- And you'll learn the astrological signs and dates associated with each card, which you can use to help determine the timing of your predictions.

This book was written for anyone who wants to see what the cards hold in store, no matter what their level of experience. If you come across information that you already know—or information you'd like to study later—feel free to skip over it.

But for now, the cards—and your future—are waiting.

All you need to do is start reading.

Madame Sosostris, famous clairvoyante,
Had a bad cold, nevertheless
Is known to be the wisest woman in Europe,
With a wicked pack of cards. Here, said she,
Is your card, the drowned Phoenician Sailor,
(Those are pearls that were his eyes. Look!)
Here is Belladonna, the Lady of the Rocks,
The lady of situations.
Here is the man with three staves, and here the Wheel,
And here is the one-eyed merchant, and this card,
Which is blank, is something he carries on his back,
Which I am forbidden to see. I do not find
The Hanged Man. Fear death by water.
I see crowds of people, walking round in a ring.
Thank you. If you see dear Mrs. Equitone,
Tell her I bring the horoscope myself:
One must be so careful these days.

—*From* The Waste Land *by T. S. Eliot*

Before We Begin:
Questions and Answers About the Cards

Everyone who reads tarot cards has questions. Sometimes, those questions are about the cards themselves. Here are some of the most frequently asked questions—and answers—about the tarot.

What exactly is the tarot?

The tarot is a deck of seventy-eight cards, which are commonly used for meditation and reflection, self-development, problem solving…and, of course, fortunetelling.

What do you mean by "fortunetelling?"

The art of fortunetelling is the art of prediction. Both terms mean the same thing: to tell, or foretell, the future, before it happens. Both terms literally mean "to say before."

A prediction can take the form of a prophecy, which is divinely inspired, or divination, in which someone accesses information from a divine, supernatural source. Tarot cards are one way to tap into that source.

Patricia Telesco, a prolific author of New Age books and guides, defined it well. "Divination," she said, "opens a spiritual window through which we can see our present situations more clearly and peek into possible futures."

Where do tarot cards come from?

Tarot cards first made an appearance in the 1400s, when a card game called "tarocchi" swept through the royal courts of Italy and France. It was a complicated game, played something like bridge: every card in the tarocchi deck had a point value, and the cards with the highest ranks trumped cards of a lower rank.

Tarocchi cards were illustrated with a host of literary and mythic figures, as well as allegorical images of virtues and ideals, like justice, temperance, and fortitude.

The images naturally lent themselves to some lighthearted banter among players. By the early 1500s, some tarocchi players were using the cards to improvise clever rhymes and poems about the others in the game. The resulting sonnets were called *tarocchi appropriati*. After a while, some tarocchi enthusiasts even started skipping the game itself, and simply passed out five or six tarocchi cards to everyone in the group so they could interpret the images for themselves.

Tarocchi appropriati was a form of divination. It was never as popular as other fortunetelling methods of the time, which included palm reading and geomancy, or the interpretation of mathematical and geometric figures. Some fortunetellers also used divination wheels, which would lead readers to a fortune in a book. Others used dice. In fact, a mathematical correspondence has led some scholars to wonder if early fortunetellers paired dice with tarot cards. A pair of dice can land on any of twenty-one combinations; there are twenty-one numbered cards of the major arcana. Three dice, rolled together, can land on any of fifty-six combinations; there are fifty-six cards in the minor arcana.

At any rate, the structure and the symbolism of tarocchi cards did lend themselves to use as a fortunetelling tool.

When did tarot cards come to be used as a fortunetelling tool?

While people obviously played with the tarot as a fortunetelling device for years, the first professional tarot reader and teacher in history was a Parisian named Jean-Baptiste Alliette—a fortuneteller who learned the art of tarot divination from an old Italian man. In fact, Alliette actually coined the word cartomancy—the art of divination with cards.

Alliette was born in 1738. When he was nineteen, he began studying divination with a man from northern Italy, where the cards had been used since the Renaissance. He studied with the Italian for eight years—even after he married in 1760, and while he tried to support his wife by selling seeds and grain. When Alliette's marriage failed in 1767, however, he went to work as a card reader, an astrologer, and an alchemist. He also changed his professional name to Etteilla, which is Alliette spelled backward.

In 1770, he wrote *Etteilla, or a Method of Entertaining Oneself with a Pack of Cards*—a how-to book for telling fortunes with ordinary playing cards. He followed that in 1785 with *A Way to Entertain Oneself with a Pack of Cards Called Tarots*.

In 1789, at the age of fifty-one, Etteilla commissioned a tarot deck to be used for divination. His was the first tarot deck to incorporate astrological and alchemical symbolism and to link the four suits to the four elements. At that point, he had been studying occult philosophy and telling fortunes for thirty-two years. In the deck he designed, he equated the first twelve trumps with the twelve signs of the zodiac, he assigned planetary gods to some of the cards, and he equated the coins to magic talismans. Today his deck, the *Grand Etteilla*, is still in print.

Subsequent tarot enthusiasts and scholars tried to denigrate Etteilla's work. A. E. Waite was probably the harshest: he called Etteilla an "illiterate but zealous adventurer." Even so, Waite didn't mind borrowing from Etteilla's interpretations when he developed his own tarot deck—and many of those interpretations are still considered standard, even to this day.

Waite also borrowed heavily from one of Etteilla's successors, Eliphas Lévi. Lévi was a tarot scholar and theorist who picked up where Etteilla left off, and continued to combine the tarot with alchemy and astrology in the 1800s. Just for good measure, Lévi also threw in some Hebrew Kabbalah, Pythagorean number symbolism, and ceremonial magic.

Lévi was a familiar figure in the secret societies that were popular during the nineteenth century. His work was eventually picked up by a group that would become the Hermetic Order of the Golden Dawn.

One member of that group, S. L. MacGregor Mathers, was the first person to formally introduce the art of tarot divination to England, with his 1888 book *The Tarot: Its Occult Signification, Use in Fortune-Telling and Methods of Play*. Mathers later developed his methods even further, with the help of his friend Dr. William Wynn Westcott. Together, they wrote *Book T*, a treatise for the Golden Dawn. In that work, they re-ordered the cards in the major arcana. They also named the four suits wands, cups, swords, and pentacles—the same nomenclature that most tarot readers use today.

Their work lives on in the tarot decks in this book.

Can tarot cards predict the future?

Yes—but that answer comes with a disclaimer.

Obviously, tarot cards do offer a glimpse of the future. Tarot cards are an especially good way to see into the very near future—particularly if you ask clear, concise questions and set the terms for a usable answer. And when you combine the insights you get from the cards along with your experience, your intuition, and your common sense, you can astonish yourself with the accuracy of your predictions.

Unfortunately, it's also true that most tarot readings don't make total sense until after they play themselves out in the real world. That's because the tarot speaks a symbolic language that can be hard to decode. Often, it's only in hindsight that most readings seem clear.

However, your predictions will get better with practice. The more you work with the cards, the more attuned you'll be to the imagery and symbols on the cards. Reading the cards can help you learn to pay attention to signs and symbols in your everyday life. They can help you focus your observations and judge your experiences. They can confirm the conclusions you make about other people and events.

Ultimately, reading tarot cards can help you learn to trust your intuition. The more you see your predictions play out in real time, the better you'll become at interpreting the cards in new situations.

Tarot cards are also really, really good at helping you prepare for new developments in your life—including monumental occasions like meeting your true love. Tarot cards can suggest situations in which you might encounter new opportunities, and ways in which you can make yourself attractive, confident, and make the most of new opportunities. Tarot cards are also a valuable way to get a bird's-eye view of any situation, and see yourself and other people from an objective standpoint.

And, of course, trying to see the future in the cards is fun.

How accurate are tarot predictions?

It depends. The further you try to see into the future, the more things can change. The future is never set in stone, and any action you take—even as a result of a tarot reading—can alter the course of subsequent events.

Just remember that the tarot is not a mysterious, all-knowing oracle that can reveal your inevitable fate. You are not obligated to entrust your fate to anyone but yourself, and you shouldn't base any major decisions solely on the cards. After all, your interpretations could be wrong—and your situation can and will change if you simply choose a new direction.

Treat the tarot as you would a trusted friend and advisor. But realize, as in astrology, the cards impel, they do not compel. As German tarot expert Hajo Banhaff has said, the tarot makes an excellent servant, but a bad master.

Do you need to be psychic to use tarot cards?

No. You can read tarot cards based solely on the images and symbols on each card.

However, reading tarot cards will probably make you feel more psychic. In fact, the more you use tarot cards, the more comfortable you'll be trusting your intuition. That's because the simple act of reading a tarot card forces you to use your intuition to zero in on important messages and symbols. The cards gently prompt you to tune out the mundane and tune in to the metaphysical.

The structure of the tarot deck does double duty as a structure for your thoughts and observations, and serves as a framework for your intuition. Tarot cards make it easier for the logical left side of your brain to work with the more creative and intuitive right side of the brain. Your rational, logistical self can study the numbers and the titles of the cards, and access the stories and symbolism associated with each one. At the same time, your psychic mind can tune in to the spiritual significance of the cards.

Oddly enough, tarot cards are also useful tools for people who are extremely psychic—the kind of people who tend to pick up on the emotions and thoughts of other people, even when they don't want to. If you find that psychic background noise interferes with your everyday life, you can train yourself to block those distractions during the course of your ordinary day, and tune in only when you're using the cards.

How do tarot cards work?

Tarot cards often seem magical and mysterious. Even when you pull cards at random, they often seem to zero in on the issue or question that's on your mind. Every tarot reader seems to have his or her own theory about why tarot cards work. Some of those beliefs are pragmatic. Others are scientific. Some are wildly speculative.

Here are some of the most popular conjectures:

Symbolism

Tarot cards could work simply because they have something for everyone. Most cards are illustrated with a wide range of images and symbols—which makes it possible to find signs and symbols that apply to any situation. Once the cards are on the table, people are inherently drawn to the images and symbols that are most important to them. In that case, the real power of the cards isn't necessarily its power to display signs, omens, and portents—it's in the thought, discussion, and action the images inspire.

Systemic study

Some people study the tarot as a purely academic pursuit. For centuries, the cards have been thought to hold the key to synchronizing a wide range of Western thought and tradition—everything from philosophy to psychology, with a little mythology, astrology, numerology, alchemy, and Kabbalah thrown in for good measure. In fact, if you were a trained tarot scholar, you could offer a powerful reading based on nothing more than a strict review of the cards' historical significance and traditional interpretations.

Unconscious observation

Tarot cards could help you access the information that your unconscious mind has stored in reserve—like snippets of overheard conversation, fleeting facial expressions, body language, and physical reactions to comments and images.

Intuition and psychic ability

Some people believe that the tarot works because it helps them access their psychic ability. They use the cards as a tool to channel their psychic impressions and tap into the underlying bond of energy, emotion, and shared experience that unites us all. Tarot cards often seem to trigger psychic ability in some readers—even those who don't necessarily think of themselves as particularly gifted. Some people notice that images and symbols on the cards seem to shimmer, move, and come to life during a reading. Others find that random words and phrases pop into their heads when they look at the cards. Still others point out that the cards seem to serve as a conduit for information that simply strikes them as impressions or gut feelings.

Synchronicity

The groundbreaking psychologist Carl Jung coined the term "synchronicity" to describe the meaningful coincidences that tend to occur during a tarot reading. Synchronicity is at work, for example, when we're thinking about an upcoming court case and the Justice card falls on the table. Jung believed synchronicity is a sign of a higher power at work.

The collective unconscious

Tarot cards might help us tap into humanity's "collective unconscious"—a sort of energy field that Jung also explored in his studies. According to his theory, the collective unconscious is a reservoir of shared emotion and understanding that unites all people on a psychic level. It also serves as a well of shared myth, history, and legendary associations that help us understand the human condition.

Quantum physics

We live in a world of Newtonian physics, where time is linear, and every occurrence—even those we can't explain—somehow conforms to the laws of nature. Give us an effect, and we'll find the cause. A newer branch of physics, however—quantum physics—suggests that time doesn't unfold just as we perceive it. In quantum physics, time seems to flow in every direction, and events in the future seem to travel back to influence the present. As those events bounce back and forth through the time stream, they even seem to communicate with each other—which could explain how tarot cards are able to depict events that haven't yet occurred.

Are tarot cards magic?

The cards are not inherently magic, but when you use them, you may find yourself making magical transformations in your life. That's because the tarot allows you to see your situation in a new light—from the perspective of an observer, rather than a participant. Tarot cards allow you to step outside yourself for a moment, and assess your situation objectively. When you spread out a handful of tarot cards, you don't need to imagine the people and places in your life when you look at tarot cards: you can literally see them, all laid out on the table in front of you. You'll also find yourself surveying any number of scenes and landscapes that remind you of your past, present, and future.

Of course, some people do use the cards in magical ways. Just as letters and words can spell out previously unspoken dreams, wishes, and desires, you can use tarot cards to explore your hopes and fears, and describe the life you want to create for yourself. You can even use the cards to experiment with alternate courses of action and their corresponding outcomes.

The cards have also been shown to correspond with several esoteric systems, such as Kabbalah, alchemy, and astrology, which are often thought of as magical because they've been kept secret.

While the cards may be mystical, you should never treat them as more sacred or more important than yourself. They are an extension of your understanding and analytical abilities—nothing more, nothing less.

My grandmother used to tell fortunes with playing cards. How is that different from tarot?

The two systems are probably similar. In fact, some very popular divination decks, like the *Gypsy Witch Fortunetelling Cards*, are basically decks of playing cards.

The main difference is the structure of the deck: a tarot deck has four suits, like a playing card deck, as well as the twenty-two major arcana cards.

What's more, most modern tarot decks are fully illustrated. In a deck of ordinary playing cards, most of the cards are simply illustrated with a simple repeating pattern of clubs, hearts, spades, and diamonds. In a tarot deck, however, every card has a distinctly separate illustration.

Those illustrations—along with the titles printed on each card—make it easier to use tarot cards for divination. While it's true that some people can read playing cards based solely on intuition and psychic impressions, most have to memorize the meanings of each card in a playing-card deck, or write them on each card. When you read tarot cards, you can interpret the symbols on each card, and use the images as a reminder of traditional interpretations.

It's interesting to note that historically, traveling gypsies used playing cards—not tarot cards—to tell fortunes. Some switched to tarot cards with the passage of time, but only when their customers began to expect tarot cards on the table.

Why do so many fortune tellers focus on the past and the present? Isn't fortunetelling all about the future?

You'd think so … until you realize that past, present, and future are all connected. Just as one moment flows into the next in our everyday lives, the full continuum of time takes its place on the tarot reader's table, too.

In a fortunetelling reading, the cards that fall in the past and present positions tend to illustrate a range of themes and motifs that will continue to play out—and they help us spot trends and predict what will happen in the future.

The cards that represent the past and present also help validate the accuracy of a reading. If we know we can trust the accuracy of cards that describe our past and present, we can also put our faith in the cards that depict our future.

Are tarot cards evil?

No. Tarot cards are simply pieces of paper. They have no intrinsic power, either for good or bad. They are merely a tool.

Like any other tool, however, they can be used for a wide range of purposes.

It's no secret that tarot cards have been used by unscrupulous readers to frighten and misguide other people. Unfortunately, that means that once you start reading tarot cards for friends and family members, you might find yourself battling an image problem. You might also find that you need to protect yourself from well-meaning people who express theological concerns about your immortal soul.

Some people—especially those who come from a Christian background—do think the cards are evil. They've heard that the Bible prohibits tarot cards, or that the Catholic Church forbids their use. Some people have even called the tarot the "Devil's Picture Book," and they claim that tarot cards are used by Satan worshippers.

In fact, most of today's tarot decks incorporate a wide range of religious images and symbols, such as the crucifix, the dove, the olive branch, angels, priests, and bishops. That's because much of the tarot was developed by Christian scholars and philosophers, who based a lot of their work on the work of even earlier Jewish mystics. Since then, other religious groups have redrawn the cards to reflect their own spiritual beliefs and practices—but no tarot decks depict images designed for evil purposes.

The Bible does not mention tarot cards, specifically, because they were invented long after the Bible was written. Scholars look to other passages to determine whether God allows for divination.

In some biblical passages, divination seems to be presented as an acceptable practice. Genesis reports that Joseph—otherwise famous for his coat of many colors—actually rose to prominence in Egypt because of his fortunetelling skills. He used a silver cup for scrying, a form of divination similar to reading a crystal ball, and he interpreted dreams. He's the one who told the Pharaoh of the seven years of record harvests, which would be followed by seven years of drought and famine.

In Numbers, the High Priest used two objects, the Urim and Thummim, to determine God's will. Scholars have speculated that the priest rolled the two objects like dice. Saul, the first king of Israel, was said to have visited a medium to consult with the spirit of the prophet Samuel. The king of Babylon also shook arrows, looked for signs in the liver of an animal, and consulted the teraphim, which were images used for the giving and receiving of oracles. The Old Testament's Daniel was said to have been filled with the light, understanding, and wisdom of the Holy Spirit—which enabled him to interpret dreams, explain riddles, and solve problems. In fact, his skills prompted the king of Babylonia to make Daniel the chief of the "magicians, enchanters, Chaldeans, and astrologers." The prophets Elijah and Moses received divine information and instructions through visions. So did the disciples Peter, Paul, and John. The three wise men who visited the newborn baby Jesus were astrologers. In Corinthians, prophecy is listed as one of the gifts of the Holy Spirit, along with healing, the working of miracles, discerning of spirits, and speaking in tongues.

On the other hand, some religious scholars have also found that the Bible prohibits divination. They point out that Jesus told his followers not to worry about the future, but to put their trust in God.

Many people who practice divination, however, believe that the word "divination" itself defines the scope of their work. They believe that they are in touch with the divine. They would tell you that their divinatory methods and practices are a form of prayer and meditation, and that God would not reveal information that he does not want them to access.

Even so, some critics believe that divination subverts God's will. They insist that divination is different from prayer, because it goes around the "natural" ways that God reveals his will. Any answer you need, they say, can be found through prayer, the Bible, and the church. They point to Isaiah 8:19, which says, "And when they say to you, 'Consult the mediums and the wizards who chirp and mutter,' should not a people consult their God? Should they consult the dead on behalf of the living?"

Most of the prohibitions against divination appear in the book of Leviticus. For example, Leviticus 19:26 says, "You shall not practice augury or witchcraft." Leviticus 19:31 warns, "Do not turn to mediums or wizards; do not seek them out, to be defiled by them: I am the Lord your God." Leviticus 20:6 says, "If a person turns to mediums and wizards, playing the harlot after them, I will set my face against that person, and will cut him off from among his people," and Leviticus 20:27 says, "A man or a woman who is a medium or a wizard shall be put to death; they shall be stoned with stones, their blood shall be upon them."

But consider those warnings in context. In the same passages, Leviticus also calls for regular animal sacrifices, burnt offerings, and sin offerings as a condition of worship. Leviticus bans women from entering the sanctuary after menstruation and childbirth. Actually, Leviticus prohibits anyone with a physical handicap from defiling God's house with his presence. Leviticus outlines a long list of prohibited activities that God considers an "abomination"—such as touching dead insects or seeing your relatives in the nude. Leviticus would keep you from eating steak—because meat with blood or fat is prohibited. Forget shellfish, pork, and rabbit, too. They're all abominable in the eyes of Leviticus' god. Leviticus also demands that men take a shower and wash their sheets immediately after having sex, and orders them not to shave or cut the hair around their temples. Leviticus prohibits tattoos, sleeping late, working on a Saturday, weaving cloth from two kinds of thread, planting two different kinds of plants in the same bed, or harvesting an entire crop. And if mere prohibitions aren't enough, Leviticus suggests that sinners should be stoned.

The book of Deuteronomy also uses strong language to discourage divination. However, it's important to note that the form of divination that Deuteronomy describes is objectionable because it incorporates black magic, the raising of the dead, and child sacrifice. And in the next breath, God promises his people that he will send a new prophet their way, so they will have access to information about the future.

In fact, even now there are fundamentalist churches that regularly encourage congregants to speak in tongues—a form of prophecy. Bibliomancy, the practice of opening the Bible to a random passage for guidance, is a time-honored form of divination. Even prayers that ask God for a sign or an answer could be considered a form of divination.

Can using tarot cards open you to evil forces?

Some church leaders believe that divination encourages practitioners to gain knowledge or information that's hidden or forbidden—information that comes from supernatural sources, such as angels, demons, and the dead. They also believe that divination takes place outside God's protection, which clears the way for evil spirits and demons to trick and mislead gullible individuals—or even to possess them, physically, and work their evil on the physical plane.

However, many of those who practice divination live very spiritual lives. In fact, they believe that they are working through the grace of God—and they take steps to pray, ask for guidance, and dispel negative energy from their lives and their tarot readings.

Some critics also believe that divination diverts one's focus from God, and forces people to place their trust in inanimate objects. Here they may have a point. Tarot cards can be addictive. It can be tempting to turn to the cards for guidance on routine matters or even on a moment-to-moment, day-by-day basis. In extreme cases, tarot cards can become an obsession or a compulsion—and that's simply not healthy. There's a world of difference between pulling a single card in the morning as a meditative device and conducting a full-fledged Celtic Cross reading to see if today would be a good day to go to the grocery store.

If you use the cards conscientiously, however, with hope and goodwill, you will have good results.

Tarot Basics: The Building Blocks of the Tarot

Some people spend years trying to memorize the meanings of all seventy-eight cards, studying the symbols and signs of each image, and attempting to decode the hidden meanings encoded in the deck.

You don't need to devote countless hours to your study of the cards before you can read them, however. You just have to understand the structure of the deck.

Normally, a tarot deck has seventy-eight cards, divided into two groups: the *major arcana*, which is Latin for "greater secrets," and the *minor arcana*, which means "lesser secrets."

The major arcana cards are the big-picture cards. They depict monumental, life-changing events and experiences, like falling in love, giving birth, starting a new job, or finding a new home. Sometimes, because the major arcana cards are so dramatic, the experiences they depict seem like they're outside our control.

The minor arcana cards, on the other hand, are the everyday cards. They picture ordinary people doing everyday things, like dancing, drinking, eating, and sleeping. The minor arcana cards are divided into four suits, just like a deck of ordinary playing cards. Each suit has ten numbered cards and four court cards, and each suit represents a separate area of life: spiritual, emotional, intellectual, and physical. As a whole, the minor arcana cards are just as important as the major arcana cards, because they show us how we live out big events on a day-to-day basis.

Together, the major and minor arcana cards combine to form a cosmology—a framework for seeing the world, and for categorizing the human experience.

The structure and the symbolism of the tarot deck make it easy to study the human condition—and even to grasp some of life's greatest mysteries.

The Major Arcana

The major arcana cards are the cards you'll recognize from movies and television shows. They're also the cards most people remember after a tarot reading.

That's because major arcana cards are forceful and dramatic. They feature figures and characters that seem larger than life. And they're familiar to everyone—even to people who've never seen a tarot deck before.

The figures on the major arcana cards are archetypes—cosmic stereotypes that transcend the limits of time and place. They are the heroes of ancient myth and legend, and they still populate the lead roles in contemporary movies, television shows, plays, and books. Artists, writers, and musicians regularly tap into the waters of the collective unconscious for inspiration and explanations of the human condition. Jung believed that the symbols, myths, and archetypes that regularly appear in our dreams, our myths, and our stories all spring from that same source, which explains why so many people and cultures share similar legends and make use of the same symbols, regardless of time and place.

The major arcana archetypes include:

1. The Fool, the happy wanderer who sees the world through the eyes of a child
2. The Magician, the skilled and cunning master of all he surveys
3. The High Priestess, the enigmatic keeper of spiritual secrets
4. The Empress, Mother Nature, the source of all creation
5. The Emperor, the authoritative protector and provider who rules the civilized world
6. The Hierophant, the head of a hierarchy that preserves his religious and cultural traditions
7. The Lovers, who embody the twin principles of opposition and attraction
8. The Chariot, a vehicle for forward motion and change
9. Strength, the lovely lady with the heart of a lion
10. The Hermit, the recluse who can't get away from his followers
11. The Wheel of Fortune, the spinning Wheel of Destiny and fate
12. Justice, the ultimate arbiter, who balances a double-edged sword
13. The Hanged Man, the visionary who sacrifices one life to be rewarded with another
14. Death, the Grim Reaper who clears away all that cannot survive
15. Temperance, the archangel of moderation
16. The Devil, the dark and shadowy side of our existence
17. The Tower, a forceful clearing of pent-up, overbuilt energy and ideas
18. The Star, the blithe spirit who offers hope, inspiration, and guidance
19. The Moon, the ever-changing mirror of life on earth
20. The Sun, the source of heat, illumination, and life on earth
21. Judgment, the call to consciousness
22. The World, the never-ending, spiral dance of life

The major arcana cards all depict major, life-changing events. While we can classify them as cosmic mysteries, they're not inexplicable puzzles: in a sense, each card also represents a life lesson that makes those mysteries clear. On a symbolic level, the major arcana cards are also mentors, teachers, and guides: they hold the keys to understanding, and they help guide our passage through every station of the journey.

The Minor Arcana

The minor arcana is divided into four suits, just like a deck of ordinary playing cards. Those four suits are usually called wands, cups, swords, and pentacles. The names aren't always the same: sometimes, depending on the deck you use, wands can be called rods, batons, or staffs. Cups may be called chalices. Swords may be called blades, and pentacles may be called coins, disks, stones, worlds, or stars. Those subtle variations, however, don't make any difference in how the cards are read.

While the major arcana cards depict the mysteries of life, the minor arcana cards show you how you experience those mysteries on a daily basis. In fact, the minor arcana cards can tell you a great deal about how you live your life—and how you manage the separate areas of your existence.

Spheres of Influence

Some people call the minor arcana cards "pip" cards, because pips are the marks that indicate the suit or numerical value of a playing card—the six hearts, for example, or seven diamonds.

In the tarot, however, pip cards take on a significance that most poker players would never dream of: in the minor arcana, each one of the four suits corresponds to a separate area of life.

- *Wands* cards symbolize spiritual life and inspiration.
- *Cups* hold the secrets of emotional affairs.
- *Swords* cards illustrate intellectual concepts.
- *Pentacles* cards represent the realities of physical and material existence.

There's also a second, equally important layer of symbolism to consider—one that's so simple, it's elementary.

The Four Elements

You've probably heard of the four elements—fire, water, air, and earth. They've played an important role in science and philosophy for thousands of years, ever since the ancient Greeks established them as fundamental components of the physical world.

Obviously, modern science has changed our understanding of the physical world. Even so, the four elements still serve as a useful psychological model. We often describe people as "fiery," "airy," or "earthy," for example. Elemental associations are also essential to an understanding of astrology, and they're a fundamental component of some Eastern beliefs, too, such as feng shui.

In the tarot, each one of the four suits of the minor arcana is associated with one of the four elements, and each element corresponds to a separate area of life. The imagery on each card makes those associations easy to remember.

Wands: The fiery cards of spirit, are associated with passion and inspiration. In most tarot decks, wands look like wooden branches that could be set on fire. Wands can be a source of illumination, and sometimes they can spark an entire conflagration of ideas.

Cups: The watery cards of emotion, are associated with deeply felt affairs. Cups can hold water, of course. We also use cups to hold other liquids with emotional significance: we toast each other in celebration. We commune with others during religious ceremonies, and sometimes, we even try to drown our sorrows.

Swords: The airy cards of the intellect, are associated with conscious awareness and communication. Swords symbolize our thoughts, ideas, and attempts to communicate. Swords, like words, move through the air. We even compare our words to the double-edged weapons when we say "The pen is mightier than the sword."

Pentacles: The earthy cards of material existence, are associated with the physical realities of life in a four-dimensional world. In most tarot decks, pentacles look like coins with star-shaped designs. That pattern is symbolic of the physical form. Think of Leonardo da Vinci's Vitruvian Man: his body, with arms outstretched and legs spread wide, creates the shape of a five-pointed star. Pentacles symbolize the tangible realities of physical existence: the things you can touch and feel, and the money you need to keep body and soul together. Pentacles also symbolize spiritual and emotional treasures, including the values you hold dear, the traditions you cherish, and the people you love most.

Those people, by the way, have their own place in the structure of the tarot deck.

The Four Royal Families

Each suit in the minor arcana has a set of four court cards: a page, a knight, a queen, and a king. Depending on the deck you use, the court cards could have other titles. Crowley's royal families, for example, consist of princesses, princes, queens, and knights. The cards themselves are roughly equivalent, as long as you can keep their respective ranks straight in your mind.

The four members of each royal family constitute an ideal family—at least on a symbolic level. They represent a father, a mother, a son, and a daughter. Some of the court cards are masculine, and some are feminine. Some are active, and some are receptive. Together, the sixteen court cards are well suited to reign over the four realms of the tarot—spiritual, emotional, intellectual, and physical—and to describe the unique combinations of qualities and characteristics that make up your personality.

Pages

Pages, knaves, and princesses are young and enthusiastic. They are students and messengers, children who must learn the fundamentals of the family's rule. During the Renaissance, pages were the youngest members of the royal court. It was their job to study—and to run errands, like ferrying messages from one person to another.

When pages show up in a tarot reading, they typically represent young people, students, messengers, or messages.

Knights

When pages grow to the age of knighthood, they must be tested: they're expected to embark on a quest, master a challenge, and demonstrate that they are not only strong enough and smart enough to succeed, but they can also live up to the family's heritage. Historically, knights were rescuers and adventurers.

When knights show up in a tarot reading, they may suggest that a new quest or adventure is about to begin, or that rescue is on its way.

Queens

As adults, both men and women ascend to the throne, where they control and reign over the monarchy. Generally speaking, the tarot's queens are all mature women who tap into their feminine qualities to safeguard, nurture, and protect their realms. Queens are also stereotypically female; they represent ideal women. They are compassionate, creative, receptive, empathic, and intuitive. They also are able to exert their power behind the scenes, convincing—or cajoling—others to adapt their point of view.

When queens show up in a reading, they often suggest that a similarly caring person will be working to safeguard, nurture, and protect your realm.

It's interesting to note that in Crowley's tarot, the transfer of power from one generation to the next takes on a complicated, soap-opera quality, as the court cards battle it out for power and authority. In an endless, overlapping cycle, the princes fight the kings for the throne. When a prince vanquishes the king, he marries the princess, and she assumes the throne of her mother, the queen. And then, the cycle repeats.

Kings

The tarot's four kings are protectors, providers, and seasoned, experienced leaders. All four successfully managed to complete the mission and quest they undertook as knights. They are skilled commanders, confident in the knowledge they acquired during their quests. They are also stereotypically masculine: they are authoritarian, assertive, and alert. They can even be aggressive. They guard their kingdoms with passion and force, and they're not afraid to make executive decisions.

When kings show up in a reading, they may suggest that someone is willing to mount an aggressive defense or even wage war on your behalf.

Your Own Royal Court

Obviously, the court cards are more than characters in a renaissance drama. The court cards also represent aspects of your personality, whether you're young and enthusiastic, or savvy and experienced.

Court cards sometimes represent other people in your life, such as family members, friends, employers, and co-workers. But at the same time, they also depict the facets of your own personality. The connection is forged in a psychological principle called projection. When you like or dislike other people, it's often because they remind you of your own strengths and weaknesses.

When you find yourself dealing with people—or court cards—that you like, it's probably because they remind you of your strengths—your clever sense of humor, your keen intelligence, and your spirit of fun. You share similar ideas about the state of the world, and similar plans for the future.

When other people or court cards rub you the wrong way, it might be because they reflect aspects of your personality that you normally keep hidden—like your occasional selfishness, laziness, or bitterness. (But don't worry. Those weaknesses are between you and the cards.)

By the Numbers

In the major arcana, the numbered cards are often said to represent stations on the journey through life. The numbered cards of the minor arcana also symbolize a progression of events. Aces represent beginnings, and tens represent conclusions. The suits, of course, indicate which events are unfolding: wands symbolize spiritual experiences, cups represent emotional affairs, swords depict intellectual issues, and pentacles suggest physical realities.

Obviously, the tarot deck is meant to be shuffled, so minor arcana cards rarely turn up in sequential order during a reading. You might be surprised, however, by how often you'll see some of the same numbers pop up in a tarot reading: it's not uncommon to find a preponderance of early, middle, or end cards in a tarot spread.

All in all, if you can remember the significance of each suit, as well as the fact that each numbered card represents a separate stage in that area of life, you'll be able to interpret the cards without memorizing the individual meanings of all seventy-eight cards in the deck. The Ace of Wands, for example, often symbolizes the beginning of a spiritual quest. The Five of Wands suggests the halfway point of a spiritual experience, and the Ten of Wands would typically signify the conclusion of a spiritual journey.

The Symbolism of Numbers

In tarot, the numbers don't merely suggest a stage of existence. Each number also has an inherent symbolism. Here is a brief guide to help you start thinking in numerological terms:

Zero

Most of us think of zero as a starting point, from which we count our way up—or down, into negative numbers. Because zero seems to precede all of the other numbers, it symbolizes the period before existence—the great void that existed before the world was created, before the Big Bang when the universe burst into existence.

The circular shape of the number 0 is also a reminder of the cosmic egg, the legendary source of the universe. It suggests the outward growth of the universe from a single point in space. It also symbolizes the shape of the world, the orb of planetary motion, the Wheel of the Year, and the cycle of life. It's even a reminder of the womb, the birth canal, and the cells that make up our substance.

One

One is the first number, so it symbolizes leadership. It's an obvious symbol of unity and singularity. The number one can even be thought of as a *thesis*—an original statement of thought, belief, and perception, still unchallenged by other competing ideas. One also represents the source of all existence. In the tarot, every numbered card in a minor arcana suit is said to originate within the ace of that suit. As such, the number one symbolizes fertility, and the potential and possibility of every new beginning. That symbolism is reinforced by the graphic nature of both the Arabic numeral 1 and the Roman numeral I. Both shapes resemble phallic symbols. Even as a geometric figure, the number one is illustrated as a single point—a dot, which could represent either an egg or a sperm.

Two

Twos represent duality and choices. The number two suggests pairs and combinations, as well as relationships, partnerships, and the attraction between two people. Twos also represent conversation and debate—the point and counterpoint of two opposing ideas, or the antithesis that rises up in response to almost every thesis. The very nature of the number two also signifies a wide range of concepts that come in pairs: heaven and earth, male and female, active and passive, conscious and unconscious, and day and night. Written as a Roman numeral II, the number suggests a gateway or a doorway, as well as female genitalia.

Three

Threes symbolize creation—the result of two separate forces combining to create a third entity. A mother and a father produce a child together. A thesis and an antithesis combine to produce a synthesis. The number three can also represent body, mind, and spirit, or past, present, and future. Many religions believe in a holy trinity, such as Father, Son, and Holy Spirit, or Maiden, Mother, and Crone, or the triple goddess of the New, Full, and Old Moon.

Four

Fours symbolize structure, stability, and security, because four points come together to form a solid. There are four walls in a room, and four corners to a house. There are four dimensions: width, length, height, and time. There are four cardinal directions: north, south, east, and west. There are four seasons, four winds, and four phases of the moon. There are four elements, and four corresponding suits in the minor arcana.

Five

Fives represent a halfway point in the progression from one to ten. In the tarot, the five cards often symbolize a crisis: they're the midway point, when events can either take a turn for the better or go horribly awry. Fives also symbolize the five senses, the five points on a star, and the five vowels in the English alphabet. Some metaphysicians suggest that five is important because it symbolizes a fifth element—spirit.

Six

Sixes historically symbolize the human being, because man was said to be created on the sixth day. Six also symbolizes the sixth sense—psychic ability—as well as the six directions of space: left, right, forward, backward, up, and down.

Seven

Seven is a mystical, magical number. Classically, there were seven days of creation. There are seven gifts of the Holy Spirit: wisdom, understanding, counsel, fortitude, knowledge, piety, and fear. There are seven deadly sins: envy, sloth, gluttony, wrath, pride, lust, and greed. There are seven virtues: faith, hope, charity, fortitude, justice, temperance, and prudence. (You can see most of them in the major arcana.) Alchemists had seven metals: gold, silver, iron, mercury, tin, copper, and lead. There are seven visible planets: the Sun, the Moon, Mars, Mercury, Jupiter, Venus, and Saturn. There are seven days of the week, seven notes in a musical scale, seven colors of the rainbow, and seven chakras, or energy points of the body. Because the seventh day is a day of rest, seven is the number of self-reflection and philosophy. To fully randomize your tarot deck before a reading, shuffle it seven times.

Eight

Eights represent infinity, because they resemble the lemniscate, the sideways symbol of infinity. There are also eight points on the Wheel of the Year. To Christians, eight is a symbol of baptism and spiritual rebirth; many baptisteries and baptismal fonts have eight sides. Eight also represents the eternal spiral of regeneration.

Nine

Because there are nine months of pregnancy, nines symbolize selflessness, compassion, universality, humanitarianism, and spirituality.

Ten

The number ten has primal, deep-seated significance for all of us. When babies are born, parents immediately do a quick count of fingers and toes. When we learn to count as children, we use our ten fingers as tools. Ten is the number of culmination, completion, and perfection. There are also ten spheres on the Kabbalistic Tree of Life and ten numbered cards in each suit of the minor arcana.

Eleven

Numerologists consider eleven a master number. It amplifies the power of a single "one."

Twelve

The number twelve is a reminder of other significant twelves—such as the twelve tribes of Israel, the twelve apostles, the twelve months in a year, and the twelve signs of the zodiac.

Thirteen

There are thirteen lunar months, or thirteen full moons, in every calendar year. Thirteen is sometimes thought to be an unlucky number, because there were thirteen diners at Jesus's last supper. In the tarot, the Death card is number thirteen.

Twenty-two

Twenty-two is another master number, which amplifies the power of two. Humans have twenty-two pairs of chromosomes. There are twenty-two letters in the Hebrew alphabet, twenty-two paths on the Kabbalistic Tree of Life, and twenty-two cards in the major arcana.

The Symbolism of Color

One other factor to consider when you're reading tarot cards is color. Once you've spread the cards, you may notice a preponderance of red—or blue, or green, or even gray. Each hue symbolizes a whole range of meanings.

Red, the color of wine or blood, symbolizes passion, love, and sex. Red is also the color of Mars, the planet of energy and aggression. It can represent danger, anger, and alarm.

Pink, a lighter shade of red, indicates passions that have cooled. Shades of pink and rose are soothing, calming, and symbolize acceptance, friendship, forgiveness, love, romance, peace, and harmony.

Orange, like a blazing fire or a sunset on a tropical island, symbolizes the flames of desire and burning passions. Orange typically represents vitality and enjoyment, vigor, physical health, enthusiasm, and enjoyment.

Yellow, like the sun, symbolizes energy, clear thinking, and consciousness. Yellow is also the color of Mercury, the planet of speed and communication. Yellow represents optimism, radiance, and brilliance. Yellow can sometimes symbolize cowardice and weakness.

Green is the color of nature, growth, healing, and fertility. It symbolizes creativity and prosperity. In the United States, green is the color of money and financial success. Green can also symbolize envy, jealousy, and greed.

Blue, like the sea and the sky, symbolizes depth and calm, a tranquil environment for meditation and reflection.

Indigo, like the midnight heavens, symbolizes cosmic mysteries. Lost in its inky depths, indigo inspires contemplation, wisdom, spiritual realization, and cosmic wisdom.

Violet, the traditional color of royalty, symbolizes leadership and divinity, as well as luxury, wealth, and sophistication.

Black, the color of night, is linked to darkness and sleep, when our consciousness fades and our unconscious thoughts and emotions take control of our dreams. Black is mysterious. It can even be elegant and authoritative. Black is also the color of mourning, depression, darkness, and anxiety, and it can symbolize the darker forces of nature, like upheaval and destruction.

White, like the clouds, symbolizes innocence, pure spirituality, intuition, and psychic ability. It can also seem sterile, cold, clinical, and easily marred.

Gray, a mixture of black and white, is the color of shadows and shade, along with fog. It can symbolize depression and confusion, or simply a steady drizzle.

Brown, the color of bare earth, symbolizes the potential of fallow soil. It can represent grounding, stability, and practicality. Brown can also symbolize poverty and dirt.

Silver, the color of the moon, symbolizes reflection.

The Art and Practice of Tarot Reading

What's in the cards for you?
The only way to find out is to start reading.

Phrasing the Question

Sit down at the tarot reader's table. Shuffle, and let the cards fall where they may. One by one, they'll reveal your future.

Provided, that is, that you ask the right question.

In fact, defining your question might be the single most important part of getting a good tarot reading. Solomon Ibn Gabirol ben Judah, a ninth-century philosopher, put it best. "A wise man's question," he said, "contains half the answer."

Here are some tips for phrasing your questions:

- Focus on a single issue.

- Try to avoid yes or no questions, which can be difficult to answer with tarot cards, and go for more open-ended inquiries, like "What can I expect from my relationship?" or "Where is my career headed?"

- Be as detailed as possible in your queries. Zero in on specifics, like who, what, when, where, why, and how. If you have trouble narrowing the focus of your question, try to put it in writing.

- Don't assume that the cards will intuit your intention. Clarify the background of the question, as well as the type of response you would like in return.

- Define your terms. The cards can be literal in their response. If you ask whether you'll have a date for your cousin's wedding, for example, the cards may give you an unequivocal yes. As the wedding draws closer, however, you may find yourself heading off to the ceremony by yourself. Were the cards wrong? Not if you think back to the question you asked. In all probability, you did have a date for the wedding. It was printed right on the invitation, next to the time and place. But that wasn't the kind of date you meant. You wanted a charming companion on your arm, not a circle on the calendar.

- Include a time frame for the response, such as a week, a month, six months, or a year.

Rephrasing the Question

Most people ask questions that seem straightforward. Sometimes, however, their questions merely hint at the real issue—the secret hopes and fears that they hardly know how to put into words.

After all, every question you ask of the cards secretly embodies a *quest*. Every person who sits down for a tarot reading has a dream, a desire, or a mission in mind. Your job as a tarot reader is to uncover that quest. Once you know what's really at the heart of the matter, you can plan a reading that will help you chart a course for the probable future.

How to Phrase the Question

Here are some empowering questions that can both reveal the path you're on and help you steer a course for the future you truly want. Feel free to adapt these suggestions to fit your situation.

1. What is the most likely outcome of my current path?
2. What should I expect along the way?
3. What would surprise me about this situation?
4. What don't I know?
5. What should I know?
6. What should I prepare for?
7. How should I prepare?
8. What could I do to change this situation?
9. What should I do?
10. What alternatives do I have?
11. How can I change course?
12. What would happen if I change course?
13. How would I feel if I change course?
14. If I were to leave this situation alone, how would it resolve itself?
15. How might this situation change?
16. Should I _____?
17. How would I feel if _____?
18. What would it take to _____?
19. What would happen if _____?
20. What started this?
21. How will it end?
22. What am I supposed to learn?

23. What will I learn?

24. Who is involved?

25. Where can I find comfort?

26. Where can I find advice?

27. Who can I trust?

28. Who can help me?

29. What can help me?

30. What gifts and talents do I have to help me through this situation?

31. How will I feel when this situation concludes? (Alternately, you could also ask, How will I feel in a week, a month, or a year?)

Significant Figures

Many tarot spreads begin with a significator—a single card that signifies the question or the situation at hand. Most tarot readers choose the significator before the rest of the cards are shuffled and spread.

The Obvious Choice

Sometimes, the choice is obvious: the Justice card, for example, is a natural significator for readings about lawsuits or court cases. In other cases, you might want to use an all-purpose significator like the Fool, who represents every man, woman, and child on the journey of life.

Sixth-Sense Significators

You might want to let your intuition guide you to your significator. Simply hold the deck in your hands, or fan the cards face down on a table. Without looking at the cards, find the one that "feels" right to you.

Alternatively, you can let the deck choose your significator: just shuffle, lay the first card down as the significator, and proceed with the rest of your spread.

The Historical Method

Historically, many tarot readers used court cards as significators. They used pages to represent children, knights for young adults, and kings and queens for mature men and women. They also took physical appearance into account, and based their court card choices on coloring.

They chose:

- Wands for people with fair skin, blonde or auburn hair, and blue eyes;

- Cups for those with light to medium skin, light brown, blonde, and gray or blue eyes;

- Swords for people with olive skin, brown hair, and hazel or gray eyes;

- And Pentacles for people with dark skin, very dark brown or black hair, and dark eyes.

The Astrological Method

You might want to choose a major arcana significator based on the sun sign of your querent, the person who's getting the reading:

- Aries: The Emperor or the Tower

- Taurus: The Hierophant or the Empress

- Gemini: The Lovers or the Magician

- Cancer: The Chariot or the High Priestess

- Leo: Strength or the Sun

- Virgo: The Hermit or the Magician

- Libra: Justice or the Empress

- Scorpio: Death or Judgment

- Sagittarius: Temperance or the Wheel of Fortune

- Capricorn: The Devil or the World

- Aquarius: The Star or the Fool

- Pisces: The Moon or the Hanged Man

Birthday Gifts

If you'd like to narrow the significator down even further, you can choose by birth date:

Birth dates	Court Cards	Minor Arcana
March 11–March 20		10 of Cups
March 21–March 30	Queen of Wands	2 of Wands
March 31–April 10		3 of Wands
April 11–April 20		4 of Wands
April 21–April 30	Knight of Pentacles	5 of Pentacles
May 1–May 10		6 of Pentacles
May 11–May 20		7 of Pentacles
May 21–May 31	King of Swords	8 of Swords
June 1–June 10		9 of Swords
June 11–June 20		10 of Swords
June 21–July 1	Queen of Cups	2 of Cups
July 2–July 11		3 of Cups
July 12–July 21		4 of Cups
July 22–August 1	Knight of Wands	5 of Wands
August 2–August 11		6 of Wands
August 12–August 22		7 of Wands
August 23–September 1	King of Pentacles	8 of Pentacles
September 2–September 11		9 of Pentacles
September 12–September 22		10 of Pentacles
September 23–October 2	Queen of Swords	2 of Swords
October 3–October 12		3 of Swords
October 13–October 22		4 of Swords
October 23–November 2	Knight of Cups	5 of Cups
November 3–November 12		6 of Cups
November 13–November 22		7 of Cups
November 23–December 2	King of Wands	8 of Wands
December 3–December 12		9 of Wands
December 13–December 21		10 of Wands
December 22–December 30	Queen of Pentacles	2 of Pentacles
December 31–January 9		3 of Pentacles
January 10–January 19		4 of Pentacles
January 20–January 29	Knight of Swords	5 of Swords
January 30–February 8		6 of Swords
February 9–February 18		7 of Swords
February 19–February 28	King of Cups	8 of Cups
March 1–March 10		9 of Cups

Spreads and Layouts

Most tarot readers have two or three favorite tarot spreads and layouts. This chapter illustrates some of the most popular and most useful spreads for fortunetellers.

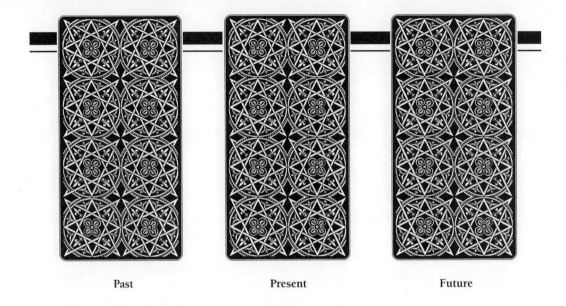

Past   Present   Future

The Past, Present, and Future Spread

Tarot spreads don't get any more basic than the past, present, and future spread. It's an all-purpose layout that's ideal when you want quick answers and a flash of insight into any situation.

Simply shuffle and cut the deck into three separate piles or deal the top three cards from the deck. Read them from left to right, just as you would read words on a page: the first card represents the past, the second card depicts the present, and the third card illustrates the most likely outcome of your current path.

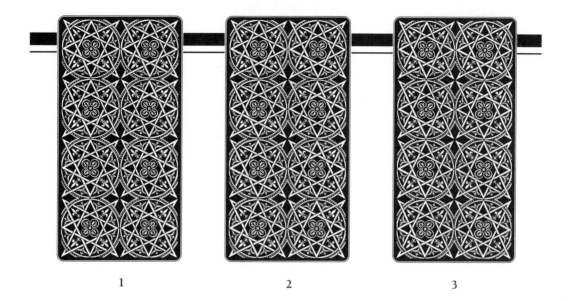

1   2   3

The Three Mysteries

The Three Mysteries spread is a three-card layout designed to address the great mysteries of life—particularly matters of love, loss, and transformation. You can try the spread with the major arcana cards alone or a full seventy-eight-card deck.

Card 1 is the mystery you understand. This is a major issue that you know well, and you have come to terms with it.

Card 2 is the mystery that eludes you. This is a life lesson that you haven't experienced, and may never fully understand.

Card 3 is the mystery you will come to comprehend. This is a revelation that will soon unfold for you.

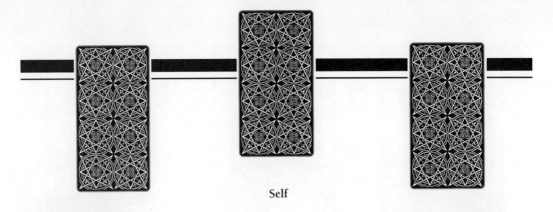

Self

Future   Friends & Family

The Horseshoe Spread

The horseshoe spread is a dramatic way to explore the details of any question or situation—all in a mystical seven-card reading.

1. The past. This card depicts the circumstances and events that led to the present situation.

2. The present. This card depicts your current situation.

3. The future. This card depicts the near future.

4. Your self. This card depicts your attitudes, thoughts, and feelings about the situation.

5. Your friends and family. This card depicts how other people close to you see and affect the situation.

6. Obstacles. The sixth card depicts the obstacles you'll need to overcome.

7. Outcome. This card depicts the most likely outcome of the current situation, if nothing changes.

Obstacles

Outcome

Present

Past

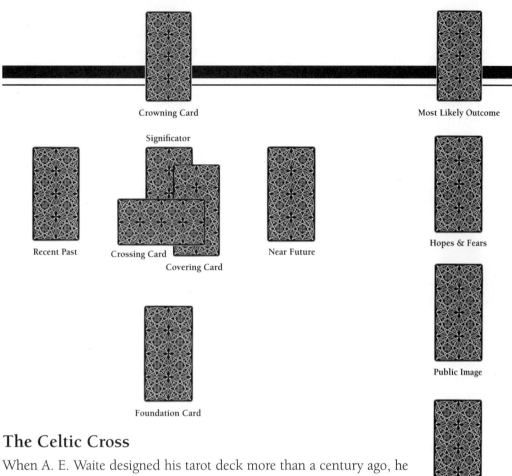

Crowning Card

Most Likely Outcome

Significator

Recent Past   Crossing Card   Near Future   Hopes & Fears

Covering Card

Public Image

Foundation Card

Self Image

The Celtic Cross

When A. E. Waite designed his tarot deck more than a century ago, he also introduced a corresponding spread. Since then, the Celtic Cross—which is pronounced "keltic," by the way—has become a perennial favorite. Here is one popular version of the spread:

1. Significator. This card represents you.

2. Covering card. This card represents your situation.

3. Crossing card. This card represents the energy of the moment and the forces that are affecting your situation.

4. Foundation card. This is the foundation of your situation.

5. Recent past. This card represents the last six months to a year.

6. Crowning card: This card represents the most ideal outcome of your current situation.

7. Near future. This card represents the next six months to a year.

8. Self image. This is how you see yourself.

9. Public image. This is how others see you.

10. Hopes and fears. This card represents your hopes and fears—the dreams you almost don't dare to dream.

11. Most likely outcome. This card represents the most likely outcome of your current path, if nothing changes.

The Wheel of Fortune

A twelve-card spread based on a horoscope chart is another popular way to read the cards. You can think of this layout as a predictive tool, and look for events in each of the time periods the signs represent. You can also read it like a standard horoscope chart, which is basically a snapshot of a single moment in time.

A horoscope chart is simply a circle divided into twelve equal sections, called houses. A horoscope spread kind of looks like the face of a clock—with one major difference. It's laid out counter-clockwise, with the first house starting at the 9 o'clock position.

The signs of the zodiac all have a home on a horoscope chart. Aries rules the first house, followed by Taurus in the second, Gemini in the third, and so on.

Just as the positions of a past, present, and future spread—or a Celtic Cross, for that matter—determine how you read the cards that fall. The same principle is at work in a horoscope spread. Every card on the table will describe the qualities associated with a separate sign of the zodiac.

You can find keywords and descriptions of each sign in any introductory book of astrology, but here are some to start with:

Aries, the Ram: Leadership, self-awareness, drive, and initiative.

Taurus, the Bull: Security, creature comforts, material resources, values, and treasures.

Gemini, the Twins: Thought, logic, and communication skills.

Cancer, the Crab: Sensitivity, emotional well-being, home life, the ability to nurture and be nurtured, and mother figures.

Leo, the Lion: Self-esteem, recreational pursuits, creative expression, children, and father figures.

Virgo, the Virgin: Health, cleanliness, and attention to detail.

Libra, the Scales: Marriage and partnerships, close personal relationships, balance and social grace.

Scorpio, the Scorpion: Sex, death, joint resources, and inheritance.

Sagittarius, the Archer: Philosophy, long-distance travel, and higher education.

Capricorn, the Goat: Career aspirations, responsibility, and public image.

Aquarius, the Water Bearer: Social groups, social causes, inventiveness, and long-term view of the future.

Pisces, the Fish: Psychological health, the subconscious mind, psychic ability, and intuition.

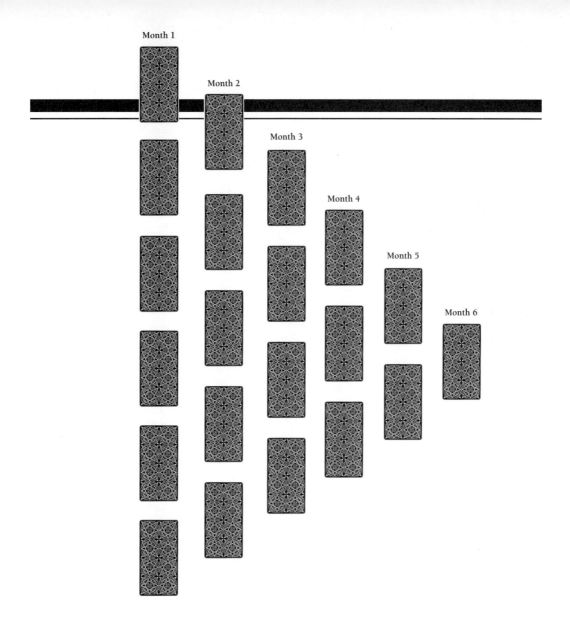

Month 1

Month 2

Month 3

Month 4

Month 5

Month 6

Six Months from Now

Use this spread to get a sneak preview of the next six months. Because predictions become less and less accurate as time goes by, this layout is designed to give you most of the information about the near future.

Wild Cards

Sometimes, you might find that you need more information than the cards on the table can provide. Getting that information is easy: just add cards as you need them, at any point during a reading.

- Wild cards. Add a wild card to any standard spread, for information that might not have had a clear-cut place in the rest of the layout.

- Clarification cards. If you need more information to interpret an individual card, cover it with a clarification card.

- Advice cards. If you get a card that seems unduly negative or alarming, deal another card for advice on how to soften the blow, negate the bad news, or change course.

- Future cards. You don't need to conclude a reading with just one "outcome" card. You can add future cards, timeline-style, to see how the situation will continue to develop.

- Alternate outcomes. Deal two or three cards to see how alternative choices could change the course of events.

- Hidden cards. Don't forget the "secret" cards in a tarot spread—the cards that never make it out of the deck, but stay hidden underneath. Simply pick the deck up and look at the bottom card. That's where you'll often find information that has been kept secret, repressed, and subconscious. If you cut the cards into three piles, as many tarot readers do, you can also check the bottom card of each stack for a quick mini-reading. You don't need to verbalize it; you can simply keep the information in mind as you put the deck back together and proceed with your reading.

Reading the Cards

Reading tarot cards isn't all that different from reading a story. Granted, you have to provide the words yourself, and the plot changes every time you shuffle the deck. But for the most part, reading the cards is simply a matter of seeing your story in the cards and following it through to its logical conclusion.

In fact, the tarot deck practically does the work for you: once you shuffle the cards, the people, places, and events in your life will all fall into place. You'll see the beginning, middle, and end of each story. You'll also spend some time identifying the main characters, deciphering their motivations, and discovering the themes and special interests that tie them together. And along the way, you'll point out a few colorful details that add drama and excitement to your delivery.

You simply need to pick up the cards and start reading.

How to Read a Single Card

Tarot reading is a simple process that can be broken down into several steps, whether you're reading a single card or working your way through every card in the deck.

- Start by saying the name of each card out loud. "This card," you might say, "is the Queen of Swords."

- If the card you're reading is from the major arcana, discuss what you know about its archetype, and the powerful life lessons that major arcana cards represent. It might help to bring up the stories and myths associated with each card.

- If the card is from the minor arcana, summarize what you know about the suit. Wands, for example, usually relate to spiritual issues, while cups are emotional, swords are intellectual, and pentacles are physical cards.

- Look at the numbers assigned to each card. They could indicate whether the issue at hand is in the beginning, middle, or end stage.

- Pay attention to the color schemes in the card. What moods do the colors convey? What accent colors are used? What do they add to the card's meaning?

- Then describe the figures or characters in each card. Describe their clothing, their posture, their expressions, and their attitudes. Imagine what they might say if you could hear them speak.

- Look beyond the characters in the card, and describe the scenery that surrounds them. Look at the earth, the sky, the background, and the foreground.

- As you study each card, your eye will probably be drawn to a single image or symbol. That image might remind you of a word, a phrase, or an expression. It might trigger a visual image or scene in your mind's eye. It might make you feel hot or cold, or inspire an emotional reaction. In fact, a card could activate any one of your senses: sight, sound, touch, scent, and even taste. Simply put your reaction into words. Don't worry about being right or wrong; just describe all of the impressions you get from the card.

- Once you start talking, don't censor yourself. Go with the flow and just keep talking, stream-of-consciousness style. Random words and phrases might pop into your head. Repeat them out loud, even if they don't seem to make sense. That's because the cards sometimes communicate through puns and wordplay. You might say "sun," for example, but the person you're reading for will hear "son," and the message will make perfect sense. At any rate, verbalizing your impressions will help you assess each card, and you may even surprise yourself with the accuracy of your insight and intuition.

- Tarot reading is a collaborative process. If you get stuck, especially if you're reading for someone else, ask them what the images could mean, and which symbols seem most important. There's no need to pretend you're psychic if you're not. Even if you do have an especially sensitive sixth sense, asking for basic information is much, much easier than trying to intuit the facts. As you look at the cards together, you may even find that your querent has a good sense of what the symbols and images portend in their lives.

Teamwork: How to Read Cards in Combination

When any number of tarot cards are laid out in a spread, you'll need to figure out how they relate to each other. Here are some tips for reading cards in combination:

- First, remember that every card in a tarot spread probably relates directly to the question or situation at hand. It's easy to get distracted during a reading and find yourself going off on tangents. Try to link the answers you receive back to the question you asked.

- It's also important to remember what each position in the spread represents. Keep the cards clear in your mind; don't confuse cards that symbolize the past, for example, with cards that represent the future.

- Do a quick count of the number of major arcana cards, minor arcana cards, and court cards that appear in your spreads. Major arcana cards tend to indicate major changes and cosmic forces that seem outside our individual control. Minor arcana cards usually represent the smooth flow of everyday life, and court cards suggest interaction with other people.

- Keep your eyes open for a preponderance of any one suit, or pairs, or runs. Their meanings will probably be obvious: wands represent spiritual issues, cups symbolize emotional affairs, swords suggest intellectual concepts, and pentacles represent physical matters. Jean Baptiste-Alliette, one of the world's first tarot fortunetellers, said that a group of wands cards could signify feasting. A cluster of cups cards would symbolize lovemaking, while swords would indicate quarrelling and trouble, and a number of pentacles cards would suggest issues with money.

- Also, check the numbers on each card. Early numbers, in both the major and minor arcana, tend to indicate beginnings, while middle numbers represent the midpoints of a cycle, and numbers at the end of a series symbolize culminations and conclusions.

- Be alert to cards that seem to stand out from the rest. Sometimes, a single card in the spread could be the key to the entire reading, while all of the other cards support or enhance its message.

- Every card in a reading could also serve to illustrate a separate facet of the issue. If that's the case, you'll get a full overview of a situation by the time you read them all.

- Look for obvious pairs and combinations of cards that seem to go together, like the Three and Eight of Pentacles. Obvious "couple" cards also work together in a spread: watch for partners like the High Priestess and the Hierophant, the Empress and the Emperor, or the King and Queen of Swords.

- At the same time, pay attention to diametrical opposites, such as the Devil and the angel of Temperance. They could be sending you a mixed message that you'll need to sort out by consulting other cards in the spread.

- Individual cards can be strengthened or weakened by the cards that surround them. Cards of the same suit, for example, tend to support and reinforce each other, while cards from other suits can cancel each other out. Elementally, the fiery wands cards are the opposite of watery cups, and the airy swords cards are the opposite of earthy pentacles. Swords are friendly with cups and wands, and wands are friendly with swords and pentacles.

Over time, you'll probably develop your own system for working with card combinations. In the meantime, you can try your hand at two systems that were developed for the Waite and Crowley decks.

Combination Platters

A. E. Waite devised the following guide for reading cards in combination:

4 Kings: great honor	3 Kings: consultation	2 Kings: minor counsel
4 Queens: great debate	3 Queens: deception by women	2 Queens: sincere friends
4 Knights: serious matters	3 Knights: lively debate	2 Knights: intimacy
4 Pages: dangerous illness	3 Pages: dispute	2 Pages: disquiet
4 Tens: condemnation	3 Tens: new condition	2 Tens: change
4 Nines: a good friend	3 Nines: success	2 Nines: receipt
4 Eights: reverse	3 Eights: marriage	2 Eights: new knowledge
4 Sevens: intrigue	3 Sevens: infirmity	2 Sevens: news
4 Sixes: abundance	3 Sixes: success	2 Sixes: irritability
4 Fives: regularity	3 Fives: determination	2 Fives: vigils
4 Fours: journey near at hand	3 Fours: a subject of reflection	2 Fours: insomnia
4 Threes: progress	3 Threes: unity	2 Threes: calm
4 Twos: contention	3 Twos: security	2 Twos: accord
4 Aces: favorable chance	3 Aces: small success	2 Aces: trickery

Crowley developed this guide:

A majority of wands: Energy, opposition, quarrel	A majority of cups: Pleasure, merriment
A majority of swords: Trouble, sadness, sickness, death	A majority of pentacles: Business, money, possessions
A majority of major arcana cards: Strong forces beyond the querent's control	A majority of court cards: Society, meetings of many persons
A majority of Aces: Strength generally. Aces are always strong cards	
4 Aces: Great power and force	3 Aces: Riches, success
4 Kings (which are called Knights in Crowley's deck): Swiftness, rapidity	3 Kings: Unexpected meetings. Knights, in general, show news
4 Queens: Authority, influence	3 Queens: Powerful friends
4 Knights (which are called Princes in Crowley's deck): Meetings with the great	3 Knights: Rank and honor
4 Pages (which are called Princesses in Crowley's deck): New ideas or plans	3 Pages: Society of the young
4 Tens: Anxiety, responsibility	3 Tens: Buying and selling (commerce)
4 Nines: Added responsibilities	3 Nines: Much correspondence
4 Eights: Much news	3 Eights: Much journeying
4 Sevens: Disappointments	3 Sevens: Treaties and compacts
4 Sixes: Pleasure	3 Sixes: Gain, success
4 Fives: Order, regularity	3 Fives: Quarrels, fights
4 Fours: Rest, peace	3 Fours: Industry
4 Threes: Resolution, determination	3 Threes: Deceit
4 Twos: Conferences, conversations	3 Twos: Reorganization, recommendation

About Face: How to Read Reversed Cards

You wouldn't read a book upside-down, and you shouldn't try to read the cards upside-down, either. You could hurt your neck. Even if you're reading for someone across the table, you should make sure that all of the cards are facing you.

That's not to say that reversed cards don't play a role in most tarot readings. No matter how careful you are when you shuffle, some cards inevitably seem to position themselves upside-down during a reading—and those reversed cards can usually put their own spin on a reading.

Some tarot readers don't read reversed cards—they simply turn them all upright. After all, every card in the deck triggers both positive and negative reactions. Every card has a good side—and a darker, shadow side.

Most tarot readers, however, do take note of the cards that fall upside-down, and then pay special attention when those cards come into play during their readings. After all, if a card is willing to vault and perform handstands to be noticed, it must be important.

While it seems counterintuitive, reversals don't necessarily reverse the meanings of the cards. Most reversals simply indicate that the card's usual significance has taken a turn—for better or for worse.

A reversed card could indicate a message that's being blocked, either consciously or unconsciously. It could represent subconscious or unconscious energy. It might symbolize situations that are developing, delayed, postponed, or cancelled. It could depict a past event that's over and done—but not yet accepted or understood.

Psychologically, reversed cards sometimes depict attitudes that are unevolved or immature, thought or energy that is either absent or excessive, or time and energy that's being wasted or misapplied. They might symbolize strengths or weaknesses that are being projected onto other people, or gifts and talents that are being misused or misdirected.

Occasionally, a reversed card simply represents a playful spirit or attitude about an issue—or a deeply private or secret activity.

Reversed cards can even be literal. They can depict a sudden, unexpected change in direction, a surprising change in position or a new perspective, or an assumption, a concern, or a fear that's completely groundless.

If you want to avoid reversed cards, make sure that all of the cards in your deck are facing the same way when you mix the cards. Most people tend to divide the deck in two, and without even realizing it, they turn half of the deck around before they start to shuffle the cards.

What Falls to the Floor

While some cards somersault and tumble to get your attention, others go a step further, and literally leap out of the deck while you shuffle or spread the cards. In those cases, you don't need to look any further for your significator, your outcome cards, or the cards you'll use for your entire reading.

"What falls to the floor," you can say, "comes to the door."

Putting It All Together

Fortunetelling, Step-by-Step

Once you have chosen your question, your significator, and your spread, you can start your reading. Here is a good, basic routine to follow when you sit down to divine with the cards.

- First, gather everything you'll need for your fortunetelling session. You'll want your tarot cards, of course. You'll also need a candle, a lighter, and a spread cloth for the cards. (Any attractive scarf, fabric, or tablecloth will do.) You might want to enhance your reading area with tokens of the four suits, such as a candle for fire, a seashell for water, incense for air, and a crystal for earth. Soft background music is also a nice touch. If you plan to keep a record of your reading, don't forget to have a pen and your tarot journal handy.

- Next, clean your reading area—both physically *and* psychically. First, clear any dirt, dust, and household debris that could be a distraction. Then clear the space mentally by visualizing it filled with white light. You can also burn incense, ring bells, or fill the room with music—whatever will help you envision your surroundings as sacred space.

- Now prepare a comfortable place to read the cards. Lay out your spread cloth, put your candle in place, and accessorize the area however you like.

- Center yourself in your reading space. Sit comfortably, clear your mind, and breathe deeply.

- Divination can be a heady experience. You'll probably want to ground yourself, to keep energy flowing *through* you, rather than simply in or out of your body, which could leave you feeling tired and achy. The grounding process is simple: Put both feet flat on the floor, or sit right on the ground, and imagine that you are a tree, with roots extending deep into the earth and branches reaching high into the heavens. If you are reading the cards for another person, have them center, clear, and ground themselves, too.

- You might find yourself slipping into a light trance, like a daydream. That's good. Your goal is to be calm, cool, and collected, and open to new ideas, flashes of insight, and intuitive wisdom.

- Light a candle to signal your intent for the reading to begin.

- When you practice divination, you'll be tapping into cosmic energy and seeking messages from a higher source. You might want to solicit divine guidance in the form of a prayer, or to request the aid of your guardian angels or guides. You can also turn to the archetypes of the cards themselves for help. Imagine yourself as the Magician, allowing cosmic energy to flow through you; that way, you won't take on the burden of carrying someone else's concerns. Or picture yourself as the High Priestess, reading from the book of secrets she holds in her lap. You might want to envision any of the figures from the major arcana—alone or in groups of two or three—standing beside you, whispering advice. You can even shuffle the major arcana cards and pull a card or two to determine which advisors will be at your side during the reading.

- Choose a question or pick a topic for your fortunetelling session. Try to avoid yes or no questions, which can be difficult to answer with tarot cards, and go for more open-ended inquiries, like "What can I expect from my relationship?" or "Where is my career headed?"

- Include a time frame in your question—a week, a month, three months, six months, or a year—so you'll be able to check your results later.

- If you're going to use a significator—a card that signifies a person, a question, or a situation—pull it out of the deck and place it, face up, on your spread cloth.

- Shuffle the cards. There's nothing wrong with a good, old-fashioned riffle-style shuffle—although you do run the risk of bending the cards, especially if they're printed on thin cardstock. Shuffle the deck seven times, and your cards should be thoroughly randomized. If you want to keep reversals to a minimum, make sure both halves of the deck are facing the same way. You can also mix the cards by holding the deck in one hand, and dropping several cards at once into your other hand. You'll need to shuffle for some time to completely randomize the cards that way. You can even scramble the cards by putting them all face down and mixing them thoroughly with both hands, but you are bound to have a lot of reversed cards in the resulting spread.

- While you shuffle, keep your mind as blank as possible. Try to put any personal bias or preconceived ideas out of your head. Be open to all possibilities.

- Cut the cards. If you're reading for someone else, have that person cut the cards for you.

- Put the deck back together and lay out the cards, face down. You can deal the cards off the top of the deck, or fan the cards out and randomly pull cards for your layout. If your spread is small—say, three or four cards—you can also just cut the deck into three or four piles.

- Turn each card face up just as you come to it during the reading. Turn them over from right to left, as you would turn pages in a book.

- Start talking about all of the single cards. As you describe them, be sure to put all of your observations in the most positive light. Avoid making negative pronouncements that could become self-fulfilling prophecies. Be kind, and predict only good things for others.

- When your reading concludes, extinguish the candle to signify that the reading has ended.

- Some readers like to clear their tarot decks after every reading, or whenever the cards start to feel tired, used, or filled with the remnants of old readings. There are a lot of ways to clear a deck: you can leave it on a windowsill overnight, where it will be washed by the light of the moon. You can put the cards back in numerical order: major arcana cards first, followed by wands, cups, swords, and pentacles. You can pass the cards through incense, or simply envision them being bathed in pure white light. You can even hold the deck in your hands, blow on it three times, and picture your breath blowing it clean.

- Keep a record of your most meaningful readings, so you can hone your skill and accuracy over time. Write your predictions down, date them, and keep them in your tarot journal. If you don't have a tarot journal, tuck your written predictions into the back pages of your calendar or organizer, or put them in a desk drawer where you can find and review them later.

Good Fortune

Not long ago, in New Orleans, a young woman, Alyssa, decided to get a tarot reading. What she described afterward is a cautionary tale for anyone who plans to read tarot cards for other people.

I sat down, shuffled the cards as directed while thinking about what I wanted the cards to answer for me—what my life would hold, would I be successful, would I fall in love—

and handed them back to the tarot card reader. As she began to lay them out on the table in their formation she sighed, and grimaced, and said "hmmm" a lot of times.

"I don't have a lot of good things to tell you," she said.

The condensed version was this: I would never be happy, I would never find love, I would never be truly successful, I would never have a family, and so on.

She said she felt bad, asked me to shuffle again, laid out more cards, one after the other, telling me she was trying to find something good to tell me, but there was nothing.

I choked back tears. The rest of my vacation was ruined. Seriously. I don't know what this "knowledge" did to me, because it certainly wasn't real, but it put a pall over everything.

And I have to tell you: each time something bad happens, I think back to the tarot card lady and think "Aren't these people supposed to give good readings no matter what?" And even though I don't believe in it, or her, I'd be lying if I said it didn't come back every time something bad happens.

For most people, a tarot reading is a special event, and they'll remember the highlights of a good reading for years.

But when a tarot reading goes bad, it's almost impossible to forget.

Your Role as a Reader

When you read tarot cards, you'll probably want to do everything in your power to offer readings that are filled with optimism, hope, and encouragement.

Happily, that's not hard to do.

Start by beginning every reading with the best of intentions, determined to relay only positive, helpful information.

As a kindness, open your readings for other people by reassuring them that they have gotten "good" cards. After all, every card has both a positive side and a negative side. Do your best to describe the positive forces that are at work in every person's life, and soft-pedal any negative information you see in the cards. Avoid making negative pronouncements that could become self-fulfilling prophecies.

At the same time, realize that information you regard as a negative might be welcome news to someone else. Let your querents decide what's "bad" or "good."

Naturally, the information you get from the cards will be colored by your own experiences, perceptions, misconceptions, and biases. Even so, you can still do your best to be objective. Try to put aside any preconceptions or judgments you have, and simply relay the information the cards have to give.

Remember that you are only a messenger. As a tarot reader, your role is simply to help other people see their lives from the objective, third-party position of the cards—and to lay out additional cards that can demonstrate their alternatives and choices, if that's what they would like. It's not your job to fix other people, heal their wounds, or solve their problems. It's also not your job to make decisions for them or to take responsibility for their situations.

Remind your querents that that the future is not set in stone, and that they can change course at any point.

One great technique to demonstrate the flexibility and variability of events is to lay out cards for two or more scenarios: what will happen if [A] vs. [B]?

Don't ever predict death, for anyone. When the Death card does come into play, remember that people experience death and transformation on many levels, in many ways, during the course of their lifetimes. Reassure your querents that the cards are symbolic. They speak a metaphorical language, not a literal one.

Try not to alarm anyone with descriptions of catastrophic illness or injury, either. If you feel that you simply must say something about a threat to someone's health or well-being, suggest that they see a doctor for a checkup, get extra rest, or pay attention to any symptoms of poor health.

Never use tarot cards to intimidate or frighten other people, or try to force them to change their behavior.

As you conclude your readings, summarize your key points, just to make sure you were heard clearly. Some people hear only what they want to hear. If you run into someone who practices selective listening, you may need to repeat, rephrase, or clarify your main points.

And finally, guard against dependence, both in your own reliance on the cards and on the part of others who might come to you for a tarot reading.

The Art of Prediction

While most people see tarot readers as magical and mysterious, with access to hidden wisdom and cosmic secrets, the art of fortunetelling with tarot cards isn't as dark and mysterious as you might think—probably because the future isn't usually as mystifying as it seems. After all, day-to-day life is almost always predictable. Even without the cards, you could probably guess—with some accuracy—how your day will unfold tomorrow. You could probably guess what your friends and family members will be doing, too.

In fact, the art of prediction is actually fairly familiar to most people. Every day we make predictions—usually based on our experience in the past, and our observations about the present. We predict the ending of a movie or a television show. We predict the course of our friends' romantic lives. We predict the weather. Our lives are filled with predictions.

The advantage of making predictions with tarot cards, however, is that the cards make it easy to see patterns, trends, and outcomes. With a deck of tarot cards, you can literally visualize coming events, conceptualize their implications, and put them into words.

The process of making predictions with tarot cards isn't much different than performing a basic reading.

- First, choose a question or pick a topic for your prediction. Most people want to know about love, money, family, and career issues, so those are all good places to start.

- Avoid yes or no questions (which can be difficult to answer with tarot cards) and go for more open-ended inquiries, like "What can I expect from my relationship?" or "Where is my career headed?"

- Include a time frame in your question so you'll be able to check your results later.

- Shuffle and draw a single card to represent the answer.

- When you look at the card, say the first thing that comes into your mind.

- Once you start talking, don't stop. Your first impressions probably won't be clear, and they probably won't make a lot of sense. That's okay. Just keep talking—even if you feel like you're spouting total nonsense. This is only a game, so don't be afraid to be wrong, and don't censor yourself.

- If you feel self-conscious, here's something to keep in mind: when you make predictions for other people, they are mesmerized by the process. As long as you keep talking, they'll be thinking of themselves—and they'll be so busy imagining their own futures that they won't have time to judge you or your performance.

- As you study each card, your eye will probably be drawn to a single image or symbol. That image might remind you of a word, a phrase, or an expression. It might trigger a visual image or scene in your mind's eye. It might make you feel hot or cold, or inspire an emotional reaction. In fact, the card might activate any one of your senses: sight, sound, touch, scent, and even taste. Simply put your reaction into words. Describe all of the impressions you get from the card. Go with the flow and just keep talking, stream-of-consciousness style.

- Once you've said everything that comes to mind, take a leap of faith and make a prediction. Simply say, "I predict that ..." Again, don't worry about being right or wrong; just take a guess.

- Put all of your observations in the most positive light. Avoid making negative pronouncements that could become self-fulfilling prophecies. Be kind, and predict only good things for others.

- Write your predictions down, date them, and keep them in your tarot journal. If you don't have a tarot journal, tuck your written predictions into the back pages of your calendar or organizer, or put them in a desk drawer where you can find and review them later.

Enjoy the process, and have fun!

Fate and Free Will

While tarot cards often show a probable future—or a possible one—the future is never set in stone. Every person is in charge of his or her own destiny. The smallest change in your course now could have a major impact on the final outcome of events. If you're traveling down the street and turn right instead of left, your destination will change. If you see something coming in the cards that you don't want to approach, a quick turn or two will change your destiny, too.

Remember, it's the choices you make that will truly determine the outcome of any situation. If you don't like what you see in the cards, you can use them to change your course—and change your destiny.

The tarot is not a mysterious, all-knowing oracle that reveals your inevitable fate. Rather, the tarot is a way for you to discover your own best road to success. The tarot can help you see your most likely future—and give you the chance to change that future, if you choose.

So go ahead. Let the cards fall where they may. But if you don't like the future they foretell, pick up the deck and shuffle it again—and this time, look for options.

A Tarot Reader's Code of Ethics

You might want to adopt or adapt the following code of ethics, which is loosely based on a similar code provided by the American Tarot Association:

- I will treat you with respect.

- I will do my best to answer any questions you have during your tarot reading.
- I will be objective. I will try to keep my own opinions and beliefs out of your reading.
- I will be truthful. I will not lie, exaggerate, or disguise what I see in the cards.
- I will be optimistic. I will use tarot cards to show you how you can make the most of your current situation.
- I will be honest. I will not use tarot cards to trick you or cheat you.
- If I charge money for a tarot reading, I will charge a fair price based on my experience and expertise. I will also tell you the full cost of the reading before we begin.
- I will keep your reading confidential. Unless I have reasonable cause to suspect that someone's life, safety, or health is in danger, I will not discuss your reading with anyone.

Types of Readings

When they sit down at the tarot reader's table, most people want to know about one of three things—love, money, and health—or any of countless variations on those themes.

Relationship Readings

Love can be a many-splendored thing, and there are as many types of romance readings as there are relationships. Single people want to know about their romantic prospects, of course. People who have relationships want to be sure that they're in the *right* relationship. Occasionally, people who have commitments come to a tarot reader seeking reassurance that their relationships are strong and their partners are faithful—or confirmation when they fear betrayal.

Many people also want readings about their relationships with their children, their family members, and their friends.

The best way to approach relationship readings is to focus on the querent's role in the relationship. If you try to conduct a reading about someone who's not there—and someone who hasn't given their informed consent—you may find yourself with cards that seem muddled and unclear.

There are a number of cards you can expect to see when you deal with relationship readings. Obviously, most people who are looking for love probably would like to see the Lovers card pop up in their reading. The Two of Cups would be an encouraging card, too, as would the Hierophant, who presides over weddings, and the Four of Wands, which seems to depict an open-air wedding under a floral canopy. The Ten of Cups and the Ten of Pentacles both seem to promise a happy home and family life, with the partner of one's choosing.

The Sun and the World cards are ideal omens in any reading, including a romance spread.

The Devil seems to be the poster child of dysfunctional relationships. It's not uncommon to find that the Devil card describes problems with drug use, alcohol abuse, chronic gambling, or physical and emotional abuse. When the Devil shows up in a relationship reading, give him his due—and then throw down a few cards for clarification and advice.

The Hermit is alone. He's not interested in a romantic relationship.

The Three of Swords is a graphic illustration of the broken heart.

Court cards are good, because they indicate a rich social life with a wide group of other people. Not surprisingly, people who are looking for love are especially glad to see the tarot's knights in shining armor. As a rule, however, the four knights each have their own peculiarities in love. The fiery Knight of Wands, for example, will inspire flames of passion, but his ardor has a tendency to burn out over time. The watery Knight of Cups is an idealist and a romantic—but he's also someone who might fall in love with every sweet young thing that crosses his path. The airy Knight of Swords will rush in and out of the picture, like a windstorm. The earthy Knight of Pentacles promises love that's solid and true, but he moves at a snail's pace.

You might think you'd have better luck with Kings. Unfortunately, most kings are already married or in a committed relationship.

The High Priestess is a virgin. The Charioteer has one-night stands.

The Hanged Man could be quite a catch; he understands the importance of patience, self-sacrifice, and communication. Temperance and Justice also illustrate the balance people need to maintain a relationship.

The Tower and the Star are sexy cards, which illustrate the passion and release that are possible in love.

The Moon is undeniably romantic, but it waxes and wanes and has been known to describe a certain amount of deception.

As with any tarot reading, how you phrase the question will have a dramatic affect on the answer you receive.

"When will I fall in love?" probably won't reveal much. But "Why haven't I fallen in love yet?" will garner some dramatic, thought-provoking results.

"How can I make myself more attractive?"

"How can I prepare to meet the person of my dreams?"

Career and Financial Readings

Money is also a popular theme for inquiries. Most relate to work and decisions about profession and career. Should I quit my job? Should I start looking for a new job? Will I be happy if I stay in my current situation, or will things only get worse? Sometimes you'll get questions about prospective employees, or clients, or business associates.

They may feel out of the loop at work, and need information about job security.

One way to handle money readings is to explore the available options: Ask the cards, "How will I feel if ...?"

In theory, you should be able to spot a career or financial reading by looking for pentacles cards. You probably won't even need to know the question: Pentacles almost always show up in readings about career and finance. Typically, the Three and Eight of Pentacles depict people who are hard at work—literally making money —while the Four of Pentacles suggests someone who is conserving, or even hoarding his resources. The Five of Pentacles is a graphic depiction of bankruptcy, poverty, or the fear of financial devastation. The Seven of Pentacles shows someone who is growing his wealth, while the Nine and Ten of Pentacles show people who enjoy a fair measure of financial security.

In practice, however, many people are completely invested in their work and careers—spiritually, emotionally, intellectually, and physically. As a result, all four suits directly pertain to career and financial questions.

The Magician is associated with sales. The High Priestess is involved in counseling. The Empress is a working mother, while the Emperor is a high-level executive, administrator, or manager. The Hierophant may be a teacher or professor. The Lovers might be business partners. The Charioteer could be involved in shipping or transportation. Strength could be a veterinarian. Justice and Judgment are connected to the legal system. Temperance may be a scientist.

Oddly enough, the Devil might have the closest connection to the career world. It's associated with the astrological sign of Capricorn, which symbolizes work, career, and being status-conscious.

The Two and Three of Wands depict businessmen, while the Ten of Wands depicts overwork.

Health Readings

Health readings may be the most difficult, because the cards don't necessarily make a distinction between physical and spiritual health. It's best to be very specific in your questions, and be prepared for answers that seem ambiguous.

One of the easiest ways to conduct a health reading is to look for astrological associations in the cards. Every astrological sign is associated with a specific part of the body—and the signs, of course, are all associated with tarot cards, too.

Sign	Body Part	Corresponding Tarot Card
Aries	The head	The Emperor or the Tower
Taurus	The neck & throat	The Hierophant or the Empress
Gemini	The shoulders, arms, hands, & lungs	The Lovers or the Magician
Cancer	The stomach & breasts	The Chariot or the High Priestess
Leo	The heart, back, & spine	Strength or the Sun
Virgo	The intestines	The Hermit or the Magician
Libra	The kidneys	Justice or the Empress
Scorpio	The reproductive organs	Death or Judgment
Sagittarius	The thighs & hips	Temperance or the Wheel of Fortune
Capricorn	The knees	The Devil or the World
Aquarius	The ankles	The Star or the Fool
Pisces	The feet	The Moon or the Hanged Man

Pentacle cards, which relate to physical existence, can offer valuable information about your physical health, while sword cards generally relate to mental health. However, occasionally some sword cards seem to pop up as painful reminders of physical discomfort, and they sometimes refer to needles, surgical tools, and medical intervention.

The King of Swords often represents a doctor or a surgeon, while the Queen of Cups typically suggests someone in a caregiving role.

The Sun is a promising card in a health reading, as is the World, Strength, Temperance, and good balance. Believe it or not, the Tower and the Death card could be very good omens in a tarot reading. They usually indicate that a health crisis will end—and end well. Not, as you might expect, in a funeral.

Many young women hope to have children, and they often ask about pregnancy during their tarot card readings. All of the Ace cards, along with the Empress, suggest that children are on the way.

While it's sometimes fun to play doctor, don't try to offer medical advice if you're not a trained physician or health professional. While the cards can offer emotional and spiritual healing, you should strongly recommend that anyone with a health question make an appointment to see a doctor.

As with all of your readings, keep your health readings light and optimistic. You should never predict illness, injury, or death, for anyone. Always remind your querents that the cards speak a metaphorical language, not a literal one. If you feel that you simply must say something about a possible health crisis, suggest that they schedule a routine physical exam, or bring their concerns to the attention of a physician.

Legal Readings

If you do tarot readings for any length of time, legal issues are certain to come up in the cards. That's because most people will find themselves before a judge at least once in their lives, for issues as routine as speeding tickets—or as traumatic as divorce and custody suits.

Most people ask yes or no questions about legal issues, and most people are satisfied with the blunt response the cards tend to offer. However, readings about legal issues involve a surprising number of emotions—especially betrayal, outrage, anxiety, and fear—so those factors also have to be incorporated in a legal tarot reading. In fact, the emotions behind a legal case may be more important than the ultimate disposition of the case. If you want a truly insightful reading, try to fine-tune your questions. You might want to ask, "What should I expect as I go into court?" "What should I know about the judge?" or "How will I look to a judge or a jury?"

When legal problems become the subject of a tarot reading, most people look for the Justice card—which is obviously the most "legal" card in the deck. Not surprisingly, it's one card that will usually show up in a legal reading, whether you choose it as the significator or not.

In general, legal readings are also filled with swords cards. We don't challenge each other to duels anymore. Instead, we rally to the cry of "See you in court!" Swords cards reflect the legal battles that play out on the courtroom floor. The King of Swords, for example, tends to make an appearance when male attorneys are involved in a situation. Female attorneys find their counterparts in the Queen of Swords.

The Judgment card can represent individual judges, as well as juries. An especially powerful or heavy-handed judge might be represented by the Emperor card, which embodies the ultimate in controlling legal authority.

The Lovers card, oddly enough, tends to symbolize the two sides of a civil lawsuit. Many legal cases get their start when love relationships and business partnerships turn sour. A sense of betrayal and disappointment can be a powerful motivating force behind a lawsuit—and spurned lovers and former friends will often recognize their antagonists in the Devil card.

The Wheel of Fortune sometimes appears as a warning that even the most justified lawsuit is still a matter of luck. No one can predict how a judge or jury will decide a case, and the Wheel of Fortune card may suggest that you should try to settle out of court.

The wheels of justice turn slowly, and the Hanged Man card often describes the inevitable delays and postponements that are a hallmark of the justice system. In a similar vein, the Eight of Cups could indicate that the quest for justice will be long and arduous, while the Four of Swords could also suggest long periods of time in which a case is at a standstill.

The Tower could portend a sudden and dramatic end to the case: a judge's ruling by default, or a settlement. That message could be reinforced if you get the Ace of Swords—in a legal reading, it's a clear indicator that the long arm of the law is coming your way.

The Moon is the classic card of deception. It's not one you necessarily want to see in a legal reading, because it could mean that trickery and deceit are in play. Still, forewarned is forearmed, and it's better to know that your opponents have a few tricks up their sleeves. Be doubly prepared for that possibility if you get the Five or Seven of Swords.

There are some clear "victory" cards in the tarot. The Sun and the World, for example, would usually suggest that you can look forward with optimism to the conclusion of a case. The Four of Wands, Six of Wands, and Three of Cups also point to a celebration.

On the other hand, you might want to prepare for legal disappointments if you get the Four of Cups, Five of Cups, Three of Swords, or Five of Pentacles.

Meanwhile, anyone who has ever had to write checks to an attorney or pore over legal documents will recognize their fate in the Five, Seven, Nine, and Ten of Wands. Most will also be familiar with the sleepless nights, worry, and anxiety depicted in the Nine of Swords.

Court cards in a court reading can be very good. Pages can represent positive news and messages regarding a case. Knights could symbolize witnesses, court officials, and attorneys who are willing to fight on your behalf. Queens and Kings could represent powerful personages administering decisions in your favor.

Obviously, people who are involved in legal issues want to know if they will "win." Unfortunately, almost no one really "wins" a court case: there are always costs, both in terms of legal fees and in terms of wear and tear on the soul. Ask questions, instead, that get to the heart of the issue, such as, "How will I feel when this case concludes?" "Will I be satisfied with the outcome of this case?" or "Will I feel vindicated?"

There is one important caveat to keep in mind when you do legal tarot readings: if you aren't a lawyer, don't give anyone legal advice. Make it clear that your role as a tarot reader is to offer insight and illumination—not strategic legal counsel. While you can use the cards to help other people deal emotionally and spiritually with legal issues, you should absolutely *insist* that your clients consult more than cards before they make decisions that could affect them in court. If your clients don't have legal representation, give them the names and numbers of a few good attorneys to make it perfectly clear that you're not in the business. It would be a shame to wind up in court yourself as the result of a tarot reading.

When Readings Don't Make Sense

Unfortunately, the cards aren't always easy to interpret, for any number of reasons. Sometimes the question might be poorly phrased. Sometimes you might ask a question based on what you think the situation is, only to find out later that your assumptions were incorrect. And sometimes, there simply is no answer to the question you seek: you'll simply have to wait and see how events will unfold.

There are any number of reasons that a tarot reading won't make sense—even for experienced, professional tarot readers.

- Maybe your question wasn't clear enough.
- Maybe you're too close to the question.
- Maybe you've asked the same question too many times.
- Maybe you aren't meant to know the answer.
- Maybe there is no answer, because events are still very much in flux.
- Maybe you're trying to force the answer one way or another.

- Maybe the cards are telling you about an issue that's more important. Sometimes you'll ask a question about work, for example, but all the cards you turn up seem to relate to love. In that case, that's the issue that needs to be addressed.

- Maybe you were distracted.

- Maybe you're taking the issue too seriously, and the cards are talking nonsense to distract you.

- Maybe the cards are for someone else in the room. Clear the room of bystanders. Shuffle and try again.

- Maybe your sense of time is off. Maybe the reading will make perfect sense in the future. If you start telling a childless woman about her children, for example, or find yourself describing a non-existent husband, your might want to ask your querents to keep the information in mind anyway, in case it will apply to them someday.

What Can You Do?

The cards are rarely wrong—but there are any number of ways to misinterpret them, and even experienced tarot readers can easily get off track.

- If the cards don't make sense when you first try to read them, try to rephrase the question. Make your inquiry as specific as you can.

- You can also narrow the focus of your reading. Try a one-card reading, and ask for a card that will show you only what you need to know.

- Ask for an advice card rather than an answer card.

- Reframe the time frame.

- Throw a clarification card or two on top of any cards that leave you confused.

- And if nothing seems to work, try the reading on another day, or if the question can wait, in a week or two.

Psychic Readings

Fortunetelling with tarot cards is an intuitive art. Whether or not you consider yourself a natural-born psychic, regular practice with the cards will help you hone and refine your sixth sense. Even if you don't believe in psychic ability, tarot cards will free you to discover, trust, and explore your own intuition.

A number of psychic abilities are associated with tarot cards:

Precognition: Obviously, when you use tarot cards for fortunetelling, you could very well find yourself gifted with precognition—the ability to know or recognize the outcome of events that have yet to transpire.

Clairsentience: Many tarot readers typically describe the information that comes to them during a reading as "impressions" or "gut feelings." They simply know or sense what's going on in another place or time. On an emotional level, some people who are clairsentient can also sense what's going on with another person, or in another place, and they occasionally experience sudden flashes of insight or understanding into other people's motivations or desires.

Clairvoyance: While you might not experience full-fledged psychic visions during a tarot reading, it's not uncommon to notice that the static, two-dimensional images on tarot cards seem to shimmer, move, and come to life as you look at them.

Clairaudience: Tarot cards seem to trigger such messages in some readers, who "hear" messages from the metaphysical or spirit world—most often, words or phrases that simply pop into their heads. You might also find that you seem to notice background noise, like wind, birds, and waves, or even the voice of the figure in the card.

Psychic guides: Some tarot readers believe that the unseen world of spirit directs them during readings, and that they are guided by ethereal messengers or angels.

Channeling: Sometimes, tarot readers even use the cards as a tool to help them channel messages from those guides.

Psychometry: Holding the cards triggers a psychometric connection with the person you're reading for—especially if they have held the deck, cut the cards, or shuffled.

Empathic ability: During a tarot reading you may experience emotions that aren't your own. They could stem from the person you're reading for, or the other people in their lives.

Telepathy: When you read tarot cards, you might also find that you can read minds by picking up on your querent's thoughts and concerns. For the most part, those thoughts will directly relate to the cards on the table.

No matter where your psychic strengths lie, tarot cards will automatically give your psychic powers a boost, because they make it easier to screen out distractions—which in turn can help you tune out the mundane and tune in to the metaphysical. If you'd like to hurry the process along, here are some card games and exercises you can play with to develop your psychic abilities.

Guidelines for Psychic Development

Before your begin any work with the tarot or with psychic development, keep a few ground rules in mind:

Cheer up: Make sure you feel enthusiastic, optimistic, and energized before you sit down to practice your psychic skills. Don't do any psychic work if you're tired, sick, crabby, or depressed. That's because "like attracts like"—and if you're in a funk, a psychic practice session probably won't be enough to pull you out of it. You might even compound the problem, because any number of sad, lonely spirits might decide to drop by and commiserate with you.

Stay sober: Don't practice your psychic gifts while you're under the influence of alcohol or drugs. When you get behind the wheel of psychic development, you will be operating heavy machinery—and a DUI on the metaphysical highway could have cosmic consequences.

Be alert: Don't feel pressured to add psychic development to a long list of "to-dos." These days, many people are chronically sleep-deprived, which can have the same effect on psychic ability as illness, drugs, and drinking. You might find you are as psychic as you need to be already—but you are also too tired to act on it. Maybe all you really need is a nap.

Ground yourself: Odd as it sounds, you need to be grounded physically before you can take off spiritually. So once you have caught up on your sleep, go for a brisk walk. Fill your lungs with fresh air. If you can see open sky or be near water, so much the better. If you really want to rejuvenate your spirit and indulge your senses: Listen to music. Visit a museum or an art gallery. Buy some new incense, a scented candle, or perfume. Take a long bath or shower. Eat something. For both practical and symbolic reasons, you should also drink plenty of water. If you're very metaphysical, you might think of it as increasing your receptivity. If you're more practical, you might just realize that any concentrated effort—even psychic work—can be physically draining.

Wear protection: Remember to shield yourself psychically. Most people don't head for the beach without sunblock and a T-shirt. You shouldn't scamper unprotected into the spirit world, either. If you don't yet have a shielding routine, start with the basics. Sit up straight and put both feet on the floor, so you are well-grounded in every sense of the word. Breathe slowly and deeply. Close your eyes and visualize a beam of white light coming down from the sky above you, encasing you in a protective, warm embrace. Announce your intentions in the form of a prayer or a meditation and ask for support. You might want to have the Temperance card nearby to represent your guardian angel or spirit guide.

Relax and ground: Find a relaxing grounding ritual that works for you and puts you into a semi-hypnotic trance, like a daydream. Use progressive relaxation, or deep breathing, or picture yourself in a peaceful place, your ideal reading area, a library, a lodge, in nature, or inside a favorite card.

Loosen up: The more fun you have with the cards—the more you loosen up, and roll with the impressions you get—the more accurate you're likely to be.

Don't censor yourself: Once you start reading the cards, don't censor yourself, and don't throw up barriers that could block your impressions. Even if the words and phrases that come to mind don't make sense to you, they could be clear to other people—or make themselves clearer as you go.

Trust your intuition: As you develop your psychic skills through the tarot, you might find that some people argue with your interpretations. It can be confusing. On the one hand, you'll probably sense that you're getting a clear picture of the issue at hand—but at the same time, the person you're reading for will object to everything you say, and deny every observation you make. Don't take it personally, It happens to every tarot reader. After a while, you'll probably learn that your instincts are pretty good—and that your readings are simply hitting too close to home for some people. At that point, don't argue. Agree to disagree, move on to other cards, and simply ask your querent to keep whatever you say in the back of their mind.

Come back to the real world: When your psychic session concludes, offer thanks for the insight and information you received, and then close up shop for the day. While you never need to let your psychic shield down, you can let it slip from your conscious awareness—at least until the next time you come to the tarot reader's table.

Keep records: When you conclude a reading, keep a record of your observations in your tarot journal. Later, you can go back to see where you hit and where you missed.

Psychic Practice

Sneak preview: Before you even start a reading, draw a card to see what the reading will be about. After you shuffle and spread the cards, you can also check the card on the bottom of the deck for a secret that relates to the reading.

Who's there?: You may have heard some experts suggest that you build your psychic sense by trying to guess who's calling whenever the phone rings. You can try a similar technique with tarot cards. Shuffle the deck, and try to guess which card you'll deal from the top of the deck. If choosing one card from the whole deck seems too overwhelming, improve your odds by guessing whether the card is from the minor or major arcana. You could also separate the majors from the minors, and work with one or the other. If you're working with the majors, now you'll have a 1 in 22 chance of guessing which one it is. Alternatively, you might want to guess whether you'll turn up a man or a woman, or predict which colors will be most predominant.

Read my mind games: Ask a friend to choose a card from the tarot deck. Without telling you which card it is, tell your friend to psychically transmit the name of the card to you. Alternately, ask your friend to focus on the image—or one part of the image, such as a face or a tree—while you focus on your friend. Have a blank piece of paper in front of you. Draw whatever comes to mind.

Guessing games: Draw a single card at random. Lay it face down on the table, without looking at it. You can hold one hand over the card, or lay your hand on top of the card, so you're actually touching it. Write down the impressions you receive.

Before and after: Choose a card that seems to illustrate your current situation. At random, draw one card to represent the events that led to your situation, and one card to predict how the situation will resolve itself. Tie all three cards together through a narrative.

Be the card: Imagine yourself as the figure inside the card. What would that character do in your situation?

Ask for advice: Relax and breathe deeply. Imagine that the borders of a tarot card are a doorway. Picture yourself walking through that doorway and into the card. Approach the characters in the card and ask them for a message. Talk to the figure in the card. You can imagine a dialogue, or write down your questions and wait for a response. You will probably be surprised by what you can hear.

Dreamwork: Forge new connections between your conscious and unconscious minds by using tarot cards to illustrate the dreams you've had.

Mood enhancers: When friends or family members come to you for a reading, try to gauge their mood, and choose a significator to represent their mood.

Tarot for the rich and famous: Practice reading cards about famous people and news of the day.

Biography: Look for cards that illustrate the beginning, middle, and end of each chapter in your life so far.

The more you use the cards, the more you'll be able to understand the meanings that each individual card holds for you.

Timing Techniques

Once you have a date with destiny, can you mark it on the calendar?

Sure. Just be sure to use a pencil, not a pen. Timing with tarot cards can be a tricky business.

For one thing, time doesn't exist in the cards the way it does in the real world. During a tarot reading, time takes on a dreamlike quality. Events can seem to occur simultaneously, or at random, or non-sequentially. You'll need to do some work to relate the cards to a clock or a calendar in the real world.

What's more, the further you try to project yourself into the future, the more things can change. A small change of direction—especially as the result of a tarot reading—can snowball over time, and radically affect future developments.

But there are ways to determine the timing of the events you see in the cards, and several techniques that can help your predictions stand the test of time.

Clarify your question: The simplest way to determine the timing of events is to specify a time frame in your question. Simply ask the cards what you can expect to happen in a week, a month, or a year.

The language of pictures: You can also look for time-related symbols in the cards. A prominent sun, for example, could indicate a time span of a year—the amount of time it takes for the earth to travel around the sun. A full moon might suggest that something will happen in a month, which is how long it takes the moon to cycle through all four of its phases, or move from one zodiac sign to the next.

In fact, images of all four phases of the moon could even help you pinpoint a time frame within a month: if no moon is visible, events could unfold during the new or dark phase of the moon. A crescent moon that's open on the left is a waxing moon. You'll recognize the full moon, of course, and a crescent moon that's open on the right is a waning moon.

As you look for signs and symbols of time in the cards, you might also spot images that relate to seasons—the budding flowers of spring, for example, or falling leaves of autumn. You might also see images that remind you of upcoming holidays, anniversaries, or special events.

The numbers game: If you simply want to ask when something will occur, you can add a timing card to any spread, and use the number on that card to specify a time frame. Decide in advance how you plan to read the number: a "Six" card, for example, could represent six days, six weeks, six months, or six years.

Numbers can also represent days of the week—starting with Sunday as number one—or months of the year, in which case January would be first.

Suit yourself: You can also use the suits to determine whether the numbered cards in your reading refer to days, weeks, months, or years. Try using wands cards to represent days, cups for weeks, swords for months, and pentacle cards for years.

Countdown: You can play a form of hide-and-seek to determine a time frame for your predictions. Simply shuffle the full deck and turn the cards face up, one by one, until you come to an Ace. Then count the number of cards it took you to reach the Ace. That number will represent days, weeks, or months.

The seasonal ace: Some tarot readers assign a season to each of the four aces. While individual preferences vary, the Golden Dawn correlated the Ace of Wands to summer, the Ace of Cups to fall, the Ace of Swords to spring, and the Ace of Pentacles to winter.

Time of month: The Golden Dawn also associated each of the four suits with a time of the month: pentacles represent the days of a dark or new moon, swords suggest the waxing moon, wands refer to the day of the full moon, and cups represent the days of a waning moon.

Time of day: If you're looking for a short-term answer about timing, or you'd like to pinpoint the time on a specific date, try using Golden Dawn associations. Pentacles represent the hours between midnight and morning, swords refer to the hours between sunrise and noon, wands suggest the time between noon and evening, and cups represent the time from twilight until midnight.

The Michelson Method: Teresa Michelsen, the author of *The Complete Tarot Reader*, has developed an intuitive method of associating the minor arcana suits with the seasons.

She associates the watery suit of cups with spring, because water is a reminder of spring rains, new growth, and creativity. She associates the fiery wands cards with summer, because fire is connected to the light and heat of the summer sun. She uses the airy swords cards to symbolize autumn—a season of harvest, cutting back, and preparing for winter. And she connects the earthy pentacles with winter, a time to live off the earth, quietly put down roots, and plan for the coming year.

Michelsen's method can even narrow time down to a specific week. In her system, every season is divided into thirteen weeks, which correspond to the first thirteen cards of the suit. The Kings—the last card in each suit—represent the transition between seasons.

Michelsen's method is designed to predict the timing of events that are likely to take place within the coming year. She says that any event that may take more than one year to occur—and relationship questions usually fall in that category—should be explored using another method. Also, Michelsen suggests that major arcana cards symbolize major issues or events that cannot be easily timed, while reversed cards may indicate a delay in the normal time frame.

Seasons of the zodiac: Tarot cards have long been associated with astrological signs:

- The fiery wands cards are linked to the fiery astrological signs of Aries, Leo, and Sagittarius.
- The watery cups cards are associated with the watery astrological signs of Cancer, Scorpio, and Pisces.
- The airy swords cards are connected with the airy astrological signs of Gemini, Libra, and Aquarius.
- And the earthy pentacles cards are matched with the earthy astrological signs of Taurus, Virgo, and Capricorn.

Major Arcana Assignations

All of the major arcana cards are assigned to a sign or a planet, which connects them to specific dates during the year. In this table, those dates are approximate, because the movement of the planets varies from year to year. You might need to check an ephemeris—a table of planetary positions—to verify the dates for a specific year.

Major Arcana Card	Sign or Planet	Approximate Dates
0. The Fool	Uranus, ruler of Aquarius	Aquarius: Jan. 21–Feb. 20
1. The Magician	Mercury, ruler of Gemini and Virgo	Gemini: May 21–June 20 Virgo: Aug. 21–Sept. 20
2. The High Priestess	The Moon, ruler of Cancer	Cancer: June 21–July 20
3. The Empress	Venus, ruler of Taurus and Libra	Taurus: April 21–May 20 Libra: Sept. 21–Oct. 20
4. The Emperor	Aries, ruled by Mars	Aries: March 21–April 20
5. The Hierophant	Taurus, ruled by Venus	Taurus: April 21–May 20
6. The Lovers	Gemini, ruled by Mercury	Gemini: May 21–June 20
7. The Chariot	Cancer, ruled by the Moon	Cancer: June 21–July 20
8. Strength	Leo, ruled by the Sun	Leo: July 21–Aug. 20
9. The Hermit	Virgo, ruled by Mercury	Virgo: Aug. 21–Sept. 20
10. The Wheel of Fortune	Sagittarius, ruled by Jupiter	Sagittarius: Nov. 21–Dec. 20
11. Justice	Libra, ruled by Venus	Libra: Sept. 21–Oct. 20
12. The Hanged Man	Neptune, ruler of Pisces	Pisces: Feb. 21–March 20
13. Death	Scorpio, ruled by Pluto	Scorpio: Oct. 21–Nov. 20
14. Temperance	Sagittarius, ruled by Jupiter	Sagittarius: Nov. 21–Dec. 20
15. The Devil	Capricorn, ruled by Saturn	Capricorn: Dec. 21–Jan. 20
16. The Tower	Mars, ruler of Aries	Aries: March 21–April 20
17. The Star	Aquarius, ruled by Uranus	Aquarius: Jan. 21–Feb. 20
18. The Moon	Pisces, ruled by Neptune	Pisces: Feb. 21–March 20
19. The Sun	The Sun, ruler of Leo	Leo: July 21–Aug. 20
20. Judgment	Pluto, ruler of Scorpio	Scorpio: Oct. 21–Nov. 20
21. The World	Saturn, ruler of Capricorn	Capricorn: Dec. 21–Jan. 20

Days of the Week: You can connect some tarot cards to days of the week, based on their associations with the planets that rule each day.

Major Arcana Cards	Day of the Week	Planetary Connection
The High Priestess and the Chariot	Monday	The Moon
The Hierophant and the Tower	Tuesday	Mars
The Magician and the Hermit	Wednesday	Mercury
The Wheel of Fortune and Temperance	Thursday	Jupiter
The Empress and Justice	Friday	Venus
The Devil and the Universe	Saturday	Saturn
Strength and the Sun	Sunday	The Sun

Minor Arcana Assignations

Like the major arcana cards, minor arcana cards are also associated with dates. In fact, the court cards are linked to specific thirty-degree segments on a horoscope wheel, while the pip cards are linked to specific ten-degree decantes.

Court Cards	Minor Arcana Cards	Zodiac Degrees	Approximate Dates
Queen of Wands	10 of Cups	20–30° Pisces	March 11–March 20
	2 of Wands	0–10° Aries	March 21–March 30
	3 of Wands	10–20° Aries	March 31–April 10
Knight of Pentacles	4 of Wands	20–30° Aries	April 11–April 20
	5 of Pentacles	0–10° Taurus	April 21–April 30
	6 of Pentacles	10–20° Taurus	May 1–May 10
King of Swords	7 of Pentacles	20–30° Taurus	May 11–May 20
	8 of Swords	0–10° Gemini	May 21–May 31
	9 of Swords	10–20° Gemini	June 1–June 10
Queen of Cups	10 of Swords	20–30° Gemini	June 11–June 20
	2 of Cups	0–10° Cancer	June 21–July 1
	3 of Cups	10–20° Cancer	July 2–July 11

	4 of Cupss	20–30° Cancer	July 12–July 21
Knight of Wands	5 of Wands	0–10° Leo	July 22–August 1
	6 of Wands	10–20° Leo	August 2–August 11
	7 of Wands	20–30° Leo	August 12–August 22
King of Pentacles	8 of Pentacles	0–10° Virgo	August 23–September 1
	9 of Pentacles	10–20° Virgo	September 2–September 11
	10 of Pentacles	20–30° Virgo	September 12–September 22
Queen of Swords	2 of Swords	0–10° Libra	September 23–October 2
	3 of Swords	10–20° Libra	October 3–October 12
	4 of Swords	20–30° Libra	October 13–October 22
Knight of Cups	5 of Cups	0–10° Scorpio	October 23–November 1
	6 of Cups	10–20° Scorpio	November 2–November 12
	7 of Cups	20–30° Scorpio	November 13–November 22
King of Wands	8 of Wands	0–10° Sagittarius	November 23–December 2
	9 of Wands	10–20° Sagittarius	December 3–December 12
	10 of Wands	20–30° Sagittarius	December 13–December 21
Queen of Pentacles	2 of Pentacles	0–10° Capricorn	December 22–December 30
	3 of Pentacles	10–20° Capricorn	December 31–January 9
	4 of Pentacles	20–30° Capricorn	January 10–January 19
Knight of Swords	5 of Swords	0–10° Aquarius	January 20–January 29
	6 of Swords	10–20° Aquarius	January 30–February 8
	7 of Swords	20–30° Aquarius	February 9–February 18
King of Cups	8 of Cups	0–10° Pisces	February 19–February 28
	9 of Cups	10–20° Pisces	March 1–March 10

Turn the page: The pages don't have astrological attributions, but some people use them to represent the four seasons. Typically, the Page of Wands represents spring, the Page of Cups represents summer, the Page of Swords represents autumn, and the Page of Pentacles represents winter.

The Cards

0. The Fool (The Unnumbered Card)

Fools rush in where angels fear to tread

Don't be fooled. The Fool is anything but foolish—and he could even be the most important card in the entire deck.

In the classic Waite design, a young man stands at the top of a cliff, eyes turned toward heaven, apparently unaware of the fact that he's standing on the edge of oblivion. He simply follows his heart and trusts that his feet will carry him wherever he needs to go. In fact, according to one mystical tradition that equates the Fool with the element of air, he won't fall when he steps off the cliff. Instead he'll float, or fly, or soar on the wings of his imagination.

The Fool wears a feather in his cap, which is a sign of honor and accomplishment, as well as a symbol of the air he represents. He also wears a colorful tunic, emblazoned with orange circles that represent the spheres of the Kabbalistic Tree of Life. He cinches his tunic with a belt made up of the seven planets of ancient astrology, which in turn correspond to the seven days of the week. He holds a rose in his left hand, symbolizing passion. He balances a walking stick in his right hand, and he has tied a pouch to the end of the stick, like a hobo.

Some tarot readers say the Fool's bag holds memories, lessons, and souvenirs of a previous life—which makes it, in effect, karmic baggage. Still others suggest that the Fool's bag contains the breath of life, which he uses to animate the world around him. Some say the bag contains tokens from the four suits of the minor arcana—a wand, a cup, a sword, and a pentacle—which will serve as tools for his journey. Some even say he's got a whole tarot deck in there.

The little white dog nipping at his heels is a loyal companion, defender, and guide whose warning bark can save lives. The dog often represents instinct, a primal form of intuition. Sometimes, the little dog also symbolizes the conscience. He could even symbolize the societal mores that reign in our most outlandish behavior.

The mountains in the distance represent obstacles to be overcome, new heights to be scaled, new challenges, and the promise of accomplishment. A bright white sun fills the corner of the card, flooding the scene with the light and energy of a higher power—guidance from a consciousness that's greater than our own.

In the Llewellyn Tarot, the Fool is Peredur—the Welsh version of Percival, the original hero in the quest for the Holy Grail. He carries his belongings in a fool's bag, too—but he's not traveling on foot. Instead, he rides a horse, a longstanding symbol of freedom, power, independence, and movement. With his cape flying in the air behind him, the Fool guides his horse in a heroic leap across a raging waterfall, traveling from shadow into light. The Fool's dog makes the jump from one rocky cliff to another, too; he is a loyal companion who never leaves his master's side. Beneath them, in the crashing roar of the waterfall, there's a prism of luminescent color. In a single bound, all three are flying over the rainbow, crossing a bridge from everyday reality into a world of magic and mystery.

In the Crowley deck, the Fool is garbed in green, symbolizing his youth—like the Green Man, the spirit of spring, or Percival, the young knight who sought the Holy Grail. He holds symbols of all four suits: in addition to a pinecone, there's a wand of fire in his left hand, a cup of water in his right, and a sword of air and a bag of stones slung over his shoulder. The stones, which symbolize the suit of pentacles, are engraved with astrological glyphs of the planets and signs.

Crowley's Fool is standing in the Nile River, the ancient cradle of civilization, surrounded by a spiral of cosmic energy that begins and ends at his heart—very much like the wreath that surrounds the dancer in the last card of the major arcana, the World. The spiraling shape of that energy symbolizes the shape of the universe. (It also happens to look a lot like the number zero.) There are several mystic creatures caught in the spiral: the vulture of Maat, the Egyptian goddess of wisdom and judgment, the dove of Venus, twin infants, and a butterfly, a symbol of transformation.

The Fool also wears a fool's cap, filled with the white light of heaven, and the horns of Bacchus, the Roman god of wine. It's no coincidence that he holds a bunch of grapes, too, symbolizing fruitfulness, celebration, and inebriation. The sun covering his groin—the Fool's root chakra—symbolizes his creative potential. There is an alligator at his feet: it's Sebek, an ancient Egyptian god of fertility, creation, and destruction. There's also a tiger biting his left leg, which is a throwback to very early versions of the Fool card.

The Fool's Journey

The Fool represents all of us—naïve travelers through life, off on a grand adventure, ready and willing to experience whatever the cards have in store. If you're looking for a standard significator, the Fool is always a good choice.

The Fool is the only unnumbered card in the deck, so he's never tethered to any one place in the cards. Instead, he's free to wander in and out of the major and minor arcana. He's the happy wanderer, too, free to step into new roles and situations, free to experiment with various personas, and free to experience all that life has to offer.

In the Fool's Journey, each card represents a separate stage of the journey, and depicts an experience of growth and transformation.

To see the Fool's Journey at a glance, divide the numbered major arcana cards into three rows of seven cards each. The three rows depict three stages of life: youth, maturity, and mastery.

First row:

As children, most of us first learn the basics of our physical existence—and like the Magician, we learn how our movements and our will can change the world around us. We also learn to relate to our parents, the Empress and the Emperor, as well as teachers and other authority figures, like the Hierophant. As we reach adolescence, we start to think of ourselves as Lovers, and we steer a course for adulthood, like the Charioteer.

Second row:

As young adults, we master other life lessons: we find the courage and strength to face our fears and insecurities. We learn to stand on our own two feet, like the Hermit. We experience the cyclical nature of luck and fortune, as well as the inevitable struggle for equanimity and Justice. Most of us also learn that we will be expected to make sacrifices like the Hanged Man, face Death in its many forms, and find balance in Temperance.

Third row:

The older we get, the more complex our lessons become. We learn that we must face our demons—the dark and shadowy world of the Devil—and we experience the dramatic, unexpected shakeups of the Tower. At the same time, however, we master the bright side: we learn to find guidance and support in the luminaries of the Star, the Moon, and the Sun. We learn to forgive and find new life, through Judgment. And we learn that the cycles—and the lessons—repeat themselves, and that every ending leads to a World of new beginnings.

Most of us don't necessarily experience the Fool's Journey in exactly the order of the cards. Instead, we tend to shuffle our way through the deck—skipping over some cards, moving quickly through others, or repeating the experiences and lessons we fail to master on our first go-round.

What Does Your Future Hold?

- Waite called the Fool the spirit in search of experience. When the Fool appears in your tarot reading, you could be on the verge of a grand new adventure—and maybe even the experience of a lifetime. You've started your own Fool's Journey toward experience, understanding, and ultimate enlightenment; now you stand on the precipice of another phase of that journey. The Fool card signals that you're now willing and able to take a leap of faith, to put theory into practice, and plunge, body and soul, into a new life.

- Experience, as they say, is the best teacher, and you might also find yourself learning new lessons. Of course, there's always a chance that you could be embarking on a fool's errand—a fruitless mission or an impossible task. Just to be on the safe side, you might want to look before you take that proverbial leap.

- You might also want to explore what it means to you to be a fool. Obviously, we can all appreciate the fool as an entertainer and a comedian. We all enjoy watching the antics of other fools. However, we dread being called fools ourselves. We resent it when other people make a fool out of us. And more often than we care to admit, we suspect that we really are fools, and that it's just a matter of time until we are found out.

- Back during the time of kings and castles, the fool was the inverse counterpart to the king. While everything the king said was automatically the rule of law, everything the fool said was a joke. Fools had no social status, no respect, and no place in high society. They were simpletons, beggars, the objects of mockery and abuse. And yet, they were sometimes the only people who could speak truth to power, concealing their wisdom in the form of a jest. A fool could confront the king when his advisors couldn't speak freely. When the Fool appears in your reading, you may be called upon to play the part of the wise fool, one who is in the exclusive position of confronting and challenging authority.

- Some people think of the Fool as the first and last card in the major arcana—like the Greek letters Alpha and Omega, the Fool represents both the beginning and the end. In that light, the Fool can be a poignant reminder that when one chapter of your life concludes, another begins.

- No matter how many times the Fool has run his course, he remains perpetually innocent and pure, unblemished and unspoiled by previous experience, untarnished by disappointment, and unscarred by experience. He's never concerned about his final destination. When the Fool appears in your tarot reading, it may be a signal that you need to slow down and enjoy your journey through life, too. After all, half the fun is getting there.

- It might also be time to pack your own Fool's bag of tricks, and take a trip—either literally or figuratively. You might want to visit a distant place in person, or as an armchair tourist. Either way, look into booking your passage.

- The Fool is always young and healthy, energetic and enthusiastic, so the Fool card bodes well for your physical and spiritual health.

- A lot of tarot cards hint at the possibility of pregnancy, and the Fool is one of them. That's because the image of the Fool, about to fall off the edge of the cliff, sometimes represents the soul at the moment of conception or birth, as it descends from heaven into human form.

For Future Reference

Keywords: Beginnings, innocence, freedom, spontaneity, originality, eccentricity, adventure, idealism, youth, folly, foolishness, carelessness, negligence

Reversed: Folly, foolishness, ineptitude, carelessness, stupidity, negligence, distraction, apathy

The mythic connection: The Fool has been compared to a wide range of figures from fables, myths, and stories, including Punch, Renaud the Fox (a medieval European trickster), the Coyote and Raven trickster of American Indians, the Green Man of spring, and Percival, one of King Arthur's Knights of the Round Table. The Fool could be a wise fool, a court jester, a carnival fool, the joker from a regular deck of playing cards, or a harlequin. The Fool can also be compared to any mythic character who undertakes a mission or a quest, or a hero's journey.

By the numbers: The Fool is the "zero" card. In everyday terms, most of us think of zero as a starting point, from which we count our way up—or down, into negative numbers. It's not, however, a "natural" number. We don't use zero for addition, subtraction, or any basic mathematical operations. Simply put, zero doesn't "count" for anything.

Since zero falls outside the sequence of ordinary numbers, it is unbound by rules of order. It floats freely, outside of time and place. In fact, the concept of zero implies a sort of nonexistence, a netherworld, a no man's land between presence and absence. It is the great divide, the vaporous border between two parallel universes. Zero can step into either world with equal grace and ease. It's not compelled to take its place in a lineup with other numbers.

That concept dovetails nicely with the thought of the Fool, free to come and go throughout the rest of the cards at will.

Graphically speaking, zero is shaped like the cosmic egg, the source—and the shape—of the cosmos. All told, it implies a universe in which events come full circle, all wisdom is revealed, and the Fool gets both the first and last word.

Astrological associations: The Fool is associated with Uranus, the planet of rebellion.

1. The Magician (I)

He's got a trick or two up his sleeve

In the classic Waite design, the young master of magic looks very much like his modern-day counterparts, the stage magicians who still make their way across Vegas stages and plasma TV screens. He's dramatic, larger than life, with a steely gaze and a firm resolve. He wears flowing robes that frame his handsome face and accentuate his slender frame. Magically, he even belts his tunic with an ouroboros—a snake that eats its own tail, a symbol of eternity.

Waite's Magician holds his right hand high over his head, and points his left hand down toward the earth, illustrating the philosophic principal "as above, so below." That's the theory that life on the physical and material plane is a mere reflection of life on a higher, more spiritual level. The Magician channels cosmic energy through his body, and through the sheer force of his will, he's able to change the physical world around him.

The Magician stands under an arbor of roses and lilies, a floral motif pops up repeatedly throughout the tarot deck. It's reminiscent of a reference in the Old Testament's Song of Songs, "I am the Rose of Sharon, the lily of the valleys." In general, red roses symbolize passion, and white lilies symbolize purity. The emblems of the tarot's four suits are spread on the table before him: a wand, a cup, a sword, and a pentacle. Wands correspond to fire and spirit. Cups correspond to water and emotion. Swords correspond to air and intellect. Pentacles correspond to earth and physical existence. The figure-eight shape above his head is a lemniscate, the symbol of infinity.

In the Llewellyn Tarot, the Magician is Gwydion, a gifted storyteller from northern Wales, where storytelling is a centuries-old art form. Unfortunately, Gwydion also had a history of misusing his gifts, tricking and cheating others who believed the stories that tripped off his tongue. In the card, Gwydion stands behind a rough-hewn stone altar in the middle of a wooded glen. He had to climb at least four steps to get to that position, symbolizing his mastery of a number of elements—including earth, air, fire, and water. Those four elements are also represented by the four tools at his disposal: the hazel wand in his right hand, and the sword, pentacle, and cup on the altar in front of him. Like Waite's Magician, Gwydion's arms are perfectly balanced and aligned: his right hand is pointed toward heaven, and his left hand is pointed toward earth. His purple robes symbolize a royal, even spiritual connection. They're embroidered with golden lemniscates, which are symbols of infinity, and trimmed with feathers—a reference to his shamanistic powers and his ability to fly between worlds.

In the Crowley deck, the Magician—dubbed the Magus—stands among crisscrossing beams of energy. He juggles a double-edged sword, a teeming cup, an Anubis-shaped wand, and a glittering pentacle, along with a sheet of papyrus, a pen, and an egg with wings—a symbol of the fifth element, ether. His feet have wings, like Mercury, the Greek god of communication. He perches on a caduceus with Ibis-headed snakes, crowned by a yoni and a lingam—Hindu symbols for male and female energy. In the bottom right corner of the card, the Ape of Thoth, the Egyptian god of wisdom, represents the Magician's shadow and his constant companion.

In other tarot decks, the Magician is sometimes called the Juggler, which hearkens back to the tradition of street performers.

What Does Your Future Hold?

- When the Magician appears in a tarot reading, magical changes are coming your way. You may soon find that you have the ability to channel cosmic energy, redirect it, and change the world around you. You might even find that you're able to create an entirely new reality.

- If you sense that the Magician card refers to other people in your life, the cards could be telling you that you will be impressed and entertained by their performance—and that they might be able to teach you a trick or two in the process.

- Most magicians practice the art of misdirection. When the Magician appears in your tarot reading, it could be a sign that you should pay attention to what's going on around you—not just where you're told to look. If you're not careful, you may be surprised by someone else's sleight of hand.

- You still hold fast to your belief in magic, a willingness to suspend your disbelief and trust that magic might be real, and mystery is an integral component of your everyday world.

- Powerful and self-assured, you are willing to take fate into your own hands and perform in front of a crowd or an audience. You know the magic words. You use a magic wand as an extension of yourself.

- A real magician never tells his secrets. The Magician card could be cautioning you to keep silent on some issue.

- Magicians have a long tradition of sharing their knowledge with apprentices, and passing their wisdom along to any students who truly want to learn. The Magician could signal that you will soon find yourself in a mentoring relationship, either as master or the sorcerer's apprentice.

- The Magician is associated with Mercury, the Roman god of communication. (In Greece, Mercury was known as Hermes.) The card may be bringing you a message about your communication skills or your exchanges with other people.

- Mercury was also the Roman god of merchants, which could indicate that a sale or trade is in your near future.

For Future Reference

Keywords: Talent, skill, will, power, cunning, self-confidence

Reversed: Misuse of gifts and talents, trickery, sleight of hand

The mythic connection: The Magician is associated with Mercury, the Roman god of communication. He was the messenger of the gods—and he himself was also the god of orators, merchants, liars, and salesmen. He was also the bringer of dreams, and a psychopomp who would lead the souls of the dead into the Underworld.

The Magician has also been compared to Merlin, as well as the mountebank of the European Carnival, and the trickster god of American Indians.

By the numbers: One is the first number, so it symbolizes leadership. It's an obvious symbol of unity and singularity. The number one can even be thought of as a thesis—an original statement of thought, belief, and perception, still unchallenged by other competing ideas. One also represents the source of all existence. Ones are also connected to the ace cards: in the tarot, every numbered card in a minor arcana suit is said to originate within the ace of that suit. As such, the number one symbolizes fertility and the potential and possibility of every new beginning. That symbolism is reinforced by the graphic nature of both the Arabic numeral 1 or the Roman numeral I. Both shapes resemble phallic symbols. Even as a geometric figure, the number one is illustrated as a single point—a dot, which could represent either an egg or a sperm.

Astrological associations: Mercury was the messenger of the gods. He was also known as the legendary Trickster of mythology. Mercury, the planet of speed and communication, was named for the Roman god; in Greece, he was known as Hermes. The planet Mercury rules Gemini, the sign of communication.

2. The High Priestess (II)
Whispered secrets

The High Priestess is the keeper of secrets, a guardian of hidden wisdom, and a sentry at the gate of intuition. She knows the secrets of life, but she shares them only with the wise.

In the classic Waite design, the High Priestess sits with a crescent moon at her feet and a lunar crown on her head. Obviously, she is closely connected with the moon, the embodiment of perpetual change and evolution. She's in tune with its phases and cyclical evolution, as it waxes to full and then wanes. The front of her gown is emblazoned with a solar cross, a symbol of balance and proportion. She holds a scroll in her lap—the Torah, the Hebrew book of the law. Part of the scroll, however, is hidden beneath her cloak, to show that some truths cannot be spoken. The High Priestess is also seated between two columns—one black, one white—which makes her a happy medium. The columns are inscribed with a J and a B, for Joachim and Boaz, the twin Kabbalistic pillars of Severity and Mercy, destruction and creation. A temple veil is stretched between the columns, separating this world from the next. It's covered with images of palms and pomegranates, symbols of male and female fertility.

In the Llewellyn Tarot, the High Priestess is Ceridwen, the goddess of the witches. She's both the maiden and the crone of ancient myth, and her dual nature is reflected in the card's two sides: the right side of her body is old and cast in a wintry shadow, while the left is young and bathed in the sunlight of spring. She is closely connected to the earthly cycles of life, death, and rebirth. Her gown, and even her body itself, is composed of earth and leaves and grass. Instead of a traditional veil, she sits in front of an ancient web, symbolizing the mysteries that divide this world from the next. She holds a book in her lap, along with a quill crafted from the feather of a magpie. She owns the cauldron of knowledge and inspiration, which is constantly filling and refilling itself and flooding the world with new life. According to legend, the poet Taliesin received his poetic gifts from her cauldron.

In the Crowley deck, the High Priestess is hiding behind an ethereal veil. She is, however, in the process of lowering the veil, revealing her face and upper torso. Like Waite's High Priestess, she wears a lunar crown, but the rest of her figure is clothed only in light, imagery that's intended to suggest her spirit shining through. The High Priestess's unveiling movements stop at her waist. She is, and will remain, a virgin, and no one will break that seal. She even has a bow and arrow in her lap, to defend her honor if she must. There's a camel in the foreground. Because camels carry their own water through the desert, the symbol suggests that the High Priestess carries her own spirit into the material world. Other shapes—trees, flowers, and crystals—are materializing on either side of the camel. They represent fertility, creativity, and the High Priestess's ability to transform ideas into reality.

In other tarot decks, the High Priestess is sometimes called the Papess or the Female Pope.

What Does Your Future Hold?

- The High Priestess is inextricably linked with the moon, and her moods ebb and flow like the tides. She represents events of a cyclical nature. The High Priestess could suggest that you're about to find yourself responding to the gravitational push and pull of heavenly bodies—or simply the push and pull of other people in your life, heavenly or not.

- If you find yourself drawn to the moon symbols on the card, you might want to plan new projects around the phases of the moon. Each month, the sky starts out in blackness, when the moon is new. Gradually, it waxes toward full. The crescent "D"-shaped moon symbolizes those early beginning stages. When the moon is full, its cycle is at its peak—it is a time of completion, maximum effect. Gradually, it wanes, which represents closure, cleaning up loose ends, and preparation for the next cycle.

- The moon also symbolizes the cycle of a woman's body, as well as the predictable physical effect of pregnancy, as a woman moves from thin, to round, and back to thin again.

- For the High Priestess, life is an open book—or an open scroll, depending on the artist's interpretation. In many renditions of the card, you can even read the title on the High Priestess's book: TORA. Some people read that title as part of the word "Torah," the Jewish holy book. Others point out that the word is an anagram of "tarot." The High Priestess's book might be a Book of Shadows—a magical diary of rituals, spells, recipes, and records. In any case, when the High Priestess appears in your reading, you might want to find a good book to read—or write your own, in the form of a journal, a memoir, a guidebook, a handbook, poetry, or prayer.

- When the High Priestess shows up in a tarot reading, it may be time to turn to wise counsel in your own life—a trusted teacher, a spiritual leader, an advisor—or anyone who might be found with a book in her hand.

- The High Priestess is a symbol of female spiritual authority. She moves easily and silently between the worlds. She symbolizes psychic ability, intuition, and oracular skills. When she shows up in a tarot reading, you can be assured that your intuition is also on the mark. You can trust your instincts. You should also pay attention to signs and symbols that pop up in your everyday life—whether they are omens of good fortune or red flags of warning and concern.

- In most tarot decks, the High Priestess wears a Mona Lisa smile—one that's knowing, wise, almost teasing. She has mastered the wise woman's maxim: to know, to will, to dare, and to keep silent. She's a powerful reminder that you should share your wisdom, experience, knowledge, and expertise only with those who seek your insights.

- The High Priestess knows when to stop talking. Many people are afraid of silence, but silence can be a powerful tool. It can help you gather knowledge and information, as others rush to fill the void in conversation.

- Staying quiet can also help you keep your plans and preparation on track; don't dissipate your energy, don't dispel your focus, don't open yourself up to criticism and critique before you are ready to put your plans into action. Your plans and ideas are like the seeds in the pomegranate. Expose them to the elements only when they're ready, and plant them in fertile soil that can help them take root and thrive.

- The High Priestess is a keeper of secrets. Like a faithful confidant or confessor, the High Priestess is sworn to uphold the confidentiality of her clients. So, too, are tarot readers. When you get the High Priestess in a tarot card reading, you may find that the card represents you in your role as a keeper of secrets.

For Future Reference

Keywords: Secrets, mystery, the unrevealed future, silence, tenacity, mystery, wisdom, science

Reversed: Passion, moral or physical ardor, conceit, surface knowledge

The mythic connection: In early decks, the High Priestess was sometimes depicted as Juno, complete with a peacock companion, to avoid offending the Catholic Church. In other decks, she was a priestess of Isis. The High Priestess is also connected to the vestal virgins of ancient Greece, the Sybil oracles, and all of the goddesses of the moon. Historically, the High Priestess has been compared to a high priestess of the Eleusinian Mysteries, an annual celebration of the mysteries of death and rebirth as related in the story of Demeter and Persephone. The High Priestess has also been associated with Sister Manfreda, the Visconti Papess who was supposed to usher in a feminist new age for the Italian Catholic church. She didn't fulfill that mission: instead, she was burned at the stake in 1300. She has also been compared to Pope Joan, the legendary woman who disguised herself as a man and ascended to the highest position in the church—until her true sex was revealed when she reportedly gave birth on the steps of the Vatican.

By the numbers: Twos represent duality, like the black and white pillars behind the High Priestess. They may stand in opposition to each other. They may be complementary, and work together as partners, or oppose each other as adversaries. The Roman numeral "II" on many renditions of the cards looks like the two pillars that stand behind her. It also looks like female genitalia—the gateway to life when a child is born.

Astrological associations: The High Priestess is associated with the Moon, the luminous orb of cyclical change and reflection. The Moon rules Cancer, the sign of home and family.

3. The Empress (III)

Mother Nature

The Empress picks up where the High Priestess leaves off, nurturing and protecting all of nature's creations.

In the classic Waite design, the Empress is visibly pregnant. She is the archetypal mother of all creation—the creative life force, and the loving, caring nurturer. She sits in a meadow-like garden of green trees and vegetation, like the earth goddess Demeter of ancient Greece. Her garden is a refuge and a paradise. She is young, blonde, and beautiful. There's a heart-shaped shield with the symbol of Venus next to her, representing the planet of love and attraction. She also holds a scepter with a globe, a symbol of her earthly realm. The waterfall in the background symbolizes her connection to life, fertility, and emotional well-being.

In the Llewellyn Tarot, the Empress is Rhiannon, the fairy goddess who married a mortal. She first appeared to her future husband riding on a white horse, like the one carved into the back of her throne. He chased her down, but he wasn't able to catch her until he finally asked her to stop. Several birds, the messengers of air, were her constant companions; according to her legend, they could wake the dead and lull the living into a dream. Sadly, Rhiannon is also associated with a measure of grief. Her infant son was kidnapped, and until he was recovered she was unfairly blamed for his disappearance. Her shield is inscribed with two swans, symbols of love and fidelity.

In the Crowley deck, the Empress wears a crown that reflects three phases of the moon—waxing and waning crescent moons, set on either side of a full moon. She herself sits between two larger moons, one waxing, one waning. The Empress's moons symbolize the cycles of life and creation, as well as the shape of a pregnant woman's body as she carries a child and then gives birth. The lunar imagery is also a subtle nod to Isis, the ancient Egyptian goddess who was honored for her fidelity in marriage. She holds a blooming lotus in her right hand, a symbol of fertility because of its thick stem and its receptive, open petals. Two sacred birds perch on her throne—the sensuous sparrow of Aphrodite and the pure white dove of the Holy Spirit. In front of her, there's a pelican, which once was believed to feed its young with its own blood. The Empress also has a belt decorated with astrological glyphs, and a shield with a double white eagle, an alchemical symbol of transformation and rebirth.

What Does Your Future Hold?

- While the Empress is the mother of us all, she also symbolizes fertility for individuals, too. When she shows up in a tarot reading, pregnancy is a definite possibility.

- If you're not in a position to physically give birth to a child, the Empress often refers to enhanced creativity in work or artistic pursuits.

- The Empress is closely connected to concepts of love, marriage, and motherhood. In a tarot reading, the Empress often relates to your relationship with your mother or your children.

- Because we can assume that the Empress is married to the Emperor, the next card in the major arcana, she symbolizes partnership, joint efforts, shared aspirations, and common goals, hopes, and dreams.

- Pay attention to the river of emotion and intuition that flows through the Empress card. In the card, that river helps her cleanse herself of the energy and emotions of others. Picture the same thing happening to you when you're doing tarot readings for other people: let energy flow through you, and release it back into the universe when you're through.

- Venus rules the sign of Taurus, a sign that appreciates comfort, luxury, and the finer things in life. When the Empress appears in a reading, you might be concerned with issues relating to your home: furnishings, decor, color and fabric, or you might be dealing with acquiring and maintaining possessions.

- You may be working with a Taurus person. Taurus is the sign of the bull ... and bulls are stubborn. The card could portend a period of stubbornness, or issues with stubborn people.

- Taurus is very connected to home, so the card could indicate a period of nesting, entertaining, or caring for others in the comfort of your home.

- The Empress card sometimes suggests that your question or concern will come to fruition in about nine months from its conception—the length of an average pregnancy.

- Because of the Taurus connection, you might also be looking at events that will take place in May, the Taurus month.

For Future Reference

Keywords: Beauty, happiness, pleasure, success, comfort, creativity, fruitfulness, pregnancy, abundance, sensuality

Reversed: Stubbornness, laziness

The mythic connection: The Empress is associated with Venus, the goddess of love; Juno, the wife of Jupiter; Hera, the wife of Zeus; and just about every other married or pregnant deity, including Freya, Ishtar, Isis, Gaia, Rhea, Demeter, Brigid, Inanna, and even Kali. You might also know her as Mother Earth, Mother Nature, Eve, or the Virgin Mary.

By the numbers: Threes symbolize creation—the result of two separate forces combining to create a third entity. A mother and a father produce a child together. A thesis and an antithesis combine to produce a synthesis. The number three can also represent body, mind, and spirit, or past, present, and future. Many religions believe in a holy trinity, such as Father, Son, and Holy Spirit; Maiden, Mother, and Crone; or the triple goddess of the New, Full, and Old Moon.

Astrological associations: The Empress is associated with Venus, the planet of love and romance. Venus rules Taurus, the earthy sign of stability and material comforts. On an astrological chart, Taurus rules the second house—the house of home and family.

4. The Emperor (IV)
Father figure

The Emperor is an authority figure. He's the archetypal protector and provider who rules the civilized world.

In the classic Waite design, the Emperor sits on a cubic throne of solid stone—the essence of structure and stability. The armrests and the back of his throne are carved with rams' heads, which symbolize his Aries-style leadership and drive. He wears a jeweled crown and a long white beard, like a figure in a child's drawing of God. Underneath his velvet robes, he's wearing a full suit of armor, which means he is always ready to rise up, protect, and defend his empire. His scepter, the symbol of his rulership and authority, is shaped like a crux ansata, a symbol of life that dates back to ancient Egypt. He also holds a globe in his left hand, like a scale model of his dominion. While the Empress held court in a lush and fertile garden, the Emperor rules from a stern and austere desert landscape, surrounded by mountains and made livable with only the slightest hint of rivers and streams in the background.

In the Llewellyn Tarot, the Emperor is Bran the Blessed, the legendary giant king. His red robes symbolize his potency and Aries-style leadership and drive. He too is armored for battle, and protected by a prominent shield. According to legend, he could wade across seas, and at one point he laid down across a river so that his army could use his body as a bridge. After his death, his men cut off his head and kept it with them; it told stories, offered guidance, and protected them from the harsh realities of life for eighty-seven years.

In the Crowley deck, the Emperor is predominantly red, like his ruling planet Mars, which symbolizes energy and aggression. (The red also serves as a complement to the blue of the Empress's card.) This Emperor is flanked by rams' heads, too, and a third ram's head is mounted on the scepter in his right hand. In his left hand, he holds an orb with a Maltese cross. His right leg is folded across his left, in the shape of the numeral 4, the number of the card. It's also a lot like the alchemical symbol for sulfur, which makes it a reference to the Emperor's fiery, masculine energy. The bees embroidered on his tunic symbolize the structure and routine of a colony. There is a lamb at his feet—a baby lamb that could also be a sacrificial animal—as well as a shield with the double eagle that symbolized the Holy Roman Empire.

What Does Your Future Hold?

- The Emperor is the epitome of leadership. He is a mighty ruler—the king of the world. Emperors rule more than a kingdom: they rule an empire. They have vision. They know how to delegate their authority, form alliances, and measure allegiances. When the Emperor card shows up in a tarot reading, it could indicate that your leadership ability will soon be put to the test. Either that, or you may find yourself in an encounter with a strong authoritative figure.

- The Emperor is also a father figure, which could indicate that you will be dealing with your father, or serving as a father figure for someone else.

- The Emperor is associated with Aries, the first sign of the zodiac. For that reason, Aries is often called the leader of the zodiac—and there is no clearer leader than the Emperor. The connection is even designed into the card: his throne is often embellished with rams' heads, the symbolic icon of Aries. In a tarot reading, the Emperor card could be referring to your leadership skills and abilities.

- Aries rules the first house of the zodiac, which is the natural domain of the self: ego, identity, first impressions, physical appearance. The Emperor's appearance in a tarot reading could indicate that you are strong and self-assured—and that you probably don't realize what a strong first impression you make.

- Aries rules the head, which would tend to indicate that you are a thinker. You're logical and intelligent, and you rule mostly with your head, rather than your heart.

- The Emperor and the Empress don't necessarily symbolize marriage, but they do represent a kindred spirit. While the Empress sits in a lush, green garden, the Emperor sits in an arid desert. Obviously, opposites attract.

- The Emperor is clearly virile, and his masculinity is a suitable counterpart to the Empress's fertility. Symbolically, that makes the Emperor a seminal thinker, too.

- The Emperor also sits on a throne that looks hard and unyielding—and he seems perfectly comfortable on the unforgiving platform. His cube-shaped throne is a symbol of stability.

For Future Reference

Keywords: Stability, power, control, dominion, authority, protection, reason, logic, confidence, war, conquest, victory, strife, ambition, leadership, power

Reversed: Tyranny, abuse or misuse of power, poor leadership

The mythic connection: The Emperor is often compared to the Greek god Zeus or the Roman god Jupiter. Historically, he's related to other, real-life emperors, like Charlemagne, Jason, Alexander the Great, Napoleon, and Caesar.

By the numbers: Fours symbolize structure, stability, and security, because four points come together to form a solid. There are four walls in a room, and four corners to a house. There are four dimensions: width, length, height, and time. There are four cardinal directions: north, south, east, and west. There are four seasons, four winds, and four phases of the moon. There are four elements, and four corresponding suits in the minor arcana.

Astrological associations: Aries is the first sign of the zodiac, so those who are born with a prominent Aries in their natal charts are natural-born leaders. They have a lot in common with the Emperor: they are commanding, forceful, bold, courageous, and confident. Like the Aries ram—an integral part of many Emperor cards—they can also be headstrong. Aries is ruled by Mars, the red planet of action and aggression, war and self-defense. In the tarot, Mars is associated with the Tower card, which offers one illustration of the Emperor's warlike nature. The Aries association could mean that your question will be answered during the month of March.

5. The Hierophant (V)
Holy father

The Hierophant—the head of a religious hierarchy, like the pope—is a symbol of traditional authority and influence. Like the High Priestess, he serves as a spiritual link to humanity's higher powers. His focus, however, is on the theological tenets and hierarchical doctrine of external religion, while the High Priestess focuses on internal spirituality. He is exoteric; she is esoteric.

In the classic Waite design, the Hierophant card depicts a pope, wearing full vestments and a triple crown. His right hand is raised in blessing, and his left hand holds a triple cross, which symbolizes the Father, Son, and Holy Spirit. Like his spiritual counterpart, the High Priestess, the Hierophant is seated between two pillars. There are two crossed keys on the floor in front of him, symbolizing the keys to heaven. Two tonsured monks, their heads shaved as a sign of their vows, kneel at his feet. One wears a tunic with the red roses of passion, while the other wears a tunic with the white lilies of purity.

In the Llewellyn Tarot, the Hierophant is Taliesin, the bard whose heroic poetry later served as Arthurian legend. Like other bards of his time, he was a member of the intellectual elite, and he was responsible for offering historic analysis and a prophetic vision of the future. He is pictured in a mountainous rugged landscape, surrounded by standing stones that evoke the pillars in other Hierophant cards. His harp symbolizes traditional law, and a string of feathers in the background represent a shaman's flight. Just as the traditional Hierophant has a set of keys, Taliesin has a branch adorned with silver bells, the Celtic symbol of his office as a visionary, prophet, and poet.

In the Crowley deck, the Hierophant is surrounded by apocryphal creatures from the book of Revelations: an eagle, an angel, a lion, and a bull, one in each corner of the card. The four creatures symbolize the four fixed signs of the zodiac—Scorpio, Aquarius, Leo, and Taurus—as well as the four seasons, the four elements, and the apostles Matthew, Mark, Luke, and John, who wrote the first four books of the New Testament. The Hierophant is also flanked by two elephants and a bull, which are all earthy symbols of the Hierophant's sign, Taurus. He holds a key-like staff with three rings, symbolizing the past, present, and future, as well as tripartite gods—particularly the Father, Son, and Holy Spirit, although the same symbolism could also apply to god as youth, father, and sage, or maiden, mother, and crone. There's a five-pointed star on his chest that embodies a human form—his inner child, as well as Horus, the magical child of Isis and Osiris. The Hierophant himself is seated in the center of a larger pentagram that symbolizes the human body. Down at the bottom of the card, there's a spectral image of Isis, the Great Mother, who keeps perpetual watch over her son. The Hierophant's head is encircled by a halo, surrounded by a snake of kundalini energy, and touched by a dove.

In other tarot decks, the Hierophant is sometimes called the High Priest or the Pope.

What Does Your Future Hold?

- The Hierophant is very much like the Pope. He's a moral authority, a religious and spiritual leader, a pillar of the church, and an intermediary between man and God. For millions of people, the Pope is a comforting figure: they are relieved to find a fellow human who has the power and the ability to assure you of God's loving nature, willingness to forgive, and opportunity to begin each day as a new person.

- Some people don't like the Hierophant, and they scowl when he shows up in a tarot reading. He reminds them too much of the rigid authority symbols who dominated their lives as children—the teachers, principals, and ministers who tried to impose their hierarchical views on the young impressionable wards who were entrusted to their care. More importantly, they feel, the Hierophant symbolizes a social construct that's badly out of date, in which one-size morality was supposed to fit everyone.

- It's true that the Hierophant represents traditional religious and spiritual authority. But that tradition, in its purest form, represents the bedrock of civilization. It served generation after generation, and it still serves as the foundation for many of today's spiritual practices and beliefs. It hardly makes sense to abandon those traditions completely out of anger and disillusionment. Instead, look for ways that the Hierophant's principles can be incorporated into your own spiritual structures.

- Take, for example, the Hierophant's hand, raised in blessing. It's a simple gesture, but it's remarkable for its impact and effect. There is a simple, profound grace, both in the act of blessing and in being blessed. The Hierophant can be a sign that you have been blessed, you are about to be blessed, or that you should bless others with your gifts and talents.

- Traditionally, priests like the Hierophant have the power to perform sacraments: baptism, communion, forgiveness and reconciliation, confirmation, marriage, holy orders, and last rites. When the Hierophant appears in a tarot reading, any of those sacraments may be on the horizon—but marriage is especially indicated. Not only are most weddings performed by ordained clergy, but the Hierophant's blessing refers to society's blessing on couples who follow traditional marriage and family structures.

- The Hierophant can also suggest that you may be involved in a hierarchical system. You may be in a position of authority—a committee chairmanship, or a promotion at work, or entrusted with responsibility of mentoring and teaching others.

- When the Hierophant appears in a reading, it might symbolize a new course of formal study, or a return to your religious and spiritual traditions.

- The Hierophant is a spiritual authority, but his authority is based on written tradition and formal study, as opposed to oral tradition and informal training that distinguishes him from intuitive counselors who model themselves after the High Priestess. The Hierophant often represents licensed teachers, academics, priests, and psychologists.

For Future Reference

Keywords: Education, knowledge, hierarchies, social and religious institutions, conservative values, discipline, social conventions, tradition, formality, groups, conformity, orthodoxy, obedience, blessing, marriage, alliance, assembly, servitude, mercy and goodness, society, social contracts and agreements, tradition, theology

Reversed: Judgmental attitudes, intolerance, criticism, fear, guilt

The mythic connection: Historically, a hierophant was the high priest of Eleusinian Mysteries, an ongoing ritual celebration of death and rebirth in ancient Greece. When Christianity began to spread, church leaders condemned the mysteries, but the rites continued for hundreds of years and greatly influenced early Christian teachings and practices.

By the numbers: Fives symbolize the five senses, the five points on a star, and the five vowels in the English alphabet. Some metaphysicians suggest that five is important because it symbolizes a fifth element—Spirit.

Astrological associations: The Hierophant card, like the Empress, is associated with the astrological sign of Taurus. Step into any traditional church, and you're likely to find reminders of Taurus sensibilities everywhere you look. Carved furnishings, larger-than-life sculpture, and jewel-toned stained glass all suit Taurus's sensuous tastes. Like the church, people with a strong Taurus sign also value faithfulness, monogamy, and procreation. The sign is usually represented by a bull—a solid, earthy creature that's incorporated in many versions of the Hierophant card. Taurus is ruled by Venus, the planet of love and romance. In the tarot, Venus is assigned to the Empress card. When the Hierophant and the Empress appear together in a tarot reading, like a minister and his church, they offer a powerful message of dedication and devotion.

6. The Lovers (VI)
All the world loves a lover

While an appearance by this couple could encourage any hopeless romantic, the Lovers card also signifies a choice to be made between two equally strong desires. The Lovers card illustrates the twin principles of opposition and attraction.

In the classic Waite design, Adam and Eve stand naked and unashamed in the Garden of Eden, in front of two trees—the Tree of Life on the right, and the Tree of Knowledge of Good and Evil on the left. The serpent of temptation is winding his way up the Tree of Knowledge, whispering seductively in Eve's ear. You know how the story goes: one bite of the forbidden fruit will ultimately open their eyes to knowledge and understanding, and Adam and Eve won't be able to live in blissful ignorance much longer. Soon they'll be forced to leave Eden with nothing but the new clothes on their backs. For now, however, they are still under the watchful guardianship and protection of Raphael, one of four archangels in the tarot. In fact, he almost seems to be sheltering them from the overwhelming radiance of the sun, which in this case is a symbol of God.

In the Llewellyn Tarot, the Lovers card depicts the Roman Emperor Macsen Wledig and his bride Helen. The emperor first saw her in a dream, and then he dispatched men to travel far and wide—up a river, across a sea, and through mountains—to find her. It took three years, but eventually Macsen Wledig did find her. Long stretches of Roman road, still known as "Helen's Highway," were built during her reign. The card pays homage to Waite's design, too, with a guardian angel, a serpent, and a Tree of Life embroidered on the drapes in the background.

In the Crowley deck, a dark king is married to a light queen, symbolizing the union of opposites. The king holds a lance, while the queen holds a grail—two not-so-veiled symbols of the union of a man and a woman. The children who attend them are also black and white, and they too hold symbols of their undeveloped masculine and feminine qualities: flowers and a club. The king's red lion is a symbol of creative will, and the queen's white eagle represents the eternal feminine. A cloaked and hooded hermit presides over their wedding, raising his arms to shelter and bless the couple. Eros, the Greek god of love and desire, hovers above them like Cupid, about to release one of his arrows. He is flanked by Eve and Lilith, who was said to have been Adam's rebellious first wife. The entire group is positioned under a canopy of swords, a symbol of division; love and marriage is humanity's way of trying to overcome the curse of separation and loneliness.

What Does Your Future Hold?

- Most people see the Lovers as a card that represents love and attraction. At its heart, however, the Lovers card is a card of choice. Typically, the course of love implies a long series of choices: we choose how we will present ourselves to others. We choose how we will respond to them when they approach us. We choose how we will treat other people, and we choose how we will nurture our relationships—or we choose to let those relationships wither and die on the vine. Adam may have blamed Eve for his fall, and Eve may have blamed the snake, but both were ultimately responsible for their own decisions. It doesn't work well to blame others or to play the victim—especially after the fact, when you really do know better. What's more, their "fall" was not merely a fall from grace—it was a leap to another level of reality and another plane of existence and experience.

- The original Lovers, Adam and Eve, chose to sample the forbidden fruit that grew on the tree of knowledge. Once Adam and Eve knew that there was a difference between good and evil, the world changed. They were forced to see the darkness that defines the light. When the Lovers card falls in a tarot reading, it's a forceful reminder that your experience with evil is a necessary part of the big picture.

- The card symbolizes dualities on every level: male and female, yin and yang, dark and light, thesis and antithesis. The card illustrates the fact that opposites attract.
- Astrologically, the Lovers card is associated with Gemini, the sign of the Twins. While the card might refer to romantic partnerships, it sometimes refers to other relationships—particularly the relationship between brothers and sisters, as suggested by Gemini, the Twins.
- Because Geminis often seem to lead double lives, filled with varied interests, the Lovers card could suggest that you will embark on a second career. You might also find yourself moonlighting, or adopting a new hobby.
- Alternately, you may face temptation, like the forbidden fruit on the Tree of Knowledge. You might have to make some difficult, life-changing decisions. You may be a willing victim of trickery and deception. You may have unwise counsel, like the snake ... or wise, depending on how you look at it.
- When the Lovers card falls in a tarot reading, your life may be in for some changes. You might find yourself leaving the safety of a metaphorical garden, so you can see the real world outside with your own eyes.
- With any luck, you will be falling in love, or find your passion and interest renewed in an existing relationship. You could find yourself in a new partnership, or discover that you are suddenly more attractive to others.
- The Lovers card is also about communication, the foundation and bedrock of any relationship. You may find yourself in close communication with others. It could indicate that you'll need to refine your communication skills.
- Because the Lovers card is associated with Gemini, the versatile, communicative sign of the Twins, it typically indicates that you have a quick wit. You can even be a flirt.

For Future Reference

Keywords: Love, romance, attraction, desirability, flirtation, communication, choices, consideration, caring, duality, opposition, partnership, choices, discrimination (in the traditional sense of the word, implying a wise choice)

Reversed: Infidelity, suspicion, jealousy, obsession (For a quick visual of the Lovers reversed, see the Devil card.)

The mythic connection: The angel on the card is sometimes thought to be Eros or Cupid, directing love's arrows at the unaware. More often, it is said to be Raphael, one of seven archangels—and one of just three mentioned specifically by name in the Bible. (The other two, Michael and Gabriel, also appear on tarot cards: Gabriel blows his horn on the Judgment card, and Michael is the angel of Temperance. One of the four "unnamed" archangels, Uriel, is on the Devil card.) Raphael's name means "God has healed," and he is the archangel of marriage, healing, joy, happy meetings, and travel.

By the numbers: The number six historically symbolizes the human being, because man was said to be created on the sixth day. Six also symbolizes the sixth sense—psychic ability—as well as the six directions of space: left, right, forward, backward, up, and down.

Astrological associations: The Lovers card is associated with Gemini, the sign of communication. The couple in the card does look a lot like the Twins who are usually pictured in conjunction with Gemini. Gemini personalities are quick thinkers. They have excellent written and verbal skills, and a wide range of interests. They may be able to juggle two careers at once, or be deeply engrossed in a wide variety of hobbies and avocations. Gemini is ruled by Mercury, the planet of communication and speed—because it revolves so quickly around the sun. In the tarot, Mercury is associated with the Magician card. When the Lovers and the Magician appear in the same reading, they are a powerful combination. The combination of the two young lovers falling under love's magic spell could spell magic in real life, too.

7. The Chariot (VII)
Driving forces

The Chariot is a vehicle for forward motion and change, and the Charioteer is a driving force to be reckoned with. He's a visual contradiction: The chariot in the card seems to be at a standstill, but it's capable of driving at great speed. What's more, even while the Charioteer stands still, he moves ahead. He explores the world—new places and people—while maintaining home away from home.

Chariots were developed as weapons of war, but they were also tools of exploration and a pathway for trade and international relations. In many renditions of the card, the chariot isn't pulled by horses—it's pulled by a mysterious team of sphinxes, who pose riddles for travelers before they are permitted to pass into new territory.

In the classic Waite design, a young prince stands in a chariot, a victorious hero in shining armor. While real-life charioteers would lead triumphal parades upon their return from battle, Waite's Charioteer has conquered the riddle of the Sphinx. He understands the outer mystery of life: how we all go from four legs, to two legs, to three. (In metaphysical terms, the riddle also describes how a spirit manifests itself in the material world.) The canopy over his head, blue and dotted with stars, symbolizes the night sky. It's held up by four posts that symbolize the four Hebrew letters in the name of God, as well as the four elements, the four seasons, the four directions, and the four suits of the minor arcana. The Sphinx themselves also represent the four elements, because they combine four creatures: a human head, a bull's body, eagle's wings, and lion's feet. The shield on the front of the chariot depicts a yoni and a lingam, a Hindu symbol that represents the union of male and female. It's topped with a winged solar disc, which represents Horus, the Egyptian god of the mid-day sun.

In the Llewellyn Tarot, the Charioteer is Manawydan, a seasoned warrior with the wisdom and patience to triumph over otherworldly opponents. Manawydan is sometimes equated with the Irish sea god Manannan Mac Lir, who captained a self-propelled boat called the Wave Sleeper. He was said to have been a glorious sight when he crossed the waves. Some even said it looked as though he was crossing a plain of flowers. According to Welsh tradition, Manawydan was the brother of Bran the Blessed, and a seasoned warrior whose cool head and patient ways brought victory even when he battled the slippery forces of the Otherworld.

In the Crowley deck, the Charioteer sits in the center of a chariot that seems to be standing still, until you notice the concentric rings that represent the rest of the universe speeding by. He holds the Holy Grail, which in turn holds the spinning, spiraling energy of the cosmos. He is fully clothed in armor. Not even his face is visible, because Crowley said that no man could see his face and live. There are ten stars on his armor; each one represents a sphere on the Kabbalistic Tree of Life. There's also a crab on his helmet, which symbolizes his association with the sign of Cancer and his link to the High Priestess via Cancer's ruling planet, the moon. Like Waite's design, the Chariot's canopy is blue like the sky, and it's supported by four posts. Crowley reinforces the symbolism of four, however, by tying the chariot to four sphinx-like creatures. They're all made up of various amalgamations of human, bull, eagle, and lion features, but each one is arranged in a different way. Crowley designed them to embody sixteen different combinations of the elements—just like the court cards, in which the pages, knights, queens, and kings embody varying mixtures of earth, air, fire, and water. The Chariot's wheels are red, which symbolizes a burning energy, drive, will, and intent.

What Does Your Future Hold?

- The Charioteer in the Chariot card is a driving force—and he's one to be reckoned with, determined and constantly moving forward. He has the courage of his convictions and the will to follow his dreams, no matter how far from home those dreams may lead. Girded in armor, ready for battle, he is a warrior and adventurer, king of the open road.

- When the Chariot appears in a tarot reading, travel is definitely indicated. On a metaphoric level, you may need to change direction or speed, and you might want to avoid running roughshod over other people.

- The Chariot is associated with the sign of Cancer, and it's a good representation of some of the most puzzling attributes of the sign. Cancer is the sign of house and home, of close family ties and motherhood. It rules the fourth house of a horoscope, which astrologers look to for clues about home and family life, as well as maternal influences. One rarely thinks of Cancerians as adventurers. And yet, Cancerians are more than happy to travel and see the world—as long as they can take all the comforts of home with them. They are sentimental and nurturing. Who does a soldier fight for, if not to protect his family back home? What warrior doesn't carry a reminder of loved ones?

- Because of the Cancer influence on this card, you might be feeling nostalgic. You might also be thinking of traveling to your childhood home. You may be dealing with your mother, grandmother, or maternal figures from your past. You may be called upon to nurture others, or you may be engaged in creating a homey environment away from home.

- The Charioteer guides his team through sound commands, the spoken word, without relying on reigns to tighten or pull. Like all good horsemen, he feeds and takes care of his team before he takes care of himself. The card could be a reminder that you should take care of your team, too.

- Like the Charioteer, with a walled city behind him, you might soon be called upon to leave the safety of a fortress in order to protect and defend those you leave behind.

- In a tarot reading, the Chariot card could indicate a move—especially if it comes up with another card of dramatic transformation, like the Tower.

- It could suggest a new car, or travel, too.

- You might need to leave your comfort zone to fight for your principles and beliefs. If you find yourself in the driver's seat, remember to check your spiritual map, and don't be afraid to ask for directions.

For Future Reference

Keywords: Movement, forward motion, travel, speed, war, warriors, battle, conquest, triumph, victory, parades, your chariot awaits, will and control, direction

Reversed: Delays, opposition, stasis, objects at rest that tend to remain at rest

The mythic connection: The Charioteer is sometimes compared to the Greek god Apollo, who drove the chariot of the sun, or the prophet Elijah, who was carried to heaven in a chariot of fire. In many versions of the card, the Charioteer wears the two faces of Janus as an emblem on his uniform. Janus was the Roman god of gates and doors, beginnings and endings, and transitions—particularly the transition from the past to the future, youth to adulthood, and between peace and war.

By the numbers: Seven is a mystical, magical number. Classically, there were seven days of creation. There are seven gifts of the Holy Spirit: wisdom, understanding, counsel, fortitude, knowledge, piety, and fear. There are seven deadly sins: envy, sloth, gluttony, wrath, pride, lust, and greed. There are seven virtues: faith, hope, charity, fortitude, justice, temperance, and prudence. (You can see most of those in the major arcana.) Alchemists had seven metals: gold, silver, iron, mercury, tin, copper, and lead. There are seven visible planets: the Sun, the Moon, Mars, Mercury, Jupiter, Venus, and Saturn. There are seven days of the week, seven notes in a musical scale, seven colors of the rainbow, and seven chakras. Because the seventh day is a day of rest, seven is the number of self-reflection and philosophy. To fully randomize your tarot deck before a reading, shuffle it seven times.

Astrological associations: The Chariot is associated with Cancer, the sign of motherhood and homemaking. While the combination might seem unlikely at first, the link makes sense when you realize that Cancerians make anywhere they travel feel like home. In fact, their emblem, the crab, travels with his home on his back. Like crabs—and warriors—people who have a strong link to the sign also seem tough and resourceful on the outside, but inside they are soft and sentimental. Cancer is ruled by the Moon, which is assigned to the High Priestess. When the Chariot and the High Priestess appear together in a reading, they are a powerful combination.

8. Strength (VIII)

The courage of your convictions

The Strength card is one of the most beautiful cards in the tarot—a simple, striking image of a self-possessed young woman with the heart of a lion.

In the classic Waite design, a brave young maiden gently closes the jaws of a lion, patiently controlling a force that could otherwise eat her alive. The lion symbolizes passion, confidence, and liberation from fear. Historically, the card was called Fortitude—one of four cardinal virtues, three of which make an appearance in the tarot. (The others are Justice and Temperance, but Prudence is missing from the deck.) There is a mountain castle in the background, which symbolizes refuge, watchfulness, and royal or divine guidance and sovereignty. Waite switched the order of the cards, trading Strength for Justice, in a change that made the deck's esoteric structure fit better with his metaphysical worldview.

In the Llewellyn Tarot, the Strength card depicts Twrch Trwyth, the wild boar from the story of Kilhwch. He was the young hero who chose to undertake a series of challenges in order to win the hand of Olwen—a woman so beautiful that white flowers grew in her footsteps. Like Hercules' labors, Kilhwch's tasks seemed both improbable and impossible.

In one of his adventures, he was supposed to retrieve a razor, comb, and scissors that balanced between the ears of a fierce wild boar named Twrch Trwyth—a former king who had been transformed, along with his family, into a wild beast. The card shows one of Kilhwch's men following Twrch Trwyth into the Severn River in pursuit of the boar's precious things. The lion on the horse's harness is a nod to the traditional imagery in other tarot decks.

The Crowley version of the card is a lot deeper—and darker—than either the Waite or the Llewellyn images. Crowley didn't go with the uplifting image of a courageous young woman or an adventurous legend. Instead, he seems to have abandoned the virgin for the whore. In the Crowley deck, the Strength card is called Lust—and it switches place with Justice, to better suit Crowley's esoteric philosophy. Crowley's lion is an apocryphal beast, like the lion of Revelations. Its tail is a serpent, a symbol that unites the mystic feminine with the masculine symbology of the lion. It also has seven heads—a lion, of course, as well as a saint, an angel, a brave man, an adulteress, a satyr, and a poet. All told, the strange menagerie symbolizes the uneasy coexistence of our human and animal natures. A scarlet woman rides the lion's back. In her left hand, she holds a pair of reins that symbolize the passion that unites them. In her right hand, she holds an anatomically correct version of the Holy Grail, filled with the flames of love and death. The woman is drunk and more than a little mad, and the lion is burning with animal lust; both have been overtaken by primal, creative energy. Above the grail, ten seminal serpents writhe, ready to destroy the world and then renew it. There are also ten spheres in the background, symbolizing fallen stars from heaven. At the bottom, underneath the lion's paws, are very faint images of the souls of the saints, victims of those who trample above them.

In some decks, especially older decks, the card was called Fortitude, one of the classical virtues.

What Does Your Future Hold?

- The Strength card represents your control over your animal nature—your primal needs and desires, your instincts for food, sleep, procreation, and self-preservation.
- Those drives are not only instinctual, they are perpetual and ongoing, symbolized by the lemniscate—a symbol shaped like a figure eight, which means infinity. The lemniscate seems to float just above the woman's head, constantly in range of her consciousness.

- When the Strength card falls in a tarot reading, you might want to ask yourself just who is the main character in the card—the maiden, the hero, or the beast. Of course, the image could be a metaphor. The two figures in each image may actually be two separate aspects of a single personality. One is civilized, the other is an example of the most primal creatures on earth. Lions, however, have their own social hierarchy, a suggestion that what we think of as civilization is merely a pantsuit on a pig, a guise, a veneer, a costume, easily shed or removed in times of strife.

- The young person in the card seems strong and self-assured, daring enough to stand outside the safety and protection of the castle in the background. In a reading, the card could reflect your own courage, self-control, and strength: you are not afraid to tackle opponents and issues that intimidate others.

- If you adopt Crowley's vision of the card, a new or more passionate chapter in your relationships or love life could be about to unfold.

- The Strength card is associated with the astrological sign of Leo, a sign of courage and strength. It's a good sign if your question happens to concern health—especially heart health, which is ruled by Leo.

- Leo rules the fifth house of the horoscope chart, where astrologers look for information about your father. When you get the Strength card in a reading, you might expect some playful interaction with your father or a male authority figure—especially if you are a father yourself. The Leo connection typically refers to recreation: As a general rule, fathers tend to play harder with their children than mothers. Fathers are usually more physical, more sports minded, and more apt to bond with their children through games and play.

- If you are a man, you may soon experience fatherhood in a new and exciting way.

- Like Leo, the lion, you can also expect to be admired. You will be the center of attention, and you will enjoy the experience.

For Future Reference

Keywords: Strength, power, energy, force, fortitude, heart, lust, life force, will, self-esteem, animal nature, self-preservation, instinct, magnanimity, heroism, ability, mastery

Reversed: Weakness, cowardice, fear, embarrassment, self-criticism, shyness, reluctance

The mythic connection: The Strength card is reminiscent of several myths, legends, and stories about lions. There's the legend of Hercules, who managed to kill the Androclean lion. There's the fable of Androcles, the slave who pulled a thorn from a lion's paw. There's also the biblical Daniel, who was shut into a lion's den. All relate the importance of courage and perseverance in the face of seemingly insurmountable danger.

By the numbers: Eights represent infinity, because they resemble the lemniscate, the sideways symbol of infinity. There are also eight points on the Wheel of the Year. To Christians, eight is a symbol of baptism and spiritual rebirth; many baptisteries and baptismal fonts have eight sides. Eight also represents the eternal spiral of regeneration.

Astrological associations: The Strength card is associated with Leo, the sign of courage and showmanship. The card perfectly illustrates the association: you've probably been to a circus yourself, and thrilled to the sight of a beautiful lady in the center ring, astounding an audience with her ability to tame a wild lion. Leo people are typically courageous and strong, brave and inspiring. They can be proud, at times, but it's usually well earned. Leo is ruled by the Sun. The combination of the beautiful young lady standing in the bright light of day relates directly to Leo's love of the spotlight.

9. The Hermit (IX)

Time out

Far removed from the hustle and bustle of everyday life, the Hermit reflects on spiritual concerns. He carries his light of wisdom as a beacon for others to follow. He is a recluse who can't seem to get away from his followers.

In the classic Waite design, an old man stands on the peak of a mountain, which could be the distant mountain peak we first saw in the background of the Fool card. He's dressed like a Capuchin friar, a member of an order that takes a vow of poverty and ascetic living. The Hermit holds a lantern high in his right hand—a symbol of light and leadership. In his left hand, he holds a tall walking stick, which is actually a magic wand, and he leans on it for support. The light in his lantern is actually a six-pointed star, which is also used to symbolize the Star of David, Solomon's Seal. Historically, the shape also symbolized the polarity of opposites, such as fire and water, masculine and feminine, and heaven and earth.

In the Llewellyn Tarot, the Hermit is Myrddin, more commonly known as Merlin. Like Taliesin in the Hierophant card, Myrddin was a sixth-century bard, as well as a prophet. After a traumatic battlefield experience, essentially shell-shocked, he lived alone in the

Caledonian forest. He feared that he was a hunted man, and he often hid beneath the cover of an apple tree. At one point, he was found, subdued with music, and taken back to King Arthur's court. The presence of other people made him panic, though, and he returned to the forest, where he found a therapeutic spring that healed him of his post-traumatic stress. He lived out the rest of his life in a forest observatory, seeking wisdom from nature, the forest animals, and the stars.

In the Crowley deck, the old man is Thoth, the Egyptian god of wisdom. (Crowley named his deck in Thoth's honor.) The Hermit holds a diamond-shaped lamp with eight sides, which represents the two worlds of heaven and earth connecting. The lamp casts a beam of light up toward an orphic egg, which symbolizes the mysteries and secrets that surround the origin of the universe. The snake wrapped around the egg is Ophion, a Greek serpent god who once ruled the world. Down at the bottom of the card, Cerberos, the three-headed hound of hell, accompanies the Hermit—just like the little white dog who follows the Fool. Occasionally, the Hermit serves as a psychopomp, and guides the souls of the dead to the Underworld. During those journeys, Cerberos is his companion. A giant sperm in the left-hand corner of the card symbolizes creation.

What Does Your Future Hold?

- Who wouldn't want a kindly old mentor or spiritual guide to shepherd them along life's path, or a spiritually evolved master to advice them? The Hermit is both a seeker and a guide, and he represents both you and the people you look to for advice.

- The Hermit is protected from the elements and shielded from the wind by his cloak. In many ways, his cape might actually act like a cloak of invisibility. Old hermit-type personalities—solitary wanderers—are often overlooked by society and can easily get lost and go unnoticed in a crowd. In a reading, the Hermit might be a suggestion that you lose yourself in the crowd, too, and merely observe the human condition.

- In very old versions of the card, the Hermit's lantern was actually an hourglass. As time passed, however, and the cards were reinterpreted, that hourglass evolved into the lantern that most artists draw today.

- The six-pointed star inside the lantern often symbolizes the union of male and female, or of heaven and earth. A partnership may be in the offering for you, too.

- The Hermit wants nothing more than solitude, so that he can discover and contemplate the great mysteries of life. His desire to live apart from society, however, is often an irresistible draw. In a move that tends to be self-defeating, followers seek him out for wisdom and advice on how they, too, can withdraw from society. In a tarot reading, the Hermit could symbolize a similar retreat—or the sense that you are attracting a crowd, despite your best efforts to be alone.

- The Hermit could be an advice card, suggesting that you spend some time alone in meditation and reflection.

- The Hermit preaches a message of austerity and asceticism, and suggests that a simpler lifestyle could be more conducive to the development of your soul.

- The Hermit is also closely connected to the passage of time, and the aging process. In fact, some tarot readers suggest that the Hermit is an older version of the Fool. Having traveled the world, he has reached the mountaintop we first saw in the Fool's card—and he is older and wiser for the experience.

- The Hermit is associated with Virgo, the sixth sign of the zodiac, and the ruler of the sixth house in an astrological chart. In a tarot reading, the Hermit may be related to Virgo issues—especially mental and physical health.

- Because Virgo is ruled by Mercury, the planet of communication, the Hermit might also have a message about your communicative skills and abilities.

For Future Reference

Keywords: Solitude, isolation, introspection, meditation, withdrawal, wisdom, philosophy, mysticism, prudence, deliberation, disguise

Reversed: Paranoia, introversion, agoraphobia

The mythic connection: The Hermit has been compared to Father Time—who, over time, has also been known as the god Saturn, as well as Cronos, the god who ate his own children. The Hermit has also been compared to the ancient Greek philosopher Diogenes, who reportedly carried a lantern through the marketplace during daylight, searching for an honest man.

   The Hermit also seems to embody the legend of Merlin the Magician, and the wounded healer, Chiron.

   In many versions of the card, the Hermit is dressed like a hooded and bearded Capuchin friar. The Capuchins were an offshoot of the Franciscan brothers, who lived like hermits and believed that lives of solitude and penance would bring them closer to God.

By the numbers: Because there are nine months of pregnancy, nines symbolize selflessness, compassion, universality, humanitarianism, and spirituality.

Astrological associations: The Hermit is associated with Virgo, the sign of mental and physical health consciousness. Virgos are rational, practical, and analytical. They have high standards. They tend to isolate themselves from people who don't share their values—but mostly, they isolate themselves in an effort to live up to their own high standards. In Latin, Virgo means "unmarried" or "self-possessed." Virgo is ruled by Mercury, the planet of speed and communication. In the tarot, Mercury corresponds to the Magician card. The combination of the wise old Hermit and the brash young Magician relates directly to Virgo's desire to mentor and teach other people.

10. The Wheel of Fortune (X)

What goes around, comes around

The Wheel of Fortune turns in rhythm with the perpetual motion of the universe. As it spins, it reflects the constant flux of human experience and serves as a measure of life, time, destiny, and fate.

In the classic Waite design, the Wheel of Fortune is one of the most lavishly illustrated cards. The four corners feature the four living creatures the prophet Ezekiel saw in his vision of "Ezekiel's Wheel"—an angel, an eagle, a lion, and a bull. The four creatures symbolize the four fixed signs of Aquarius, Scorpio, Leo, and Taurus. There's a riddling Sphinx at the top of the wheel, guarding the mysterious turns of fate. The serpent Typhon is on the left, and the Anubis, a jackal-headed god who represented the Egyptian priesthood, is on the right. The Wheel itself is divided into eight sections. The divisions symbolize the four cardinal directions—north, south, east, and west—along with the midway points, northeast, southeast, southwest, and northwest. It's also a graphical representation of the Wheel of the Year, with the spring, summer, winter, and fall equinoxes, as well as the cross-quarter midpoints of the year. There are four letters printed on the rim of the wheel; they are the same four letters that were inscribed on the High Priestess's scroll TARO. When you read them clockwise all around the wheel, they spell *tarot*. Read them counterclockwise, they spell *tora*. And if you start at the bottom and read clockwise, the letters spell *rota*, which is Latin for wheel. There are Hebrew letters on the wheel, too. The four letters, Yod, Heh, Vau, Heh, make up the name of God—pronounced "Jehovah" in English. They show that God is at the center of everything. The symbols inside the wheel are alchemical symbols: that's mercury at the top, sulfur on the right, salt on the left, and dissolution at the bottom.

In the Llewellyn Tarot, the Wheel of Fortune is represented by Arianrhod, whose name means "silver wheel" or "queen of the wheel." Arianrhod was a beautiful, goddess-like maiden who repeatedly cast hateful, binding fates upon her son, simply because his birth embarrassed her and stripped her of her status as a virginal young woman. (Happily, her brother Gwydion took charge of the young boy, and helped him outsmart his mother.) The Welsh named a constellation for her, Caer Arianhod, and associated it with the Wheel of Fate.

In the Crowley deck, the Wheel of Fortune is a wheel within a wheel. The center wheel, with the ten-pointed star, symbolizes the finite lifespan of our earthly existence, while the outer wheel symbolizes the eternity of infinite time and space. The star itself symbolizes the eye of Shiva, which would destroy the universe when it opened. As in Waite's design, there are three creatures on the wheel—again, it's the Anubis, Typhon, and the Sphinx. They represent the creator, the protector, and the destroyer gods, which rule the movement of time. The Typhon's tail is wrapped around the wheel in the shape of a lemniscate, the symbol of infinity: he is tied to the wheel for all eternity. He holds an ankh, a symbol of life, in his right hand, and the magic staff of Osiris in his left. The ten spokes on the wheel symbolize divine order and the ten spheres on the Kabbalistic Tree of Life. The lightning bolts in the background are Zeus' thunderbolts, and the swirling energy is a result of the constant movement of the wheel.

What Does Your Future Hold?

- In very old versions of the card, four kings rode the Wheel, and each one described his position with a Latin phrase: *Regno, regnabo, regnavi*, and *sum sine regno*: "I reign," "I shall reign," "I reigned," and "I am without a kingdom." It was a clear expression of the fact that no one's place in life is secure. Change happens.

- In a tarot reading, the Wheel of Fortune often serves as a reminder that what goes up, must come down—and in a karmic way, what goes around, comes around.

- When the Wheel of Fortune falls in a tarot reading, it's often a clear sign that your luck is on the upswing. Because you're also responsible for making your own luck, though, you should pay special attention to the world around you—opportunity may be knocking on your door.

- The Wheel of Fortune can also suggest that it's a good idea to buy a lottery ticket.

- Remember to stay centered. From the midpoint of the wheel, you'll be less likely to lose your balance and fall.

- The Wheel of Fortune also illustrates the cycle of life. In some cases, it's designed to reflect the Wheel of the Year. In others, it almost looks like a clock with spinning hands.

- In some renditions of the card, the Wheel of Fortune looks like a horoscope wheel. It may even remind you of the circular path that the planets follow in their annual paths around the sun … and you might notice that the measure of a year differs from planet to planet, just as people follow their own paths through life, and time passes in accordance with each individual's journey.

- The Wheel of Fortune is associated with Jupiter, the planet of luck and expansion. Jupiter has a twelve-year cycle, so the card could symbolize the start of a new twelve-year cycle in your life.

- Jupiter rules the sign of Sagittarius, which is connected with philosophy and long-distance travel. In a reading, you might find that your world is going to expand, either through formal thought and study, or contact with people from far-away places.

- Jupiter is also associated with benefactors and presents, so the card could indicate that you are in a position to give or receive gifts.

For Future Reference

Keywords: Fortune, destiny, luck, chance, karma, perpetual motion, cycles, the Wheel of Life, the Wheel of the Year

Reversed: Reversal of fortune, bad luck, standstills, delays

The mythic connection: In myth and legend, three female goddesses—the Fates—are responsible for spinning the Wheel of Life.

By the numbers: The number ten has primal, deep-seated significance for all of us. When babies are born, parents immediately do a quick count of fingers and toes. When we learn to count as children, we use our ten fingers as tools. Ten is the number of culmination, completion, and perfection. There are also ten spheres on the Kabbalistic Tree of Life, and ten numbered cards in each suit of the minor arcana.

Astrological associations: The Wheel of Fortune card is associated with Jupiter, the planet of luck and expansion: expansion, because Jupiter is the largest planet in our solar system, and luck, because Jupiter was the god of good fortune. Jupiter represents the process of expanding your worldview, through travel to distant lands or armchair travels through books, documentaries, or conversations with other people. It's a philosophical card. It's also generous and optimistic. Traditionally, Jupiter is known as the "greater benefic"—it's like the Santa Claus of the tarot.

Jupiter also rules Sagittarius, which is associated with the Temperance card. When The Wheel of Fortune appears alongside Temperance in a tarot reading, it's a powerful combination, and each card will reinforce the message of the other.

11. Justice (XI)
Justice is served

The Sword of Justice is a double-edged sword, and her scales are perpetually balanced.

In the classic Waite design, Justice looks like the figure we see in courtrooms and attorney's offices—except for the fact that she wears no blindfold. Her eyes are wide open: she sees the whole story, and she's not forced to rule based on technicalities. As a result, she dispenses spiritual and karmic justice, which is a lot more reliable and fair than legal justice. She holds the Sword of Justice in her right hand; it's a double-edged sword, ready to cut through distractions and delays and get right to the point. She holds the scales of balance in her left hand, ready to weigh the two sides of any case. She sits between pillars, like the High Priestess and the Hierophant—but, as Waite wrote about the card, "the pillars of Justice open into one world and the pillars of the High Priestess into another."

In the Llewellyn Tarot, Lady Justice is the Lady of the Fountain, a figure of sovereignty and a personification of the land itself. Sovereignty appears in traditional tales to test the ability and weigh the merits of would-be suitors or champions. She was an impartial judge who placed principle above personality, and set emotion aside for the higher good.

One of the young people she tested was a young knight named Owaine who left King Arthur's court to find her fountain. When he did, he was caught up in a fierce battle with the Lady's husband, the Black Knight. As they fought, Owaine inflected a mortal wound on the Black Knight, who barely made it back to the Lady's castle before he died. Owaine followed, but he was trapped by the castle gates. Luned, a young woman from the castle, rescued him. She gave him a ring that could make him invisible and smuggled him into her chambers. From Luned's window, Owaine saw the grief-stricken Lady of the Fountain for the first time, as she marched in her husband's funeral procession. Despite the morbid circumstances, it was love at first sight for Owaine. Luned decided to play matchmaker. Even though the Lady of the Fountain knew that Owaine had killed her husband, she agreed to marry him, because he had proved that he was a champion who could guard and defend the fountain—and, by extension, her realm.

In the Crowley deck, the card is called Adjustment, not Justice, and Crowley switched its place in the major arcana with Strength. The card design itself is perfectly symmetrical and perfectly balanced. In the image, a masked young woman balances on tiptoe. She's dressed in a cloak of feathers, like those the Egyptian goddess Maat used to weigh against the hearts of the dead. She stands inside a diamond of light, a geometric design that symbolizes harmony. She seems to lean on her sword for support; its tip is planted in the earth. The scales of justice are hanging from chains that are attached to the top of her head, and they're inscribed with the Alpha and Omega, the first and last letters of the Greek alphabet.

What Does Your Future Hold?

- Most people assume that Justice is a "good" card, one that will guarantee them their own just desserts. When the Justice card appears in a reading, however, it doesn't necessarily mean that you're home free. Justice carries a double-edged sword, and truth cuts both ways. There are two sides to any dispute, and the Justice card could indicate that you will be held fully responsible for your role in any misunderstandings, miscommunications, or misjudgments that have affected your life.

- The Justice card can be literal. It can often signify a quest for legal justice, or an oncoming legal issue such as a lawsuit or court date.

- Justice delayed is justice denied. In most court systems, however, the wheels of justice turn exceedingly slow, and grind exceedingly fine. When the Justice card shows up in your reading, you might want to look at nearby cards to determine whether or not you can expect a long wait for Justice.

- Justice is associated with Libra, which rules the seventh house of the horoscope. There it's connected with marriages and partnerships. In a reading, the Justice card could have a message about your significant other.
- The sign of Libra is also concerned with social grace. In that case, the Justice card could relate to your social life, and could symbolize a renewed sense of balance in your interaction with other people.
- The Justice card could serve as a reminder for you to weigh your options and to make a decision that you've been delaying.
- The Justice card could even suggest that it's time to recognize your own authority and ability to hold court.

For Future Reference

Keywords: Justice, karma, equality, equilibrium, equity, legal action, contracts, lawsuits, trials, judgments

Reversed: Injustice, abuse of power, imbalance, justice delayed, justice denied, red tape, complications

The mythic connection: The Justice card is sometimes associated with Themis, the Greek goddess of Justice who helped keep the infant Zeus safe from his father Cronos, or Time. She was also a gifted prophet who served for a time at the Oracle of Delphi. The Justice card can also be associated with the Egyptian goddess Maat, who would measure a dead man's heart against the weight of a feather before he could be allowed to continue on into the afterlife. The Justice card can even be connected to the biblical judge Solomon, who threatened to cut an infant in half in order to determine his true mother.

By the numbers: Numerologists consider eleven a master number, because it amplifies the power of a single "one."

Astrological associations: Justice is associated with Libra, the sign of balance and grace. Libra rules the seventh house of the horoscope, where it is connected with marriages and partnerships.

Librans have an innate need to balance themselves through relationships with others. They are typically friendly, gregarious, and charming. They are exceptionally social creatures, with visionary and humanitarian ideals.

Like living versions of the goddess on the card, most people born under the sign of Libra spend their lives trying to find a balance between extremes. First and foremost, they need balance, beauty, and harmony in their lives, not conflict. They are skilled at solving problems, compromising, and arranging diplomatic solutions for any conflict. Occasionally, their need to see both sides of any issue makes them indecisive.

Libra is ruled by Venus, the planet of love and beauty. Venus is also associated with the Empress card.

12. The Hanged Man (XII)

A change of perspective

The Hanged Man is a visionary who sacrifices one life to find another. He readily relinquishes his comfort, for a time, knowing that better things will occur as a result.

In the classic Waite design, a young man hangs upside-down in a tree, suspended by a rope tied around his ankle. His arms are tied behind his back, and his left leg is crossed behind the right. The shape of his legs suggest a fylfot cross—a type of solar cross with "feet" that represents harmony and movement. Meanwhile, the leafy branches of the tree form a T-shaped cross, like the Greek letter tau that's used to symbolize life. Oddly enough, the Hanged Man doesn't seem to be suffering. He looks peaceful, even happy; there's a halo-like nimbus around his head, and he's in a mystic trance. He's not going to die as a result of this hanging, but as long as he stays suspended in the tree his life will be suspended, too. Once he's back on his feet, he'll experience a resurrection of sorts.

In the Llewellyn Tarot, the Hanged Man is Pryderi, who found himself drawn into an enchanted castle in Dyfed. As he wandered through its interior, he came across an ornate fountain with a golden bowl hanging above it. When he reached out to touch the bowl, his hands stuck to the sides and he was paralyzed. His mother, Rhiannon, went looking for her son. When she found him, she too reached for the bowl. Thunder roared, and the castle vanished. Pryderi and Rhiannon were suspended between worlds for the next seven years. As it turns out, the two were simply the hapless victims of a vengeful magician who years before had been trapped in a bag and physically beaten by Pryderi's father.

In the Crowley deck, a faceless, anonymous man is suspended from an ankh. He literally hangs on to life by a thread. A snake binds his left foot to the ancient Egyptian Tau Cross, a symbol of energy and life force. His right foot and hands are nailed to green discs. His right leg is crossed over his left, in the shape of an upside-down figure 4. His arms are stretched out at a 60-degree angle, forming an equilateral cross. According to Crowley, the triangle surmounted by the cross symbolizes the descent of light to redeem the darkness. His head and body are shaved—he is completely hairless, like a defenseless, helpless child. A second snake, black as death, is waiting for him in the open grave beneath his head. The background is a grid that symbolizes a table of the elements, as well as the unforgiving matrix of social structure and expectation.

What Does Your Future Hold?

- While no one relishes the prospect of being hanged, the Hanged Man card normally represents a period of willing self-sacrifice, and the suspension of everyday cares and concerns.

- In most versions of the card, the Hanged Man doesn't seem to be suffering. Instead, he seems to be entering an altered state of being, and possibly even a state of enlightenment.

- When the Hanged Man card falls in your tarot reading, it could suggest that you, too, could benefit from some time away from your ordinary concerns, or a new perspective. The change, in fact, could do you good.

- Historically, the Hanged Man was sometimes called "The Traitor," because traitors like Judas were hung upside-down. The practice isn't dead, either: as recently as World War II, for example, the Italian leader Mussolini was hanged upside-down for his corrupt rule.

- The Hanged Man's legs are often crossed in the shape of the numeral 4—just like the Emperor. The pose is designed to suggest a certain stability, even though the ground is swept away.

- The position of the Hanged Man's head sometimes represents a descent into the underworld. Lucifer, the dark angel, was said to have been cast out of heaven head-first, straight into hell. The upside-down posture might also remind you of an unborn child, suspended in the womb. As a result, the card occasionally symbolizes rebirth and transitions from one life to another. In initiation ceremonies, new members of mystical groups are sometimes suspended upside-down.

- The Hanged Man also symbolizes revolution and reversal. When the Hanged Man card falls in your tarot reading, it could suggest that you're in for a shakeup or two.

- Because the Hanged Man is associated with Neptune, the planet of illusion, it could symbolize a period of vivid daydreams or lucid nighttime dreams.

- It could also be a warning, or sorts, against self-deception.

- The Hanged Man is also associated with runes—an ancient alphabet that could represent your language skills. If you need to write something, this is the time.

For Future Reference

Keywords: Voluntary withdrawal, sacrifice, restraint, foresight, wisdom, meditation, rebirth, transition, initiation

Reversed: Unwilling sacrifice, punishment, imprisonment, treason

The mythic connection: The Hanged Man is often compared to Judas, who betrayed Jesus Christ for 40 pieces of silver. In fact, some versions of the card actually depict Judas, hung upside-down, with 40 pieces of silver falling out of his pocket or purse. The Hanged Man has also been compared to Saint Peter, who was crucified upside-down to avoid being compared to Jesus—who was, of course, the world's most famous hanged man.

Many tarot readers compare the Hanged Man to Odin, the Norse god who hung himself from Yggdrasil, the world tree. In return, he was rewarded with runes, the gift of written language.

By the numbers: The number twelve is a reminder of other significant twelves—such as the twelve tribes of Israel, the twelve apostles, the twelve months in a year, and the twelve signs of the zodiac.

Astrological associations: The Hanged Man is associated with Neptune, the planet of illusion. Neptune is ruled by Pisces, the sign of mysticism and intuition.

13. Death (XIII)

Don't fear the reaper

Not the frightening specter that most of us expect, the card of Death is one of transition. It foretells the completion of one stage of life and the beginning of a new phase. Death is simply the reaper who clears away all that cannot survive.

In the classic Waite design, a pale rider on a white horse marches across the battle-field of life, mowing down all those in his path. Your frightened friends will all recognize him immediately: he is the Grim Reaper. He is the ultimate equalizer, a democratizing force, and he cuts down the king, the bishop, the maiden, and the child alike. He has been this way before: the field is littered with body parts. He carries a black banner emblazoned with a mystic rose—a symbol of life and resurrection. The sun of immortality gleams on the horizon, between two pillars that are reminiscent of the pillars behind the High Priestess, Justice, and the Moon. In every case, the pillars represent a gateway, a passage to another world.

In the Llewellyn Tarot, the Grim Reaper is Arawn, the gentle lord of the Otherworld, accompanied by a pack of hounds. According to legend, Arawn once traded places with a mortal leader—Pwyll, the lord of Dyfed—for a year. Together, the two devised a plan to defeat another Otherworld king, Hafgan. Every year, Hafgan would challenge Arawn to a battle for control of the Otherworld. Pwyll agreed to the switch, and the two kings magically assumed each other's form. When the year was out, Pwyll was both forewarned and forearmed for his battle with Hafgan. Arawn had told him that he could strike Hafgan once, but that a second blow would lead to his opponent's death *and* resurrection. Pwyll struck Hafgan once, wounding him. When Hafgan begged him for the sweet release of death, Pwyll refused. Hafgan's men carried him away, and Pwyll returned control of the Otherworld to Arawn. Pwyll returned to his own kingdom, and learned that Arawn had wisely ruled his domain for the last year. From then on, the two kings were close friends and allies.

In the Crowley deck, a nimble, double-jointed skeleton performs his own dance of death. He swings his scythe, curved like the waning crescent moon, and harvests all those who have slipped through the web of fate. Their bodies fall into a pool of death, where they swim with a bottom-feeding fish, a snake, and a scorpion, a symbol of death. There in the darkness they decompose alongside the wilted blossoms of a lotus and a lily. Eventually, they will disintegrate completely, so their essence can float back up the thread of time and space to create new life.

What Does Your Future Hold?

The Death card is usually the one card most people fear most in a reading. Contrary to public opinion, however, the Death card almost never refers to an actual, physical death.

The Death card, like all of the cards in the tarot deck, is an allegorical image. It's probably based, to some extent, on similar images that were developed during the fourteenth century, when the Black Death swept across Europe. It suggests the danse macabre, the allegorical images of dancing skeletons that were generated as a result. Even now, the black-robed figure reminds some people of the priests who perform last rites at the bedsides of those who are very ill.

Most of the symbols on the Death card don't need to be explained. The skeleton, for example, has always represented the bare bones of the matter. A scythe can only mean harvest, even if it's the harvest of souls. The rising and setting sun has symbolized death and resurrection since the time of ancient Egypt.

It is, however, still a card that inspires fear. While the transition from life to death can be fearful, most people are afraid that they're going to be caught by surprise.

Happily, when you get the Death card in a reading, your odds of falling out of the chair, dead, are very, very low.

That's because most people don't pass away unexpectedly. While we all know of people who have died in accidents, or young people who succumbed to unexpected illness, almost everyone else dies of old age. With any luck, death won't come as a surprise to most of us.

- The Death card does imply one inevitable fate, however: change. It suggests the endless cycle of creation and destruction, and it symbolizes the change of consciousness that occurs as a result.

- We all encounter death, every day, in a million different ways. Sleep has been compared to a form of death. Sex has been called a "little death." Even experience can be a form of death, as our innocence is destroyed by experience, and replaced with knowledge, and wisdom, and understanding. Not all death is bad.

- When the Death card rears its ugly head in a tarot reading, it frequently refers to something in you that's already dead. You may simply need to acknowledge it.

- The card could indicate a release, a change of form, transformation, or the little deaths of sex and sleep. The card could suggest finality—and the fear of endings and closing doors. It could represent a passage to a new life.

- The Death card could also refer to a change in our focus. According to the laws of physics, energy can't be created or destroyed—it simply is converted from one form to another. The Death card could foretell a change in your consciousness—a higher, more evolved understanding of the universe.

Sometimes, people sit down for a tarot reading and want to know if they're going to die. The answer, obviously, is yes. Death is a certainty. But can you see it coming in the cards? Not very often—and definitely not based only on the appearance of the Death card.

For Future Reference

Keywords: Endings and beginnings, death and rebirth, creation and destination, change, transformation, alteration, mortality, corruption, loss, failure, annihilation, destruction

Reversed: Inertia, sleep, lethargy, loss of hope

The mythic connection: The Grim Reaper is one variant on the ancient psychopomp, a conductor of souls. The Death card also reflects the myth of Cronos, the ancient Greek god who was said to eat his own children. Cronos means "time," and his myth referred to the fact that time destroys all of its own creations.

By the numbers: There are thirteen lunar months, or thirteen full moons, in every calendar year. Thirteen is sometimes thought to be an unlucky number, because there were thirteen diners at Jesus's last supper. In the tarot, the Death card is number thirteen.

Astrological associations: The Death card is associated with Scorpio, a sign that's closely connected to the great, interconnected mysteries of life: sex and death. Scorpio is ruled by Pluto, the planet of transformation and the underworld.

14. Temperance (XIV)

Beauty is truth, truth beauty

With dexterity and grace, Temperance demonstrates how balance can serve as a bridge to wholeness.

In the classic Waite design, the winged angel of Temperance pours the essence of life from one chalice into another. Behind him, a winding path leads to a mountain range where the sun is rising, crowned in the glory of eternal life. According to one tarot tradition, the water that flows between the two chalices isn't flowing from the top to the bottom; instead, it flows up from the lower chalice into the higher one, like the path that leads up the mountain in the background. The archangel is Michael, one of four archangels in the tarot. (The others are Raphael, who appears in the Lovers card, Gabriel, the archangel of Judgment, and Uriel, the Devil.) In Temperance, Michael wears the astrological glyph of the sun on his forehead, and the square and triangle of the septenary on his chest. His left foot is on the dry land of logic, and his right foot is submerged in the water of emotion. Two yellow irises are blooming on the shore near his feet. Iris was said to be the goddess of rainbows, so the flowers in the card symbolize a bridge between worlds. All told, the design is meant to illustrate how we should temper and harmonize the spiritual and physical realms of our existence.

In the Llewellyn Tarot, Temperance is the Keeper of the Well, a priestess who guarded a sacred well in a land that had become known for its excess. She eventually was violated by a notorious drunkard on the Isle of the Mighty. She cried out to the gods for help, and the well waters rose to drown the entire island. Everyone died but the young woman and her dog, who continued to live on underwater in peace and safety at the bottom of the sea. As centuries passed, she was transformed into a salmon and her dog became an otter. Her story was immortalized in poetry and stories of warning told across Wales, Ireland, and Brittany.

In the Crowley deck, the Temperance card is called Art—a not-so-subtle nod to alchemists, who use the term to describe their methodology. The alchemists' goal was to combine and recombine the various elements of the natural world, constantly rectifying and refining their results. Eventually, they hoped to find the perfect balance that would allow them to transmute lead into gold. While the process never did pay off as they hoped, the study of alchemy has become a metaphor for spiritual development, as philosophers and metaphysicians attempt to describe how human beings can refine themselves over time. In Crowley's design, the king and queen from the Lovers card are no longer separate individuals. They have become one, and they work together to blend fire and water in the cauldron of life. The steam that rises up as a result symbolizes spirit. The royal companions, the lion and the eagle are there, too, but they're much larger—and they've changed color. Now the lion is white, and eagle is red. The cosmic egg behind them is inscribed with the words "Vista interiora terrae rectificando invenies occultum lapidem," which means, "Visit the interior parts of the earth; by rectification you shall find the hidden stone."

What Does Your Future Hold?

- Just as steel is tempered by fire and ice, people are tempered—made harder, more durable—by time and experience.
- In the tarot, however, the Temperance card typically refers to the process of mixing the elements. Most versions of the card illustrate that mix, by depicting a figure with one foot in water, and the other on dry land. Water is mixing between the two cups in the card, too: according to tarot tradition, the water is flowing from the lower cup up to the top, violating gravity and laws of nature.

- Some people read the card literally. Temperance is the practice of moderation. Temperance was one of the five cardinal virtues in ancient Greece, and it's one of the four cardinal virtues of the Catholic Church.

- In practical terms, the word temperance describes the process of cutting wine with water, and in today's world, the word temperance often refers to abstinence from beer, wine, and hard liquor.

- The Temperance card most often refers to a combination of opposites. It's often symbolized by the magic of the alchemical process.

- The Temperance card might also refer to the principles of proportionality, reconciliation, and unification.

- Temperance, like all of the "angel" cards in the tarot deck, could be a reassurance that you are under divine protection during times of trial and tribulation.

- The Temperance card is associated with Sagittarius, the sign of the archer. Sagittarius rules the ninth house of the zodiac, which describes your philosophy and long-distance travel.

- Historically, the Temperance card was associated with established religions and church services. Occasionally, the Temperance card was said to represent the priest who would marry the querents.

For Future Reference

Keywords: Economy, moderation, frugality, management, combinations, unification

Reversed: Intemperance, mismanagement, irreconcilable differences

The mythic connection: The angel of Temperance is the archangel Michael, the patron saint of the warrior, police officers, soldiers, and paratroopers.

    The iris flowers growing along the shoreline symbolize Iris, the goddess of rainbows, which serve as a bridge to another world.

Astrological associations: The Temperance card is associated with the sign of Sagittarius, the adventurer, the philosopher, and the explorer. Sagittarius is ruled by Jupiter, which is associated with the luck of the Wheel of Fortune card.

15. The Devil (XV)

Have we met?

He may be the personification of all evil—but the Devil is also a portrait of our shadow side.

In the classic Waite design, the Devil looks like the sum of all our fears. He's horrifying. He's horned, like a goat, and there's an inverted glowing pentagram on his forehead. Upright, the pentagram symbolizes the human form, living in balance and health. Reversed, it symbolizes a perversion of all that is whole, holy, and good. The Devil has pointed ears, an angry red face, and enormous bat wings growing out of his shoulders. The entire bottom half of his body is monstrous. His legs are covered in filthy, matted fur, and he perches on a small black altar with his scraggy, claw-like talons. That's not the worst of it, though. He has enslaved a man and a woman, and chained them to the base of his horrible throne. They are naked, like Adam and Eve, but they are clearly not in the Garden of Eden anymore. In fact, the Devil has cursed them with horns and tails, so they more closely resemble their dark master. He mocks the Hierophant by raising his right hand in a demonic blessing over their heads, grinning malevolently. He lights their dark pit with a flaming torch, held upside-down and dangerously close to his captured human.

In the Llewellyn Tarot, the Devil is called the Horned One. A nature-based god, he was part man, part beast—a supernatural blend of human and animal, and the personification of nature. The Horned One symbolized the spirit of the wild. As a herdsman and god of the hunt, he was the guardian and protector of the natural world. The wolf at his feet symbolizes his lordship over animals, not people. In stories and myths, the Horned One was said to sit cross-legged on a mound that doubled as an observation post. Over time, as church leaders began to exorcise the old gods from their new Christian congregations, the Horned One's primal, earthy nature was eventually associated with evil and the devil.

In the Crowley deck, the Devil isn't nearly so ominous. In fact, it even holds a certain fascination and appeal—especially for those of us who like men. The sly goat in the center of the design is Banebdjet, the Egyptian goat god of Mendes. He is also one version of Pan, the Greek god who embodied both human and animal nature. The goat has an enormous third eye, a symbol of his ability to perceive the whole picture, as well as grapes on his head, an homage to Bacchus, the Greek god of revelry and wine. He stands in front of a tall and sturdy tree, a symbol of growth and regeneration. At the top of the card, the tree parts the gates of heaven. Two spheres at the bottom of the card hold the seeds of future generations, as well as I Ching trigrams, which symbolize energy.

What Does Your Future Hold?

- The Devil card is obviously an ominous-looking card. It is typically illustrated with a malevolent-looking demon, with wild eyes, horns, and a tail. It perches on its talon feet, holding a hapless couple captive, in chains.

- In a tarot reading, the Devil card could indicate that you are feeling devilish, bedeviled, or like playing the devil's advocate.

- The card often alludes to Pan, the mythic figure from ancient Greece who was half-goat, half-man. Pan was the god of physical pleasures, including sexuality, as well as indulgence in food and drink. As a result, the Devil card often refers to an increased interest in the pleasures of the flesh—although it also could warn against overindulgence.

- The Devil card frequently refers to the temptation of drugs and alcohol, and the addiction that plagues some people who can't resist those temptations.

- The Devil card also warns that the darker, more negative issues you try to ignore and repress don't go away, but play themselves out in alternate venues.

- Oddly enough, many versions of the Devil card are actually a grotesque mirror image of the Lovers card, in which the pair has been trapped and enslaved by their own misplaced priorities. The Devil clearly demonstrates the shadow side of a dysfunctional or abusive relationship.
- Because the Devil card is associated with Capricorn, the sign of business and industry, its appearance in a reading could suggest big changes in your work or career life.
- The Devil card could also be a reminder that idle hands are the devil's playground. You might want to get busy on a project you've been putting off.
- The Devil is actually a depiction of Uriel, one of four archangels in the tarot. His name means "Flame of God," and he represents man's scientific nature.

For Future Reference

Keywords: Materiality, material force, material temptation, obsession, scapegoating, the dark or shadow side of an issue

Reversed: Weakness, abuse, addiction, violence, evil

The mythic connection: The card often alludes to Pan, the mythic figure from ancient Greece who was half-goat, half-man. Pan was the god of physical pleasures, including sexuality, as well as indulgence in food and drink. The Devil card can also be connected to Cernnunos, the horned nature and fertility god of the Celts, and Baphomet, the creature that's usually depicted as a goat's head superimposed on an inverted pyramid.

Occasionally, the Devil card relates to Pluto or Hades, the Roman and Greek gods of the underworld and lords of the dead.

Astrological associations: The Devil card is associated with Capricorn, the sign of business and career.

Most Capricorns are keenly aware of their social status. Like their symbol, the goat, they are constantly climbing, and constantly seeking greener pastures. They are ambitious, driven, disciplined, and industrious. They are prudent, patient, stable, and enduring.

Capricorn is ruled by Saturn, the planet of boundaries and limitations. In the tarot, Saturn is assigned to the World card. The combination is effective: the Devil is an earthly creature, firmly rooted in the material world, and closely associated with both the pleasures and pain of physical existence.

16. The Tower (XVI)

A bolt from the blue

Should we build ourselves up too high, the Tower card warns that a bolt from the blue could shake us to our very foundations. That forceful clearing of pent-up energy could come as a welcome relief, or a sudden shock.

In the classic Waite design, the inky blackness of a moonless night is illuminated with a flash of lightning. You can probably imagine the thunderclap that accompanies the bolt—as well as the sound of lightning actually striking the mountain tower. The top of the structure, symbolically shaped like a crown, is blown away. The tower catches fire, and two people, a queen and her consort, plunge or leap to their deaths on the rocky ground below. The lightning's jagged path through the sky roughly follows the path that energy takes as it flows down the Kabbalistic Tree of Life, moving from sphere to sphere. Each raindrop is shaped like a yod, the smallest letter in the Hebrew alphabet—and the only letter that is suspended in midair. Every other letter in Hebrew incorporates the shape of a yod, so it symbolizes the premise that the divine is present in everything.

In the Llewellyn Tarot, the Tower is the castle of Bala Lake, which was flooded to cleanse the land of debauchery, greed, and misuse of power. On the night it was flooded, the castle of a greedy, arrogant prince was filled with royals, all celebrating the birth of the prince's first son. The extravagant party and excessive display of wealth offended the gods, and a storm drowned the prince and his sycophant guests. Only one man survived: a humble musician. He was warned of the oncoming flood by a whispering bird, who wouldn't rest until he had led the bard to safety on a hill. To this day it is said that one can sometimes hear phantom bells and a whispered voice carrying across the lake, warning, "Vengeance will come."

In the Crowley deck, the chaos and destruction are equally vivid. The Eye of Shiva at the top of the card is open, and just as the myth foretold, the universe is falling apart as a result. A dove flies with an olive branch in its mouth, apparently fleeing Abraxas, the lion serpent of destruction. In the bottom right corner, the Roman god of the underworld, Dis Pater, opens his jaws and unleashes the fires of hell. Four bodies fall from the collapsing tower.

In other tarot decks, the Tower card is sometimes called La Maison Dieu, the House of God—a term that used to apply to hospitals.

What Does Your Future Hold?

- The Tower card is an unmistakable illustration of the shock we experience during times of crisis and change. It is a card of sudden, drastic transformation. It is a surprise ending, a dramatic twist, a rude awakening. On rare occasions, the Tower even symbolizes punishment on a biblical scale, like the retribution God inflicted on the builders of the Tower of Babel.

- The Tower is usually associated with Mars, the god of war, and the destruction and havoc he can wreak.

- If you've ever lived in tornado or earthquake country, you know the fear that the Tower card can inspire. It's the card of complete and total devastation that strikes without warning, in the middle of the night. If you get the Tower card in a tarot reading, you might want to pull your emergency survival kit together and brace for a storm.

- The Tower card isn't always a bad thing. Once the clouds part, the Tower offers you a chance to start over. For those who were trapped inside, the Tower card can even be a "get out of jail free" card. Some have compared the image to Saint Paul's miraculous escape from prison.

- The Tower card sometimes refers to breakups or breakdowns, and the disintegration or collapse of a structure you thought was stable—like a relationship, a home, or a career. In that case, however, the destruction was probably inevitable, and it ultimately clears the space for new developments.

- The Tower can also symbolize the destruction of false ideas and beliefs.

- In a tarot reading, the Tower card can represent a flash of new ideas and inspiration. It's a metaphoric bolt from the blue.

- The Tower is an undeniably phallic symbol, and it's pictured releasing a massive buildup of energy. It can be a good card if you're a man looking for physical action.

- After the Twin Towers attacks on September 11, 2001, the Tower card took on an added significance for many tarot readers, who saw a horrific, real-life version of the card play out on television news broadcasts.

For Future Reference

Keywords: Misery, ruin, adversity, calamity, fall, destruction, imprisonment, awakening, freedom, escape

Reversed: Oppression, imprisonment, tyranny

The mythic connection: The Tower has been compared to the biblical Tower of Babel, Rapunzel's tower, and the ivory towers of academia.

Astrological associations: The Tower is associated with Mars, the planet of war and aggression. Mars rules the Emperor card. When the Tower and the Emperor appear together in a reading, the two cards reinforce each other.

17. The Star (XVII)

Twinkle, twinkle

A classic image of faith and hope, the Star is a shining light in the darkness—a blithe spirit who offers hope, inspiration, and guidance.

In the classic Waite design, a yellow, eight-rayed star shines over a naked woman who kneels on the edge of a lake. The star in Waite's design is Sirius, the Dog Star, but it might also be compared to the Star of Bethlehem, the Star of the Magi, Venus, the morning and evening star, or the North Star that guides sailors through the night. The woman, who looks distinctly like a goddess of eternal youth and beauty, is kneeling. Her left knee is on solid ground, but her right foot is in the water. She holds two earthenware jugs filled with the water of life, and she leans forward to pour one of them into the lake, while the other empties on the shore and streams away. All around the central star, seven smaller white stars gleam in a twilight sky. Waite said the woman might be Truth unveiled, glorious in undying beauty, pouring on the waters of the soul some part and measure of her priceless possession. He also described her as the Great Mother, perpetually giving and sharing her wisdom and understanding with those under her guiding light. There's a tree in the background, with an ibis stretching its wings on one of its branches. The ibis was a symbol of the Greek god Thoth, a variant of Hermes.

In the Llewellyn Tarot, the Star is Branwen, a brave, considerate queen who suffered through a horrific political marriage for the sake of peace between Ireland and her beloved Wales. She was abused and made to work in the kitchens of her husband's family. While she ultimately died of a broken heart, for a time she found comfort, hope, and help in the form of a starling. She trained the bird in secret, and used it to carry a letter to her brother, Bran the Blessed. He and his men came to her aid. Even after death, her courage served as a source of hope and inspiration to her countrymen.

In the Crowley deck, the Star is Nut, the Egyptian goddess of the night. She stands on the surface of a distant star, in a landscape of healing crystals, and pours the waters of life from a golden chalice in her right hand to a silver chalice in her left hand. Roses grow at her feet, and butterflies flutter by, symbols of beauty and transformation. In the background, the earth spins in the deep blue embrace of space, surrounded by spiraling cosmic energy.

What Does Your Future Hold?

- For thousands of years, stars have been a guiding light in the heavens, helping humankind chart a course in the darkness toward the fulfillment of their dreams. Even today, the stars help us to map ourselves in space and time, by finding our position on a map of the cosmos. When the Star card falls in a tarot reading, it's a clear indication that you are being offered guidance and direction.

- Almost every star in the night sky is in itself a sun, the center of its own solar system. Of course, as more and more satellites begin to circle the earth, it's sometimes easy to mistake one of them for a star. Satellites are our new guiding lights in the sky, beaming instructions and information, so the Star could symbolize your connection to other people and places around the world.

- The central star in the card could symbolize a nova or supernova of understanding, the creation of new solar systems, and galaxies, far, far away from our experience and understanding.

- The Star card could also symbolize your unconscious wishes and desires. The Star card might remind you of shooting stars, or meteor showers, in which wishes are yours for the making.

- When you admire the stars, you are literally looking into the past. Every glimmer of starlight has traveled thousands of years, across lifetimes and centuries, to meet us in the dark. In a tarot reading, the Star card could refer to your past lifetimes and experiences.

- Stars often symbolize immortality, because the souls of the dead were once thought to be mounted in heaven.

- The Star card could also refer to astral travel, out-of-body experiences, or dreams.

- The Star's connection to futuristic Aquarius could suggest a sudden onslaught of new innovations and ideas, or the arrival of new technology and causes.

- A century ago, the Star card had a fairly negative meaning. It suggested loss, theft, privation, and abandonment—and that was in its upright position. Reversed, it suggested arrogance, haughtiness, and impotence. Those interpretations have long since fallen out of favor.

For Future Reference

Keywords: Hope, faith, wishes, dreams, promises, expectations, confidence

Reversed: Broken dreams, dashed hopes, disappointments, unfulfilled wishes

The mythic connection: Thousands of ancient myths were founded on observations of the night sky. The Star card could, however, be a depiction of Phospheros and Hesperos, two names for the rising and setting morning and evening star, Venus.

Astrological associations: What could be more astrological than the stars? Every star, nighttime planet, and constellation is represented by the Star card. Appropriately, the Star card is also associated with Aquarius, the sign of social consciousness and futuristic thinking.

Aquarians are the forward-thinking, progressive people of the zodiac. They are visionaries, revolutionaries, and pioneers. Their ability to dream of a brighter tomorrow links them closely with the Star card.

18. The Moon (XVIII)
Full moon rising

The moon, the ever-changing mirror of life on earth, reflects our unconscious needs and desires. Deeply rooted in the unconscious, the dreamlike moon symbolizes secrets and mysteries that you might not understand—or even recognize.

In the classic Waite design, a full moon shines in a twilit sky. Beneath it, a crayfish crawls out of the primordial sea, past a rocky shoreline, and onto dry land—a graphic representation of evolution in action. Two dogs—one wild, one tame—wait for him on shore, hinting at terrors both wild and domestic. There are two towers in the background; they symbolize a passageway, and in fact, they look just like the towers we saw earlier in the Death card. A path winds between the towers, weaving its way toward whatever lies over the horizon.

In the Llewellyn Tarot, the Moon card depicts Llyn y Morynion, the mountainous "Lake of the Maidens." The owl is Blodeuwedd, who had been created to serve as a wife to the sun god Llew Llaw Gyffes. Unfortunately, Blodeuwedd fell in love with another man, and then tried to murder her husband. She didn't succeed. When she realized that her efforts to kill him had failed, she and her maidens ran for the hills. Fearful and distraught, the women looked backward as they ran. Blodeuwedd's companions fell into the lake and drowned. When Blodeuwedd's creator, Gwydion, eventually caught up to her, he turned her into an owl who could only show her face at night.

In the Crowley deck, two night watchmen guard the towers of the moon, each armed with a jackal-headed staff. They are a twin version of the Anubis, who symbolized the Egyptian priesthood, along with two black jackals. The moon rises between the towers, embodying both its full and crescent phases. A stream of blood and water winds its way across the surface of the moon, and nine yod-shaped drops of blood also fall—one for every month of a woman's pregnancy. The moon has always been a symbol of pregnancy, because the phases of the moon reflect the changing shape of a pregnant woman's body as she grows larger with a child, gives birth, and then returns to her pre-pregnancy figure. In fact, an image of pregnancy and birth is woven into the card: behind the towers, in blue, you can see the shape of a woman's legs, bent at the knees, with the birth canal and an infant's head crowning between them. At the bottom of the card, there's a scarab, an ancient symbol of resurrection. He crawls upward, carrying another symbol of resurrection—the astrological glyph of the sun.

What Does Your Future Hold?

- The Moon is a reflective, feminine counterpart to the active, masculine energy of the sun, and it symbolizes the need for reflection, meditation, and contemplation.

- Waite said the Moon card represents the life of the imagination, separate and apart from the life of the spirit. The path between the towers, he said, winds its way toward an unknown horizon. The path is lit, however, by a calm and peaceful moon, suggesting that you won't have to travel in darkness or fear.

- The Moon card often describes a process of emotional or social evolution, because it depicts a crab crawling out of the primordial sea onto the dry land of civilization.

- There are thirteen full moons in a year. That means that once a year, one of the months will actually have a second full moon—the so-called "Blue Moon." Check your calendar. When the Moon card shows up in a tarot reading, the date of the Blue Moon could be significant for you.

- The full moon has always been linked to wild and erratic behavior. The card could refer to a little lunacy on your part, or on the part of the other people in your life.

- Tides rise and fall in answer to the beckoning call of the moon. In a tarot reading, the Moon card could suggest that you, too, tend to get carried away by the gravitational pull of your emotion.

- There's an unusual saying among some tarot readers: "The Moon reveals what the High Priestess conceals." When you get both cards in a spread, you might be able to discern one of the High Priestess's secrets.

- Because the Moon tends to mirror the twenty-eight-day cycle of a woman's fertility, it may be a suggestion that you pay attention to your fertility and creativity, too.

- Some people plan their work around the phases of the moon, beginning new projects when the moon is new, rounding them out as the moon is full, and concluding them as the moon wanes into the night. Before the next cycle, when the moon is still dark, they plan their next projects.

- The Moon symbolizes the intuition and the unconscious, because most people sleep when the moon is high.

- Historically, the Moon card was linked to deception and subterfuge, as truth could be hidden in the shadows.

For Future Reference

Keywords: Cycles, moonlight, reflection, hidden enemies, shadows, deception

Reversed: Deception, shadows, danger

The mythic connection: The Moon card is associated with Diana, the goddess of the hunt, who was normally accompanied by her hounds. The Moon is also linked to the goddess in all her forms: dark, maiden, mother, and crone.

Astrological associations: The Moon card is associated with Pisces, the sign of intuition and psychic ability.

Pisces is often said to be the most mystical sign of the Zodiac. While most people live entirely on the dry land of observable reality, the Pisces fish are usually most comfortable swimming through the deep waters of intuition and spiritual transformation. On land, the Pisces individuals can be restless, changeable, and self-destructive.

In water, they become adventurous, compassionate, intuitive, empathetic, sensitive, receptive, imaginative, and poetic.

Pisces is ruled by Neptune, the planet of mystery and illusion. In the tarot, Neptune is assigned to the Hanged Man. The combination of the Moon and the Hanged Man reflect the mesmerizing appeal of alternate realities.

19. The Sun (XIX)
Solar flair

The Sun, the source of heat and light and life on earth, symbolizes the energy and force that keeps the universe in motion.

In the classic Waite design, a beaming toddler rides a white pony through a walled garden, under the warm rays of an anthropomorphic sun—childlike symbol of happiness and joy. He wears nothing but a garland of flowers around his head, topped with the red feather of the Fool. He's naked, because his enthusiasm is innocent, unbridled, and pure. As he rides, he waves a red banner, signaling the joy and exuberance of youth. The banner—technically, a standard, or a symbolic flag mounted on a pole—represents a rallying point and an inspiration to victory. The child is ready to serve as a standard bearer, leading a procession of followers out of the garden and into the world beyond the wall.

In the Llewellyn Tarot, the Sun is Llew Llaw Gyffes, the "bright one of the skillful hand." He was a sun god, often equated with the Irish Lugh, who started life as a perfect child who grew twice as fast as any other child. He was handsome, strong, and able to manage any horse, and as an adult he was also a warrior, bard, magician, and healer. His unfaithful wife, Blodeuwedd, was pictured in the Moon card.

In the Crowley deck, two children, naked except for butterfly wings, dance with their arms upraised. The boy symbolizes soul, and the girl symbolizes mind, both united in a dance of joy. A rose and a cross are at their feet, a symbol of their source and their support. The field they dance in is lush and green, with gentle hills and a red wall in the background. What's most notable, however, is the circle of protective cosmic energy that envelops them. It flows out from the sun, the center of the universe and the hub of creation. As it surrounds the children and the earth with light and energy, its rays encircle them with a rainbow of color. Orange and yellow sunbeams divide the sphere into the twelve houses of the zodiac, complete with images for all twelve signs.

What Does Your Future Hold?

- The sun is the center of our solar system. It's the source of heat, light, and life on our planet.

- In astrology, the sun represents the true center of every person's universe—themselves. No matter how perceptive or empathic you might be, it's still impossible to see the world from someone else's point of view. We can only see the world from our perspective, at the center of our own existence. As a result, the sun symbolizes your consciousness, self-awareness, and ego.

- The Sun also illustrates your need to shine, and to find a moonlike companion who can reflect your radiance.

- For the most part, the Sun card is a good card to get in any tarot reading. It can often symbolize good health and renewed energy.

- Because nothing can hide in the bright light of day, the Sun card also suggests a time when even the most dour individuals will come out to play.

- The sun isn't reflective, like the moon, but active. It embodies masculine principles of energy and action.

- In a tarot reading, the Sun card could refer to annual events like solstices and cross-quarter days.

- Once a year, the sun comes back to the same place in the sky that it was when you were born. On that day—your birthday—you should feel like you're the center of the universe.
- The Sun card can also suggest a certain innocence, along with cosmic safeguards and protection that can help shield that innocence.

For Future Reference

Keywords: Material happiness, fortunate marriage, contentment, joy, enlightenment, light, clarity, glory, heat, passion, radiance, optimism, the active principle, masculinity, enthusiasm, a source of light and heat and the source of life, the center of the universe, the ego, full consciousness, brightness, eclipses, life and death on a symbolic level as the sun rises and sets, riding off into the sunset, blinding truth, success, happiness, joy, celebration

Reversed: Sunburn, overexposure, drought, global warming

The mythic connection: The sun symbolizes the light of the world—and in myth and religion alike, the sun symbolizes the gods who die and are reborn. The Sun card is especially related to Apollo, the god of the sun, whose sister Diana was goddess of the moon.

Astrological associations: In astrology, the sun takes center stage, as the symbol of the ego and the self. In tarot, the Sun card corresponds to its namesake, the sun, and symbolizes many of the same things in astrology that it does in tarot—like the self, the ego, and consciousness.

The sun rules Leo, a fire sign that's associated with a sense of play, fun, and unabashed showmanship. Leo is associated with the Strength card.

  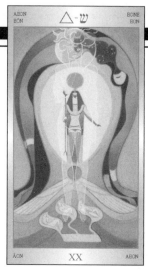

20. Judgement (XX)

Rise up and live again

All is revealed, as the Judgment card reminds us to forgive and be forgiven.

In the classic Waite design, the angel Gabriel blows his horn and a heavenly host of the dead and buried rise from their graves. The key figures are a man, a woman, and a child—a family unit—but they're not the only ones who thrill at the sound of the trumpet. All of the figures seem to be expressing wonder, amazement, adoration, and ecstasy. They have heard a higher calling, and they responded. Now they're undergoing the transformation of their lives—literally.

In the Llewellyn Tarot, the Judgment card depicts "The Sleepers"—the fallen King Arthur and his knights, safely entombed in an enchanted cave, sleeping until the day when their country needs them again. They rest on their shields in full battle dress, with swords close at hand and spears planted at their sides. In the distance is an intruder, a cowherd who stumbled across the cave with a magician and couldn't resist ringing the bell that could awaken the warriors. When they began to stir, the magician urged them to go back to sleep. He and the cave both disappeared, and the cowherd suffered poor health for the rest of his life. Sleeping heroes are a common theme in folklore, because they provide common people with the hope of salvation in the resurrection of a hero who will come to their aid. Such tales also served to dissuade would-be grave robbers with threats of dire consequences should the heroes be woken without cause.

In the Crowley deck, we see two versions of the same Egyptian god: Horus the elder, in the center of the card, as well as the ghostly outline of Horus the child, with his index finger in his mouth. Horus was the child of Isis and Osiris; he was conceived after Osiris was murdered and Isis brought him back to life. Crowley believed that Horus' death and rebirth, in turn, would symbolize the dawning of a New Age. In the background there's an egg-shaped globe of light and energy, resting on the winged solar disk that symbolizes death and resurrection. The egg is surrounded by the blue embrace of Nut, the goddess of the night. At the bottom of the card, the three branches of the Hebrew letter Shin hold three human figures, the seeds of future creation. It's superimposed over the astrological glyph for Libra, the sign of balance.

What Does Your Future Hold?

- Anyone who's familiar with Christianity will recognize the story behind Waite's Judgment card: it's a picture of Judgment Day, when the dead will rise, the gates of heaven will open, and there will be no further separation of heaven and earth.

- The Judgment card, however, embodies much more than the simple story of judgment and resurrection on the last day—although that, in itself, would be enough. The card is also a symbol of a new lease on life, and a calling loud enough to wake the dead.

- In a tarot reading, the Judgment card could be a clear indication that you need to be up and about. It may be time for you to rise and face the music.

- The Judgment card is a card of ultimate transformation, during which no secret can be hidden, and all will be revealed.

- In a tarot reading, the Judgment card may be a reminder that it's time for you to reveal secrets, forgive yourself and others, or simply think out of the box.

- The card is a good one to see during health readings, because it implies a certain wholeness and return to optimum health and fitness.

- Historically, the Judgment card was said to suggest a loss in a lawsuit.

For Future Reference

Keywords: Decision, change, renewal, rebirth, consciousness, compassion, forgiveness

Reversed: An unwillingness to forgive and move on, weakness, indecision, delay

The mythic connection: The angel of Judgment is the angel Gabriel, who first revealed that Elizabeth and Mary would bear children—John the Baptist and Jesus, respectively. According to the Bible, Gabriel will also be the angel who blows the horn announcing Judgment Day.

Astrological associations: Scorpio is ruled by Pluto, the planet of death, regeneration, and unavoidable change. In the tarot, Pluto is assigned to the Judgment card. The combination of the Death and Judgment cards reaffirms Scorpio's grasp of the deep mysteries of life, as well as its appreciation for the life to come.

21. The World (XXI)

Last dance

A card of completion and success, the World is the last stop on the Fool's Journey.

In the classic Waite design, a bare-breasted woman, wrapped only in a silk scarf, dances for joy in the center of a wreath. She is clearly happy to be alive. She holds a wand in each hand—like her counterpart in the first card of the major arcana, the Magician. In a sense, the cards have come full circle. In fact, the woman in the World card is dancing squarely in the center of that circle. A circle is a symbol of eternity, because it has no beginning and no end. It goes on and on, forever. That symbolism is reinforced by the fact that the circular wreath is held together by ribbons in the shape of a lemniscate, the figure-eight symbol of infinity. Wreaths are often connected to stories of death, resurrection, and immortality. We hang evergreen wreaths at Christmas and the winter solstice as a symbol of everlasting life. We send floral wreaths to funerals. Historically, people even crowned their heroes with laurel wreaths whenever they defeated an opponent in battle or in an athletic event—both of which represented victory over death. The dancer's scarf is another powerful symbol of beginnings and ends. Newborn infants have always been wrapped in swaddling cloths, while the dead were wrapped in shrouds. Look closely, and you'll notice that the shape of the scarf also resembles a lemniscate. The World dancer is surrounded by the four creatures of the Apocalypse: an angel, an eagle, a lion, and a bull. The creatures symbolize the four evangelists, Matthew, Mark, Luke, and John, and the four Hebrew letters in the name of God: Yod-Heh-Vau-Heh.

In the Llewellyn Tarot, the card is called the Universe, and it depicts the mountain of Cadair Idris—a haunted gathering place for spirits and spectral forces in North Wales. The name Cadair Idris means "Chair of Idris," because its rock formation resembles a chair. It's believed that if people spend the night there, they will either be gifted with poetic gifts and prophetic visions—or they'll be driven insane. According to legend, the lord of the Otherworld circles its peak every Halloween, leading the souls of the dead on a wild hunt. During the rest of the year, otherworldly hounds run over its slopes and howl at the moon. People who dare to spend a night on its summit know that they'll either leave the mountain as gifted poets—or be driven insane. The mountain is a place of mystery, in which humanity can find meaning and messages for the world at large.

In the Crowley deck, the Universe card depicts a nude dancer wrapped in a serpent, not a scarf. She is reminiscent of the Greek goddess Eurynome, who danced with the serpent Ophion and produced the Orphic egg. She's also somewhat like the Old Testament's Eve, reconciling with the serpent who tempted her back in the Garden of Eden. The familiar creatures of the Apocalypse stand guard around the four corners of the card. As always, they also represent the four fixed signs of the zodiac: Aquarius the water bearer, Scorpio the eagle, Leo the lion, and Taurus the bull. While the dancer isn't encircled by a wreath, she does seem to be standing at the end of a tunnel—a tunnel that looks an awful lot like a birth canal. Above her, the eye of God shines light on his creations. Beneath her, pyramids take shape, and behind her the stars and planets swirl in an unending cosmic dance.

What Does Your Future Hold?

- As the Fool comes to the final stop of the journey through the major arcana, the World card offers a study in the close connection between endings and beginnings.

- The World card is the last card in the major arcana, but it's also a starting point for a whole new cycle of adventures and experience. The card implies the successful completion of one journey, and the celebration that's due as a result.

- When the World card falls in a reading, it's time to celebrate the conclusion of one chapter in your life and the beginning of a new world of experience.

- The card also suggests a state of wholeness, balance, and unity, as body, mind, and spirit work as one.

- You might even find yourself literally re-enacting the image of the World card, at a wedding dance, a party, or a celebration.

- Because of its connections to Saturn, the World card could symbolize limitations and boundaries that will leave you feeling confined.

- Alternately, you might find that you need to set limits and establish clear, firm boundaries for other people.

For Future Reference

Keywords: Success, completion, perfection, celebration, reward, coming full circle, center stage, endings and beginnings, world travel, unity, synthesis, oneness, wholeness

Reversed: Delays, hesitations, false starts

The mythic connection: While she doesn't look particularly masculine in most renditions of the card, the dancer is often said to be a hermaphrodite—a person who is neither male nor female, but exhibits characteristics of both sexes. According to Greek myth, Hermaphroditos was the son of Hermes, the messenger of the gods, and Aphrodite, the goddess of love. A young fountain nymph named Salmacis fell in love with Hermaphroditos, but he ignored her. She turned to the gods for help, and prayed that she would be united with him forever. Her prayers were answered: when Hermaphroditos took a bath in her fountain, they became one person.

By the numbers: The World dancer is firmly encircled by the shape of the number 0. She is dancing in the center of the universe. She is the chick in the cosmic egg, or the seed about to be implanted in the womb of the world.

Astrological associations: The World card corresponds to Saturn, the ringed planet. While those rings do imply a certain number of limitations and restrictions, they also set boundaries that can help us define our position and relate to other people without losing our own individuality. In other words, Saturn's boundaries don't merely confine us: they define us.

Saturn rules Capricorn, an earth sign that's associated with work, achievement, responsibility, and drive. Capricorn is associated with the Devil card. If you see the World card and the Devil card together in a reading, pay attention, because they reinforce each other's message.

Ace of Wands

Fire power

All of the aces represent the promise and opportunity of new beginnings, and the Ace of Wands is perhaps the most promising card of all. It represents potential in its purest form—raw, unbridled possibility, ready, willing, and able to be unleashed.

The Ace of Wands is the first card in the minor arcana, and it's the spark that starts the series off with a bang. You might even think of it as a Big Bang, like the one that created the universe.

In the classic Waite design, all four aces share a similar design: a giant hand parts the swirling mists of a silver cloud, holding the emblem of the suit. In this case, that emblem is a tree branch, still sprouting buds and leaves. Wands are an active, masculine suit: whoever is holding this wand is using their right hand, which symbolizes action. The landscape below features a mountain castle in the distance, symbolizing refuge, watchfulness, and royal or divine guidance and sovereignty. There is also a small grove of trees along a riverbank. That could be the place where this wand came from. Waite called this card the "Root of the Powers of Fire."

In the Llewellyn Tarot, the Ace of Wands symbolizes inspiration and a breakthrough in thinking. It's more introspective than Waite's version of the card; the wand is held in the left hand, instead of the right. It seems to signal a more receptive mood, which could be more open to divine inspiration. The flowing river at the bottom of the card reflects the growth of trees and shrubs along its banks, as well as the changing landscape of the seasons.

In the Crowley deck, the wand looks like a torch with ten flames, symbolizing the ten spheres on the Kabbalistic Tree of Life. Behind the flames, there's a shower of twenty-two yod-shaped sparks that represent the twenty-two letters of the Hebrew alphabet. In fact, the Hebrew word aleph—the first letter of the Hebrew alphabet—is carved into the wand itself. Like Waite, Crowley also called this card "Root of the Powers of Fire."

What Does Your Future Hold?

Like a match bursting into flame, or a stick of dynamite that's about to explode, the Ace of Wands is an exciting card. Who knows what passions are about to ignite, or what fireworks are about to go off?

- In many ways, the Ace of Wands is a card of imminent creation. The Ace of Wands symbolizes the promise and possibility of new life for you, filled with active masculine energy and potency.

- It's no coincidence that the Ace of Wands is undeniably phallic in nature. It reflects the powerful drive for creation (and subsequent re-creation) inherent in the species. The Ace of Wands embodies your power to generate—and regenerate—countless generations.

- Wands cards often symbolize work and career, so the Ace of Wands could suggest the start of a new job or business endeavor.

- When you get the Ace of Wands in a reading, you might be inspired to invent something artistic. You might be offered a new opportunity at work. You might find yourself inventing something, and imbuing it with the very essence of your spirit.

- No matter what new opportunity presents itself, you'll be fired up about it. You'll feel driven, excited, and filled with enthusiasm. You won't be able to wait to get things underway.

- Historically, the Ace of Wands was said to herald money, fortune, and inheritance.

For Future Reference

Keywords: Fire, energy, sparks of creativity, virility, vitality, potency, desire, male energy, invention, enterprise, excitement, enthusiasm, force, strength, vigor, ignition, confidence, willpower, drive

Reversed: Impotence, delays, frustration, dissatisfaction, the misuse of power, violence, cruelty, tyranny, decadence, destruction

By the numbers: All of the aces represent pure promise and possibility, because they hold limitless potential: succeeding cards in each suit stem from this single starting point. In fact, the Ace of Wands is said to be the root of the powers of fire.

Timing and dates: In fortunetelling, the ace could refer to one hour, one day, one week, one month, one year—or Sunday, the first day of the week, or January, the first month.

Astrological associations: Astrologically, the Ace of Wands is associated with all of the powers of fire—the element associated with Aries, Leo, and Sagittarius.

Two of Wands

Will power

Rub two sticks together, and what do you get? Fire—assuming that you've laid the groundwork for a blaze, and that you have fuel on hand to feed the flames and keep them burning.

The fiery Two of Wands is, in fact, all about the will—and the power—to move beyond the initial stages of creation.

In the classic Waite design, a regal-looking figure—perhaps a nobleman or a business-man—stands behind a battlement. The low wall has been decorated with a banner of the red rose of passion and the white lily of purity. He is the master of all he surveys. His power is symbolized by the globe in his right hand: he literally, and figuratively, holds the whole world in his hand. He's stationed above a protected bay or inlet, with cliffs and mountains in the distance; it's a geographic feature that helps make it easier to defend his castle. The bay also makes the castle a convenient base of operations; he's in a position to trade. He is steady and reliable, with a firm grip on one wand. While the figure is obviously well off, Waite suggested that it also hints at the sadness of Alexander amidst the grandeur of this world's wealth, sym-bolizing the harmony of rule and justice. Waite called this card "Dominion."

In the Llewellyn Tarot, the figure on the Two of Wands is a woman, not a man. She gazes into a crystal ball, hoping to catch a glimpse of her future. She is not nearly as concerned about the practical realities of the physical world beyond her walls; she has a more visionary perspective, and she sees the world through the eyes of a psychic.

In the Crowley deck, the two wands are Tibetan dorjes, which represent thunderbolts, the emblem of celestial power. They are crossed, and the friction they create sends sparks of energy out into the universe. The green, red-eyed demon who holds them symbolizes fear. He is the proverbial monster in the closet of your subconscious mind. The six flames behind the wands symbolize the will to create. The glyphs are for Mars and Aries; Aries, the sign of leadership, is ruled by Mars, planet of energy and aggression. The card symbolizes rule; Crowley also called this card "Dominion."

What Does Your Future Hold?

- The Two of Wands symbolizes influence and power over others, as well as authority, control, and dominion.

- When you get the Two of Wands in a reading, you may find yourself in a position of power over other people or property. Your managerial skills will be put to the test.

- You could find yourself richly rewarded for your efforts, but at the same time you could be watching and waiting for something more to come along.

- Your boldness and decisiveness pay off, but you know you can accomplish more.

- More than a century ago, fortune tellers said that the Two of Wands meant that marriage would not be possible, or that a young lady could expect trivial disappointments.

For Future Reference

Keywords: Strength, ambition, resolution, courage, pride, vision, dominance, domination, fierceness, generosity, sensitivity, refinement, the harmony of rule and of justice, a stronghold

Reversed: Tyranny, abuse of power, weakness, revenge, turbulence, restlessness, obstinacy, shamelessness, pride, subjugation, hesitation

By the numbers: Twos represent duality and choices. The number two suggests pairs and combinations, as well as relationships, partnerships, and the attraction between two people. Twos also represent conversation and debate—the point and counterpoint of two opposing ideas, or the antithesis that rises up in response to almost every thesis. The very nature of the number two also signifies a wide range of concepts that come in pairs: heaven and earth, male and female, active and passive, conscious and un-conscious, and day and night. Written as a Roman numeral II, the number suggests a gateway or a doorway, as well as female genitalia.

Timing and dates: In fortunetelling, the number two could refer to two hours, days, two weeks, two months, two years—or Monday, the second day of the week, or February, the second month. Astrologically, the Two of Wands is assigned to 0–10° Aries (March 21–30).

Three of Wands
Established strength

Most people spend a good deal of their time imagining the way things *could* be, if everything they plan turns out the way they hope. The Three of Wands is one card that depicts the longing and hope each one of us has for the future.

In the classic Waite design, the Three of Wands depicts a strong man on a hill overlooking the sea, watching as three ships sail across a bay. (It could be the same bay we saw just one card back, in the Two of Wands.) The man looks like a businessman, waiting and watching for his ships to come in. What riches will they bring? What precious cargo do they carry in their hold, from exotic, far-off lands? Waite called this card "Established Strength."

In the Llewellyn Tarot, those three ships are tantalizingly close, either drawing nearer or just starting off for newer, more promising waters. It's a card of speculation, new enterprise, new directions, and adventure. It's the card of a well-planned gamble, and the hope of a payoff that will be worth the risk.

In the Crowley deck, the three crossed wands are lotus blossoms that symbolize the harmony of spring. The two astrological glyphs represent Aries and the sun; the sun is exalted in Aries. The falcon-headed god in the background looks like Horus, Egyptian god of the sky; he rests his hands protectively on a stork, a symbol of the human soul. Crowley called this card "Virtue."

What Does Your Future Hold?

- The Three of Wands is a very good card. In a reading, the Three of Wands could mean that your ships are finally about to come in. You may have experienced some struggle recently, but now your success is assured—especially if you collaborate with others. Your hopes will soon be realized. You will be bold, decisive, and able to take the risks you need to pay off on the bottom line.

- The Three of Wands suggests natural leadership ability, wealth, and power.

- You may find yourself entering into a profitable partnership or relationship with a business acquaintance, or find yourself involved in a trade or business deal that will enrich everyone involved. Your negotiations will go smoothly. You might even find that a mentor or senior business manager steps in to assist you.

- While the Three of Wands suggests that you have good business sense, watch out for the dark side of this card. It can be a card of conceit, pride, arrogance, insolence, and obstinacy. It may be a warning: don't get too cocky. You will still need to think clearly to make smart decisions.

- The Three of Wands symbolizes trade. It suggests that you've put something of value out in the world, and that it will probably generate even more profit and wealth in the days and weeks to come.

- The card also serves as a reminder of the old adage, "Nothing ventured, nothing gained."

- In a reading, the card symbolizes the strength of a well-run, well-funded business organization, dedicated to enterprise, trade, and commerce. It implies a sense of adventure and discovery, not only of markets and customers, but also of new lands, new sources of goods and services, and new opportunities for partnerships and alliances.

For Future Reference

Keywords: Business leadership and acumen, trade, commerce, cooperation, discovery

Reversed: Historically, the Three of Wands was supposed to be even better when it was reversed. It heralded the end of troubles, adversity, toil, and disappointment.

By the numbers: Back in the Ace of Wands, an idea was conceived. There were some initial preparations in the Two of Wands, and here in the Three of Wands, it begins to manifest itself. Threes symbolize creation—the result of two separate forces combining to create a third entity. A mother and a father produce a child together. A thesis and an antithesis combine to produce a synthesis. The number three can also represent body, mind, and spirit, or past, present, and future. Many religions believe in a holy trinity, such as Father, Son, and Holy Spirit, or Maiden, Mother, and Crone, or the triple goddess of the New, Full, and Old Moon.

Timing and dates: In fortunetelling, the number three could refer to three hours, three days, three weeks, three months, or three years—or Tuesday, the third day of the week, or March, the third month. Astrologically, the Three of Wands is assigned to 10–20° Aries (March 31–April 10).

Four of Wands

Grab your partner

The Four of Wands is a card of harmony and completion. For the moment, all is right with the world.

In the classic Waite design, a young couple celebrates. They are dressed in complementary colors of blue and red—one water, one fire. They hold bouquets of flowers over their heads. The garland of flowers even looks like a Jewish chuppa or wedding canopy, a symbolic structure designed to represent a couple's first home together. Waite called this card "Perfected Work."

In the Llewellyn Tarot, the garlands are strung over a winding country stream. In the background, a bridge leads to an impressive hilltop castle, a symbol of reguse and protection. In the foreground, a dam holds water in a still reflective pool, which overflows in a white-capped waterfall. The card symbolizes celebrations, social events, and rewards. It promises new alliances and friendships, as well as a solid foundation for the future.

In the Crowley deck, the four wands are arranged in the shape of a circle, much like the Wheel of Fortune. When you spin this wheel, however, you'll either land on a ram's head, the symbol of Mars, or a dove, the symbol of Venus. The astrological glyphs repeat the motif: the ram's horns stand for Aries, the sign of leadership that rules Mars, and Venus, the planet of love and attraction. A goddess holds the wheel, while a godlike figure holds a sacred gold ring and wand in his outstretched hands, ready to consummate their symbolic union. Crowley called this card "Completion."

What Does Your Future Hold?

- When you get the Four of Wands in a reading, you can almost certainly expect a celebration in the near future. It could be a wedding, like the one pictured on the card. It could be a bridal shower, a bachelor party, a housewarming, or a baby shower. It could even be a casual get-together with friends or co-workers.

- Remember that weddings are celebrations, not only for the couple at the heart of the event, but also for family and friends. Weddings are one occasion in which family traditions are strengthened and passed along from generation to generation, old stories can be retold, and new stories can begin. Ultimately, the Four of Wands symbolizes social gatherings that are designed for an entire community.

- The card also suggests a firm foundation for family life, as well as domestic tranquility.

- Historically, the Four of Wands was said to symbolize unexpected good fortune—both upright and in its reversed position. It also symbolized the haven of country life.

For Future Reference

Keywords: Stability, prosperity, peace, good fortune, union, harmony, success, happiness

Reversed: Instability, shakeups, conflicts (Historically, the Four of Wands reversed was said to suggest that a married woman would have beautiful children.)

By the numbers: The number four symbolizes structure and foundation, because there are four walls to a room, four sides to a house, and four corners to a building's foundation. The Four of Wands often symbolizes the structure and foundation of marriage and family life. Fours symbolize structure, stability, and security, because four points come together to form a solid. There are four walls in a room, and four corners to a house. There are four dimensions: width, length, height, and time. There are four cardinal directions: north, south, east, and west. There are four seasons, four winds, and four phases of the moon. There are four elements, and four corresponding suits in the minor arcana.

Timing and dates: In fortunetelling, the number four could refer to four hours, four days, four weeks, four months, or four years—or Wednesday, the fourth day of the week, or April, the fourth month. Astrologically, the Four of Wands is assigned to 20–30° Aries (April 11–20).

Five of Wands
Go play outside

The Five of Wands is the halfway card in the suit, and it acts like the tipping point on a scale. It depicts a situation that could either take a turn for the better, or fall apart completely. It's a lot like the crisis we face in the middle of any big project, when we look around and wonder why we even bothered to start. Unfortunately, there's no turning back. Once you're at that midway point, it takes the same amount of effort to put things back the way they were or to forge ahead and finish the job.

In the classic Waite design, five young men are trying to work together and coordinate their efforts. They're either on the verge of creating a five-pointed star design—or they're on the brink of anarchy. They are distinctly adolescent, and their actions seem playful. At any minute, however, complete chaos could erupt. Waite called this card "Strife."

In the Llewellyn Tarot, the five young men are working from a master plan, carefully drawn out on the scroll at their feet. Just as you might expect, the card symbolizes competition, confusion, erratic energy, and inconsistent effort—and it can even hint at a communication breakdown, rebellion, turmoil, and the need to reorganize and make a fresh start.

In the Crowley deck, two of the wands are crowned with the head of a phoenix, a symbol of destruction and purification by fire and subsequent rebirth from the ashes. The other two wands are crowned with lotus flowers, a symbol of creative, motherly energy. The fifth wand, in the middle, is an Egyptian staff, crowned with the lion-headed serpent Abraxas. The astrological glyphs represent Leo and Saturn; Crowley said that Leo symbolizes the element of fire at its strongest and most balanced, but Saturn—the planet of limits, restrictions, and boundaries—weighs it down. Like Waite, Crowley also called this card "Strife."

What Does Your Future Hold?

- When you get the Five of Wands in a reading, you might find that you're suddenly part of a team at work or in a social situation. In fact, the Five of Wands has all the hallmarks of committee work. You might need to refine your leadership skills, or be prepared to serve as a willing member of the team.

- The Five of Wands could indicate a test of strength or a battle of wills. Keep your cool and watch your temper.

- Even if you're feeling comfortable and light-hearted, watch your words carefully—especially if you think you're only joking. When the Five of Wands comes up, it might not take much to turn a mock battle into a real war.

- Historically, the Five of Wands was supposed to be a good sign for anyone who wanted to engage in a little financial speculation. If you get the card, you might want to play the stock market. Just don't invest more than you can afford to lose.

For Future Reference

Keywords: Group efforts, teamwork, conversations, games, power struggles

Reversed: Quarreling, fighting, clashes, strife, disputes, litigation, legal proceedings

By the numbers: Fives represent a halfway point in the progression from one to ten. In the tarot, "five" cards often symbolize a crisis: they're the midway point, when events can either take a turn for the better or go horribly awry. Fives also symbolize the five senses, the five points on a star, and the five vowels in the English alphabet. Some metaphysicians suggest that five is important because it symbolizes a fifth element—Spirit.

Timing and dates: In fortunetelling, the number five could refer to five hours, five days, five weeks, five months, or five years—or Thursday, the fifth day of the week, or May, the fifth month. Astrologically, the Five of Wands is assigned to 0–10° Leo (July 22–August 1).

Six of Wands
All hail the conquering hero

Historically, when conquering heroes returned from battle, they led a triumphal parade—complete with all the spoils of war displayed for the crowd. Today, we still hold victory parades. Most often, they're sports figures, fresh from the field of triumph in a Super Bowl or World Series, and we hail them with tickertape and widespread acclaim.

In the classic Waite design, a triumphant horseman rides through a crowd, a laurel wreath of victory on his head, and footmen at his side. On the surface, it is a hero's welcome. The horseman could also represent great news carried by the King's courier—a message long anticipated and warmly welcomed. Waite called this card "Victory."

In the Llewellyn Tarot, a brave man on his white horse gets a hero's welcome. He has fought the good fight. He saved the day, and made it possible for the rest of his community to live in peace and prosperity—at least for the time being. The card symbolizes acknowledgement, accolades, and gratitude. It signifies the respect of the community, recognition, and honor.

In the Crowley deck, the six crossed wands also symbolize victory. Two of the wands are crowned with lotus flowers, two feature the phoenix, and two feature a sun and a moon, symbols of light and dark, day and night, action and reflection. All of the wands are perfectly balanced, and they burn steadily where they intersect. The four figures standing around the fire represent the four elements, each involved in a ritual greeting. The two astrological glyphs stand for Leo, the fiery sign of creativity, and Jupiter, the planet of luck and expansion. Like Waite, Crowley also called this card "Victory."

What Does Your Future Hold?

- When you get the Six of Wands in a reading, it could indicate that you will soon receive credit and acclaim for a job well done. News of your success will spread, and you will be heralded as a hero, greeted by praise and even a measure of adoration.

- The Six of Wands could symbolize validation, or even vindication for a stand you took much earlier.

- Be aware, however, that once you're on your high horse, someone may decide it's their job to tear you back down. You're no longer just one of the crowd.

- You might also find that the Six of Wands portends good news riding your way from a distant battlefield—news you'll want to celebrate.

- Historically, the Six of Wands suggested that servants could lose the confidence of their masters—a polite way of suggesting that an employee could be fired—or that a young lady could be betrayed by a friend.

For Future Reference

Keywords: Victory, success, acclaim, messages, messengers, parades

Reversed: Infidelity, treachery, disloyalty, disrespect, apprehension, fear, an enemy at the gate

By the numbers: Sixes historically symbolize the human being, because man was said to be created on the sixth day. Six also symbolizes the sixth sense—psychic ability—as well as the six directions of space: left, right, forward, backward, up, and down.

Timing and dates: In fortunetelling, the number six could refer to six hours, six days, six weeks, six months, or six years—or Friday, the sixth day of the week, or June, the sixth month. Astrologically, the Six of Wands is assigned to 10–20° Leo (August 2–11).

Seven of Wands

Valor

The Seven of Wands is a card of confidence and strength, even when you find yourself outnumbered and outgunned.

In the classic Waite design, a young man on a cliff defends his turf against six unseen opponents. He is fighting from a position of power: both feet are firmly on the ground, while his adversaries seem to be making their way up a steep cliff. He is outnumbered, but he has the advantage and he can certainly keep them at bay, beating them back one by one. Waite called this card "Valor."

In the Llewellyn Tarot, a brave young man also holds his challengers at bay, but he doesn't have the benefit of a solid footing. In fact, he's standing in a waterfall—which means his attackers, at least, are forced to swim upstream. The card symbolizes courage, determination, and creative thinking.

In the Crowley deck, we see the same wands we noticed in the Six of Wands, but the mood is decidedly darker. They've all been relegated to the background, and a crude weapon of war—a club—throws the rest of the scene off balance. In the background, the crocodile god Sebek presides over other creatures of the underworld, and volcanoes spew fire and ash into an already-darkened sky. The astrological glyphs stand for Mars, the planet of war and aggression, and Leo, the sign of courage and performance under pressure. The card symbolizes unbalanced energy. Like Waite, Crowley also called this card "Valor."

What Does Your Future Hold?

- Hold firm. Stand your ground. Yes, you're still in the thick of things. You're definitely embattled. And no, you're not imagining it: you are under attack. But your feet are firmly planted. You're fighting from a position of strength. It's relatively easy for you to fight back, to pick off each of your opponents, one by one, as they clamber to gain a foothold and toss you off the cliff. This battle is yours to lose. Maintain your sense of calm and your presence of mind. Don't give up your footing.

- Call for reinforcements, if you have them, so someone has your back.

- In a tarot reading, the Seven of Wands occasionally represents intellectual arguments and disagreements, discussions, negotiations, competition, and trade.

- It also can caution against a fall in power and a drop in stature. Be careful who you step on while you're on the way up, because you'll probably meet those same people on the way down.

- Historically, the Seven of Wands was said to refer to a dark child.

For Future Reference

Keywords: Courage in the face of opposition, the promise of victory, valor, persistence, advantage, strife, negotiation, barter, competition, success, gain, profit

Reversed: Vulnerability, confusion, embarrassment, anxiety, indecision, hesitation, vacillation

By the numbers: Seven is a mystical, magical number. Classically, there were seven days of creation. There are seven gifts of the Holy Spirit: wisdom, understanding, counsel, fortitude, knowledge, piety, and fear. There are seven deadly sins: envy, sloth, gluttony, wrath, pride, lust, and greed. There are seven virtues: faith, hope, charity, fortitude, justice, temperance, and prudence. (You can see most of them in the major arcana.) Alchemists had seven metals: gold, silver, iron, mercury, tin, copper, and lead. There are seven visible planets: the Sun, the Moon, Mars, Mercury, Jupiter, Venus, and Saturn. There are seven days of the week, seven notes in a musical scale, seven colors of the rainbow, and seven chakras. Because the seventh day is a day of rest, seven is the number of self-reflection and philosophy. To fully randomize your tarot deck before a reading, shuffle it seven times.

Timing and dates: In fortunetelling, the number seven could refer to seven hours, seven days, seven weeks, seven months, or seven years—or Saturday, the seventh day of the week, or July, the seventh month. Astrologically, the Seven of Wands is assigned to 20–30° Leo (August 12–22).

Eight of Wands
Swiftness

When the Eight of Wands appears in a reading, things happen fast.

In the classic Waite design, eight wands fly through the air in open country. There's a river in the background, along with a hilltop castle far in the distance. According to Waite, the wands are descending, not taking off. In other words, they'll land soon, and whatever they prophesy will soon manifest itself. Waite called this card "Swiftness."

In the Llewellyn Tarot, the eight wands soar over five members of a herd of antelope. Each one is in a different state of awareness: two are simply grazing, two are ambling along, and one seems to sense motion. The card symbolizes swiftness and opportunity, as well as the importance of thinking on your feet.

In the Crowley deck, eight rays of electricity vibrate so energetically that they either sustain or create matter, symbolized by the red, yellow, green, and blue pyramid shapes that serve as the focus of the card. A red-robed, hooded figure seems to be mixing that energy with the handle of a two-headed axe, almost as if he were stirring a magical cauldron. Behind him, the web of space and time flows out into infinity. The rainbow at the top of the card is pure light, divided into a spectrum of seven colors; it represents a bridge to other worlds. The astrological glyphs symbolize Mercury, the planet of speed and communication, and Sagittarius, the sign of adventure, higher education, and long-distance travel. The card symbolizes dynamic action. Like Waite, Crowley also called this card "Swiftness."

What Does Your Future Hold?

- Traditionally, the Eight of Wands was associated with long-distance travel, as well as the imminent arrival of letters and communications from afar. As times have changed, the card's meaning still applies: while we don't send as many letters these days, we still communicate across long distances—and we communicate almost instantaneously, via fax, phone calls, and e-mail.

- When you go with that interpretation, each wand in the card becomes another branch of communication; they all fly through the air, each one a message, parallel ports, e-mail, telephone calls, conference calls, missives from far-away people and places. That's a lot to manage, and the card could signify an array of long-distance romances, alliances, support groups, and shared-interest communities.

- Sometimes, the Eight of Wands is associated with the slings and arrows of outrageous fortune.

- Some tarot readers view the eight wands as Cupid's arrows, flying through the air to their mark.

- Historically, the Eight of Wands was said to predict domestic disputes for married couples.

For Future Reference

Keywords: Activity, speed, messages, communication

Reversed: Jealousy, quarrels, remorse, repentance, guilty conscience

By the numbers: Eights represent infinity, because they resemble the lemniscate, the sideways symbol of infinity. There are also eight points on the Wheel of the Year. To Christians, eight is a symbol of baptism and spiritual rebirth; many baptisteries and baptismal fonts have eight sides. Eight also represents the eternal spiral of regeneration.

Timing and dates: In fortunetelling, the number eight could refer to eight hours, eight weeks, eight months, eight years—or August, the eighth month. Astrologically, the Eight of Wands is assigned to 0–10° Sagittarius (November 23–December 2).

Nine of Wands
The wounded warrior

In the classic Waite design, a mustachioed man, obviously exhausted, leans on his wand. He may be wounded. There's a cloth bandage wrapped around his head, and he stands defensively, almost as though he's anticipating another attack. His back is literally against the wall: he's standing in front of a palisade of eight Wands, all in a row. Waite called this card "Strength."

In the Llewellyn Tarot, the warrior is clearly wounded. Not only is his head bandaged, but his arm is also in a sling. The card can be read as a cautionary tale, one that calls for order and control, planning, and protecting one's assets. It also suggests a certain hard-fought wisdom, as well as the growth and character development that comes only at the price of experience.

In the Crowley deck, the wands are arrows—eight in the background, and one "master" arrow in the front, with the moon as its tip and the sun as its driving force. The two luminaries are symbols of the conscious and unconscious mind. The moon in the design also incorporates the symbol for Sagittarius—which is, of course, the sign of the archer. It's a card of vigor and quick recovery, even in the face of adversity. Crowley also called this card "Strength."

What Does Your Future Hold?

- When the Nine of Wands appears in a tarot reading, it could suggest that you are a wounded warrior, and that your back is to the wall.

- At some point earlier in the day, you may have said to yourself, "today is a good day to die." However, you were focused and strong. You were brave and courageous. You took risks, and you persevered. Now you will live to fight another day.

- Granted, you're not the same fighter you were before you saw battle. You've been injured. Your wounds may heal, with time, but they might leave scars, permanent reminders of the damage wrought.

- Of course, the Nine of Wands might also represent good health and a quick recovery from illness or injury.

For Future Reference

Keywords: Strength, courage, discipline, adversity, health

Reversed: Obstacles, adversity, calamity, weakness, character flaws, fearfulness

By the numbers: Because there are nine months of pregnancy, nines symbolize selflessness, compassion, universality, humanitarianism, and spirituality.

Timing and dates: In fortunetelling, the number nine could refer to nine hours, nine days, nine weeks, nine months, or nine years—or September, the ninth month. Astrologically, the Nine of Wands is assigned to 10–20° Sagittarius (December 3–12).

Ten of Wands

Lay down your burden

A world-weary traveler, burdened with cares and concerns, needs to be careful about carrying too much baggage.

In the classic Waite design, a laborer struggles under the weight of a heavy load of timbers—the ten wands that give the card its name. His back is bent and stooped with effort. His burden is disorganized, unwieldy. The strain on his arms, back, neck, and shoulders is probably excruciating. From the looks of most versions of the card, the only way he can tolerate his burden is knowing that his destination isn't far—home is just down the road a little, at the end of a gently winding, downhill path. Waite called this card "Oppression."

In the Llewellyn Tarot, the laborer carries nine long wands on his back, and uses one strong branch as a walking stick for support. He climbs a series of steps, each one leading through a flowering meadow to a cozy cottage. He is old, and his white hair suggests the wisdom and experience he picked up along the way—along with all those wands. The card symbolizes a burden, but also the reward of rising to a challenge, and devoting time and energy to a worthy cause.

In the Crowley deck, two long dorjes are standing upright, in front of eight crossed wands in the background. The ends of those wands are hooked like claws, and they seem to have entrapped or imprisoned three hapless figures. A cruel and oppressive tyrant, dressed in full battle armor, stands over them. The design is intended to symbolize oppression and repression—a situation that Crowley described as "a stupid and obstinate cruelty from which there is no escape." The astrological glyphs refer to the unhappy pairing of the planet Saturn—material, slow, and heavy—in the sign of Sagittarius, which is spiritual, swift, and light. Like Waite, Crowley also called this card "Oppression."

What Does Your Future Hold?

- When the Ten of Wands falls in a tarot reading, it suggests that you have clearly struggled with burdens on your own. You know how difficult your responsibilities can be to manage—but you have also managed to become quite adept at juggling your duties and obligations.

- What's more, the Ten of Wands also suggests that the end of your current task is in sight. Your home is just down the road. Your friends and family might even be waiting for you inside, along with a hot dinner and a comfortable night's sleep in your own bed.

- Perhaps it wouldn't hurt for you to lay down your burden, just for a minute, so you can get organized, or search for some assistance. Ask for help if you need it. Delegate if you must. You might save time—and your back.

- Once you do get home, you'll be exhausted—but you'll have stories to tell and the dirt of distant lands on the soles of your shoes. Keep your sense of humor and good faith.

For Future Reference

Keywords: Oppression, burden, cruelty, malice, revenge, injustice, overbearing force, failure, opposition, ill will, slander, envy, obstinacy, generosity, self-sacrifice, fortune, gain

Reversed: Treachery, subterfuge, duplicity, treason, trickery, deception, cunning, disguise, hypocrisy, disloyalty, hindrance, inconvenience

By the numbers: The number ten has a primal, deep-seated significance for all of us. When babies are born, parents immediately do a quick count of fingers and toes. When we learn to count as children, we use our ten fingers as tools. Ten is the number of culmination, completion, and perfection. There are also ten spheres on the Kabbalistic Tree of Life, and ten numbered cards in each suit of the minor arcana.

Timing and dates: In fortunetelling, the number ten could refer to ten hours, ten days, ten weeks, ten months, ten years—or October, the tenth month. Astrologically, the Ten of Wands is assigned to 20–30° Sagittarius (December 13–21).

Page of Wands

If fire could take human form, it would look like the Page of Wands, the personification of fire. He literally embodies the fiery energy that connects the spirit of wands to the physical world.

In the classic Waite design, the Page of Wands stands alone in an arid desert. Because he is the embodiment of fire, he is comfortable in the heat. His face is even turned to the sun; he bathes in its light. He is confident and self-assured. Both of his feet are firmly planted on the ground, and he holds his wand with both hands.

In the Llewellyn Tarot, the Page of Wands holds a scroll of rolled-up parchment—a message, presumably, that he was entrusted to carry. He's standing in the middle of a hilly meadow, where a rabbit scurries past. The card symbolizes good news, delivered by a cheerful friend, as well as the arrival of a positive new chapter of life.

In the Crowley deck, the Page of Wands is called the Princess of Scepters. In Crowley's version of the card, an Amazonian woman and a striped Bengal tiger both float on an undulating column of flame. She is completely nude, except for an odd-looking headpiece—the plumes of justice, according to Crowley. She is muscular and lithe; she almost seems to be dancing. She holds a scepter of the sun, and there's a flaming pedestal in the background, covered with carvings of rams.

Crowley put a lot of thought into the personality profiles of the members of his royal court. According to his description, the Princess of Wands is an individualist. She is brilliant, daring, vigorous, and energetic. The sheer force of her personality makes her seem beautiful to others. In anger or love she is sudden, violent, and implacable. She is ambitious, aspiring, and enthusiastic—sometimes irrationally so. She never forgets an injury, and the only quality of patience to be found in her is the patience with which she lies in ambush to avenge. At her worst, she is superficial, theatrical, shallow, and false, yet blind to her own fickle mood. She can also be cruel, unreliable, faithless, and domineering.

What Does Your Future Hold?

- Pages typically represent students and messengers. Wands correspond to spiritual and career life. When you put them both together, and the Page of Wands falls in your reading, you can probably expect to learn a new lesson—or receive a clear message—about your spiritual life.

- Historically, the Page of Wands was said to represent a dark young man—one who might also be a messenger, such as an envoy or a postman.

- Waite said the Page of Wands is standing "in the act of proclamation"—but what, exactly, is he proclaiming? An emotion? An idea? News? The word proclamation can mean any number of things: an official declaration, a formal announcement, or praise. In other words, the Page of Wands might even be relaying a royal edict or an order. As the tarot reader, you'll have to listen carefully for his message.

- All of the wands cards are fiery, which means that the court card personalities are lively and full of fun.

- Crowley's Princess of Wands has a tiger by the tail. If she falls in your tarot reading, it could indicate that you, too, have a tiger by the tail. You might want to enjoy the experience while you can—because once you decide to let go, you'll have to be clever and fast to avoid its teeth.

For Future Reference

Keywords: A youthful person—fiery, spirited, creative, and outspoken—or a messenger with news about your career

Reversed: A rash, immature, thoughtless young person who speaks without thinking; a superficial, theatrical, cruel, and unstable young woman

Astrological associations: Pages are purely elemental. In other words, the Page of Wands is the personification of fire itself. The card isn't associated with any astrological sign, but it can be linked to the fire signs of Aries, Leo, and Sagittarius.

Knight of Wands

The four knights are all airy individuals. They combine the element of air with the element of their suit. The knight of the fiery suit of wands is a mixture of air and fire. He's self-propelled; all of that knightly air in his system feeds the fire generated by his wand energy.

In the classic Waite design, the Knight of Wands seems to be on a journey, skillfully riding along on a cantering horse. He is traveling past several pyramids, a sign that he's in the hot, arid desert that fiery personalities enjoy, and that he is part of a historical tradition.

In the Llewellyn Tarot, the Knight of Wands is ready for a tournament; he and his horse are both dressed in flowing saffron robes. He's a quick, clever man with a fiery sense of humor, a quirky outlook, and enthusiasm. The card sometimes symbolizes a journey or a change of residence.

In the Crowley deck, the Knight of Wands is called the Prince of Scepters. He wears a golden, winged crown, a corset, and armor decorated with a winged lion's head. He rides a chariot of fire, drawn by a lion, and he holds a flaming, wand-like torch. Crowley described the King of Wands as swift, strong, and impulsive. While he would normally be slow to form an opinion—and he's sometimes prone to indecision—he's also the type of person who likes to argue simply for argument's sake. Once he forms an opinion, he doesn't change it easily. He's also basically fair, keenly aware of justice, intensely noble, courageous, romantic, and generous to a fault. He has a good sense of humor, and an appreciation for a well-executed practical joke. At his worst, he is intolerant, prejudiced, cruel, sadistic, and violent—or indifferent, lazy, and fearful.

What Does Your Future Hold?

- During medieval times, knights were adventurers and rescuers, sworn to defend the weak and helpless while they journeyed to fulfill a quest. When the Knight of Wands appears in a tarot reading, the card could signal an upcoming journey or quest of your own—or a rescue—in the Wands' realm of spiritual life.

- The Knight of Wands is often said to describe a dark young man.

- Historically, the Knight of Wands was connected with departures, absences, long journeys, and even emigration to a foreign land. It was also believed to foretell marriage for a woman—but not necessarily an easy marriage, and one that could be marred by frustration.

- The Knight of Wands might also be connected to a move to a new home.

For Future Reference

Keywords: A dark young man; spiritual rescue or adventure; departure, absence, flight, emigration, a move to a new home

Reversed: Rupture, division, interruption, discord, alienation, a break in a relationship

Timing and dates: Astrogically the Knight of Wands is assigned to 20° Scorpio to 20° Sagittarius (November 13–December 12)

Queen of Wands

The four queens are all watery individuals. Each one combines the element of water with the element of her suit. The queen of the fiery suit of wands embodies the steamy combination of water with the fire, energy, passion, and heat of the wands cards.

In the classic Waite design, the magnetic Queen of Wands sits on a throne surrounded by symbols of fire and heat, like the sunflowers that grow all around her.

In the Llewellyn Tarot, the warm-hearted Queen of Wands symbolizes a self-made woman, one with courage, conviction, and high ideals. She, too, likes sunflowers; she holds one in her left hand. The card typically represents a person of intellectual influence and a steadfast supporter.

In the Crowley deck, the red-headed Queen of Scepters sits on a throne, with a steady flame burning beneath her. A leopard's head motif decorates her robe and crown, and a real-life leopard rests at her side. Crowley described her as adaptable, persistent, calm, kind, generous, loving, and friendly—but not necessarily outgoing. He said she could also be impatient whenever someone opposes her. At her worst, she could be vain, snobbish, brooding, easily deceived, easily offended, obstinate, tyrannical, and vengeful. She could snap at a friend for no reason, and break her own jaw in the process.

What Does Your Future Hold?

- The Queen of Wands typically represents someone who is friendly, outgoing, enthusiastic, energetic, and passionate. Imagine a stereotypical fiery redhead, and you'll probably be picturing a Queen of Wands personality.
- That wasn't always the case. Historically, the Queen of Wands was used to represent dark women who lived in the countryside, and who were generally thought of as virtuous, chaste, strict, and an honorable housewife.
- If the Queen of Wands card happened to fall next to a card with a man, it meant that she was friendly toward him. If it fell next to a woman, it meant that she was interested in the querent.
- The Queen of Wands is associated with money and business success, and generally portends a good harvest.
- Historically, the Queen of Wands reversed was said to represent good will toward the querent, but no opportunity to do anything with that good will.

For Future Reference

Keywords: Fiery, energetic, passionate, powerful, dynamic, generous, willful, confident, friendly, kind, outgoing, dramatic, enthusiastic, optimistic

Reversed: Fierce, domineering, jealous, deceitful, potentially unfaithful, disorganized

Timing and dates: 20° Pisces to 20° Aries (March 11–April 10)

RE DI BASTONI / ROI DE BATONS / KING OF WANDS / REY DE BASTOS / KÖNIG DER STÄBE / STAVEN KONING

King of Wands

KNIGHT OF SCEPTERS / CABALLERO DE CETROS / CAVALIERE DI SCETTRI / CHEVALIER DE SCEPTRES / RITTER DER ZEPTER / SCEPTERS RIDDER

King of Wands

The four kings are all fiery individuals. They combine the element of fire with the element of their suit. The king of the fiery suit of wands, therefore, is a sizzling blend of fire with fire.

In the classic Waite design, the King of Wands is dark and noble. He holds a flowering wand, and wears a ceremonial cap beneath his crown. A lion, his royal emblem, is carved into the back of his throne, and a salamander, the elemental creature of fire, stands nearby.

In the Llewellyn Tarot, the fiery King of Wands symbolizes status, honor, and an intellectual force—a man who has succeeded through intelligence and determination. The card symbolizes material success, achievement, and a life well lived.

In the Crowley deck, the King of Wands is called the Knight of Scepters. He's depicted as a winged warrior on a black horse with a flaming mane and tail. He wears a winged helmet and a flowing red cape, and he holds a burning, wand-like torch. Crowley described the Knight of Wands as active, generous, fierce, impetuous, proud, impulsive, and unpredictable. At his worst, he could be evil, cruel, bigoted, and brutal. Either way, he would be slow to change course, and quick to burn out.

What Does Your Future Hold?

- Kings are active rulers and protectors, willing to defend their realms and dispense justice on behalf of their countrymen. Wands cards all relate to spiritual and career issues. When the King of Wands appears in a tarot reading, you can expect your work to be defended, too—even if you have to resort to self-defense, or mete out your own form of justice.

- Traditionally, the King of Wands was said to be a dark-complexioned man. He was generally thought of as friendly, honest, and conscientious. Typically, he was also thought of as a country gentleman, usually married.

- Historically, the King of Wands has always signified honesty. The card also suggested news of an unexpected inheritance. Reversed, the King of Wands was said to represent advice that should be followed.

- Many tarot readers today believe that the King of Wands represents a strong businessman or leader, a mentor, an entrepreneur, a business visionary, and an enthusiastic captain of industry.

For Future Reference

Keywords: A strong, spiritual man; a business leader; a mentor; ambition, leadership ability, enthusiasm, optimism, entrepreneurial spirit, a self-made man

Reversed: Selfishness, severity, austerity, power-hungry, impulsive, impatient, daredevil

Timing and dates: 20° Scorpio to 20° Sagittarius (November 13–December 12)

Ace of Cups
Your cup runneth over

All of the aces represent pure promise and possibility. They hold limitless potential: succeeding cards in each suit stem from this single starting point. All of the aces also represent new beginnings, and the Ace of Cups symbolizes a new beginning on the emotional level.

In the classic Waite design, all four aces share a similar design: a giant hand parts the swirling mists of a silver cloud, holding the emblem of the suit. In this case, that emblem is a single golden chalice, balanced on an outstretched palm. It is a gift, and it's yours for the taking. Cups correspond to the watery world of emotion, and in this case, the gift is an emotional one. In fact, the cup is overflowing. Streams of water spill out over its rim and into a lake, while a white dove dips a holy wafer into the cup. As the waters of love and friendship spill over the rim, they separate into clearly defined streams—one for each of the senses. Those streams, in turn, feed a tranquil body of water filled with lily pads. Waite called this card the "Root of the Powers of Water."

In the Llewellyn Tarot, the lily pads are especially prominent, and each one is in full bloom. The hills in the background are lush and verdant, while the skies overhead are filled with the energy of swirling white clouds. The card symbolizes the beginning of a blessed, fruitful phase in life.

In the Crowley deck, a double-handled chalice rises from a lotus, which in turn floats on a fountain that rises up from the bottom of the card. It's inscribed with the word "Babalon," the name of the goddess in Crowley's philosophical system of Thelema. (The goddess herself is pictured on the "Lust" card.) A steady stream of white light fills the chalice with the Holy Spirit. Crowley actually identified the Ace of Cups as the Holy Grail, the chalice that Jesus used at the last supper. In the legend of King Arthur, the young knight Percival devoted his life to the quest for the Holy Grail. (Percival, of course, is sometimes compared to the tarot's Fool.) Crowley also called this card the "Root of the Powers of Water."

What Does Your Future Hold?

- Whenever the Ace of Cups appears in a reading, it hints at fertility and creativity. The cup is a womblike symbol; inside its mysterious depths, new life can take root and find nurturance until it's ready to come into the world, take a deep breath, and exist on its own.

- What's more, that Holy Spirit entering the cup is a not-so-subtle hint at pregnancy. It is a graphic depiction of spirit descending into matter.

- If you're not in a position to give birth to a child, you may find yourself conceiving and giving birth to a tangible creative work—a book, a painting, a sculpture, a new program at work, or some equally impressive undertaking.

For Future Reference

Keywords: A new relationship, overflowing emotions, fertility, creativity, joy, contentment, nourishment, abundance, and in the case of pregnancy, the birth of a girl

Reversed: The end of a relationship, infidelity, selfishness, female infertility, failed projects (Turned upside-down, the Ace of Cups will soon be drained, with nothing in reserve.)

By the numbers: All of the aces represent pure promise and possibility, because they hold limitless potential: succeeding cards in each suit stem from this single starting point. In fact, the Ace of Cups is said to be the root of the powers of water.

Timing and dates: In fortunetelling, the Ace could refer to one hour, one day, one week, one month, one year—or Sunday, the first day of the week, or January, the first month. Astrologically, the Ace of Cups is associated with all of the powers of water—the element associated with the signs Cancer, Scorpio, and Pisces.

Two of Cups
The Law of Attraction

"Drink to me, only, with thine eyes," Ben Johnson wrote, "And I will pledge with mine; Or leave a kiss but in the cup, And I'll not look for wine."

In the classic Waite design, two lovers gaze, mesmerized, into each other's eyes, where they swim, oblivious to the sights and sounds of the world outside. They are truly lost in each other's eyes. They each hold a cup—and they seem to be raising their glasses in a toast to each other, as well as to their health, their happiness, and the future that is about to unfold before them. Above them, there's a lion's head—with wings—perched on a caduceus, the staff of Mercury. Mercury was the god of commerce, eloquence, invention, travel, and theft. His staff here could mean that communication between the two isn't a problem; they see eye-to-eye, and talk face-to-face. It could even refer to the old cliché about having their hearts stolen. Mercury was also linked to alchemy, and the symbol here could be related to the alchemical, transformational effect that love has on people. At the same time, the lion on the staff could represent a soul, waiting for a vehicle into which he can be born.

If that couple keeps toasting each other, one thing could lead to another, and a child could result. Waite called this card "Love."

In the Llewellyn Tarot, the lovers are locked in a deep embrace—one that has lasted so long that a thicket of blossoming apple branches has grown around them, entwining the pair. The red and white serpents who climb the caduceus behind them symbolize the passion and purity of their love, as well as the fact that they are two separate people, united as one. The card is one of romance, entwined energy, and the balanced ebb and flow of a relationship.

In the Crowley deck, a lotus floats on a calm sea. Another lotus rises from the first. Twin dolphins, an alchemical symbol, wrap around the stem. Sparkling clear water flows from the top like a fountain and bounces off the dolphins, symbols of emotion. The water fills two golden cups at the bottom of the card. The card symbolizes the harmony of male and female, an ideal of perfect peace and harmony that radiates joy and ecstasy—unfortunately, Crowley points out that the more the ideal plays out in the material world, the less perfect it becomes. The astrological glyphs refer to Venus, the planet of love and attraction, in Cancer, the sign of home and family life. Like Waite, Crowley also called this card "Love."

What Does Your Future Hold?

- In a reading, the Two of Cups usually relates to romance, but it can also describe friendships and partnerships, too. It symbolizes the synergy and productivity that occur when two kindred spirits work together toward a shared goal, dream, or vision. Together, they become more than the sum of their parts.

- The partnership or alliance may be personal or professional, romantic or platonic. You might even feel that there is a past-life connection with someone, which makes your partnership in this lifetime seem almost like karmic destiny.

- The Two of Cups could symbolize an engagement or marriage.

- Reversed, the Two of Cups could suggest a friendship or partnership that's coming to an end, because its mission is complete.

For Future Reference

Keywords: Love, attraction, romance, passion, desire, marriage, union, affinity, friendship, compatibility, affection, faithfulness, harmony, pleasure

Reversed: Infidelity, jealousy, longing, loneliness, isolation, misunderstanding, unrequited love

By the numbers: An early card in the suit, the Two of Cups could suggest that you are in the early stages of a partnership, or you soon will be. Perhaps you're still in the "getting to know you" phase—or you're in negotiations. The partnership may be romantic, platonic, or business-related. All twos refer to duality, oppositions, attraction, and communication. Twos represent choices. The number two suggests pairs and combinations, as well as relationships, partnerships, and the attraction between two people. Twos also represent conversation and debate—the point and counterpoint of two opposing ideas, or the antithesis that rises up in response to almost every thesis. The very nature of the number two also signifies a wide range of concepts that come in pairs: heaven and earth, male and female, active and passive, conscious and unconscious, and day and night. Written as a Roman numeral II, the number suggests a gateway or a doorway, as well as female genitalia.

Timing and dates: In fortunetelling, the number two could refer to two hours, two days, two weeks, two months, two years—or Monday, the second day of the week, or February, the second month. Astrologically, the Two of Cups is assigned to 0–10° Cancer (June 21–July 1).

Three of Cups
The power of three

Most versions of the Three of Cups look very much like a classical artist's depictions of the Three Graces, the mythic Greek sisters. Aglaia, whose name means beauty, was "she who gave away." Euphrosyne, whose name means joy, was "she who received." And Thalia, whose name means abundance, was "she who gave back."

The three women in the Three of Cups could also be the three Norns, the Scandinavian goddesses of destiny. They lived beneath the World Tree Yggdrasil, where they wove the tapestry of fate. The first sister, Urd, spun the thread. Verdani, the second sister, wove it in her loom. Skuld, the third sister, cut the final string. The Greeks had a similar legend, with three Moirae sisters: Clotho, the spinner, Lachesis, who measured the thread, and Atropos, the inevitable, who cut the thread.

In the classic Waite design, a bevy of beautiful women link arms and raise their glasses to each other, as they dance among the fruits of a successful harvest. The three women could be sisters. They could be friends. They could even represent the three faces of the goddess—Maiden, Mother, and Crone, which embody every woman at different stages of life. The three women could also symbolize the three elements of water, air, and fire, dancing on the surface of the earth, uniting all four elements in an ancient circular web. Waite called this card "Pleasure."

In the Llewellyn Tarot, three maidens dance under a full moon. Their arms are entwined, and they raise oversized goblets high above their heads. The card symbolizes celebration and thanksgiving, along with shared happiness, pleasure, support, and encouragement.

In the Crowley deck, a champagne fountain of red pomegranate wine glasses and water lilies fills and refills a pool of crystal-clear water. In the background, the winged solar god Horus watches three couples dance on the back of a tortoise, an ancient symbol of the planet earth. The astrological glyphs refer to Mercury, the planet of speed and communication, in Cancer, the sign of motherhood, home, and family. Crowley said the Three of Cups was the card of Demeter and Persephone, the Greek goddesses who came to encompass the full spectrum of love, loss, and reunion. Persephone was the maiden, abducted by Hades; once she tasted the pomegranate in the Underworld, she was condemned to stay there. Only the fierceness of her mother's love could win her a reprieve. Crowley called this card "Abundance."

What Does Your Future Hold?

- In a tarot reading the three women could also represent three very real women in your life—your sisters, friends, or amicable co-workers.
- The Three of Cups clearly describes the companionship and company of women. The Three of Cups could also suggest an upcoming girls' night out, a bridal or baby shower, or a bachelorette party.
- Reversed, the Three of Cups could depict the petty jealousies, backstabbing, gossip, and resentments that often flare up among groups of women. The card may be cautioning you to be careful with whom you socialize, and to guard what you say—or hear—about others.
- Historically, the Three of Cups was said to foretell a promotion or advancement for a member of the military.

For Future Reference

Keywords: Parties and celebrations, dancing, drinking, girls' night out, pleasure, sensuality, happiness, conviviality, hospitality, good luck, good fortune, kindness, and merriment

Reversed: Excesses, physical exhaustion, hangovers, unplanned pregnancy

By the numbers: Threes symbolize creation—the result of two separate forces combining to create a third entity. A mother and a father produce a child together. A thesis and an antithesis combine to produce a synthesis. The number three can also represent body, mind, and spirit, or past, present, and future. Many religions believe in a holy trinity, such as Father, Son, and Holy Spirit, or Maiden, Mother, and Crone, or the triple goddess of the New, Full, and Old Moon.

Timing and dates: In fortunetelling, the number three could refer to three hours, three days, three weeks, three months, three years—or Tuesday, the third day of the week, or March, the third month. Astrologically, the Three of Cups is assigned to 10–20° Cancer (July 2–11).

Four of Cups

Is that all there is?

The process of enlightenment can be long and slow—or it can fall suddenly into your lap. The Four of Cups offers a contemplative route to conscious awareness.

In the classic Waite design, a brooding young man sits underneath a tree, arms and legs crossed defensively. He seems to be staring at three cups, all lined up on the grass in front of him. At the same time, a strange, ghostly hand emerges from a vaporous mist, and a fourth golden chalice materializes right before his eyes. It's as though he's getting a close-up, real-life view of the image from the Ace of Cups. Even so, his expression seems more discontented than amazed.

He might not realize that there is more to life than the things of this world; he has drunk from the cups of the material sphere, but he is blinded to the gifts of the spiritual realm. In any case, he seems decidedly unimpressed by the miracle that is unfolding in front of him. Waite called this card "Blended Pleasures."

In the Llewellyn Tarot, a young woman is sitting near a stream, where water flows past three golden cups. A fourth cup is suspended above her from the gnarled branches of an ancient oak. She seems oblivious to all of them. The card symbolizes discontent and isolation, doubt, and disenchantment.

In the Crowley deck, four trophy-like cups are stacked. They are so perfectly symmetrical, so stable, that water flows from the bottom to the top, but it doesn't flow any farther. Around them, the sea is beginning to move. In the background, three winged demons try to keep a turtle god from climbing into an Egyptian bark—a ship to the underworld—where four serpents wait with a cosmic egg, a symbol of the universe. In the distance, day and night embrace. The astrological glyphs refer to the Moon in Cancer, its ruling sign. Crowley called this card "Luxury."

What Does Your Future Hold?

- In a reading, the Four of Cups could be a literal depiction of disappointment or disenchantment, which could even sour you to new possibilities.

- The card could indicate that you're simply overwhelmed by the circumstances and events that brought you to that place underneath the tree.

- Another more positive interpretation stems from the tree in the background. Rather than sitting glumly, you might find yourself emulating Buddha, meditating under the Bodhi tree. You might be engaged in theoretical activity, like Sir Isaac Newton, who was said to discover gravity while he sat under an apple tree. You might even be reliving the myth of Odin, just before he climbed up the World Tree—or right after he climbed down. In any of those three scenarios, the three cups that stand, along with the fourth one in the wings, could show that you are in the process of putting two and two together and reaching enlightenment.

- We all see miracles every day, and the Four of Cups might be reminding you of that fact. If anyone who lived more than a century ago were to wake up here tomorrow, for example, he would think everything in your world was miraculous—from the buzzing digital alarm clock on your nightstand to the hot and cold water on tap in your shower. Your microwave and coffeemaker would blow him away. So would the air-conditioned car you ride to work, and the fact that you can communicate in real time with customers, clients, and co-workers around the world.

- Of course, not all of today's miracles are technology-based. The Four of Cups might also be a reminder of the miracles that have amazed and delighted people since the beginning of time: friendship, love, and the birth of a child, or miracles as simple as a hot dinner or a game of cards.

For Future Reference

Keywords: Weariness, disgust, displeasure, discontent, dissatisfaction, boredom, dejection

Reversed: New friends, new adventures, reenergizing, regeneration, refreshment

By the numbers: All fours symbolize structure and stability. In this case, however, you might be interpreting your temporary stasis as a standstill—or even an ending. You're nowhere near the end, however. Hold on. More good things are coming your way. Fours symbolize structure, stability, and security, because four points come together to form a solid. There are four walls in a room, and four corners to a house. There are four dimensions: width, length, height, and time. There are four cardinal directions: north, south, east, and west. There are four seasons, four winds, and four phases of the moon. There are four elements, and four corresponding suits in the minor arcana.

Timing and dates: In fortunetelling, the number four could refer to four hours, four days, four weeks, four months, or four years—or Wednesday, the fourth day of the week, or April, the fourth month. Astrologically, the Four of Cups is assigned to 20–30° Cancer (July 12–21).

Five of Cups

Loss and disappointment

Old wives often say, "It's no use crying over spilt milk." That may be, but sometimes a good cry doesn't hurt—and it can't make an already bad situation any worse.

In the classic Waite design, a dark-robed figure stands on the banks of a river, looking sadly at three golden cups that have tipped and spilled on the ground. Behind him, two cups stand upright. He'll need to be careful when he turns around, or the hem of his cape could tip them over, too. There's a small keep in the background—the fortified stronghold of a castle, or a jail. There's also a bridge, a symbol of connection between two worlds. The person in the card seems stooped with grief or regret. Sadness seems wrapped around him like a cloak of invisibility. Waite called this card "Loss."

In the Llewellyn Tarot, the composition is the same: three cups lie on their sides, but they're surrounded by a pool of red. What did the cups hold—was it wine, or was it blood? And how did they spill? Was there an accident, or were they a libation, poured out upon the ground as an offering to the gods? The card symbolizes disappointment, suffering, and loss.

In the Crowley deck, lotus stems weave their way through five crystal goblets, forcing them into the shape of an inverted pentagram—a symbol of the triumph of matter over spirit. There is no water in the cups, or flowing into them. The blooms of the lotuses are dying, and their petals are falling into a dry, dead sea. The astrological glyphs refer to Mars, the planet of energy and aggression, in Scorpio, its own house. Both the planet and the sign are fiery; that's one reason the water in this card has all dried up. Crowley called this card "Disappointment."

What Does Your Future Hold?

- The man in the cards obviously has a reason to mourn. When the Five of Cups appears in a reading, it could indicate that you, too, have suffered a loss. The card sometimes refers to the loss of a friendship or a relationship—perhaps as a result of treachery, deceit, or unkind behavior.

- The card might also be trying to illustrate how you collect yourself and move on after failure and disappointment.

- The Five of Cups is also a vivid reminder of the five stages of grief defined by Elisabeth Kübler-Ross: denial, anger, bargaining, depression, and acceptance.

- If the Five of Cups represents the future, it may be time to step out of your mourning clothes and your cloak of invisibility. There are two cups still standing; now pick up the three that spilled and refill them.

- Historically, the Five of Cups reversed was said to herald the return of a long-lost relative.

For Future Reference

Keywords: Disappointment, disillusionment, dissatisfaction, sorrow, loss, bitterness, frustration

Reversed: A short-lived period of mourning, soon forgotten; acceptance, recovery, hope

By the numbers: Fives represent the halfway point—the tipping point—where things could go either way. They could get better or worse. Fives represent a halfway point in the progression from one to ten. In the tarot, "five" cards often symbolize a crisis: they're the midway point when events can either take a turn for the better or go horribly awry. Fives also symbolize the five senses, the five points on a star, and the five vowels in the English alphabet. Some metaphysicians suggest that five is important because it symbolizes a fifth element—Spirit.

Timing and dates: In fortunetelling, the number five could refer to five hours, five days, five weeks, five months, or five years—or Thursday, the fifth day of the week, or May, the fifth month. Astrologically, the Five of Cups is assigned to 0–10° Scorpio (October 23–November 1).

Six of Cups

The pleasure of your company

The Six of Cups suggests a certain nostalgia—not only for childhood, but also for the care-free days of youth and innocence.

In the classic Waite design, a small boy offers a little girl a gift—a nosegay of flowers. The sun is shining. It's a beautiful late spring or early summer's day. The children are safe within the town square or in their yard, protected by a low wall. They are clean, well dressed, well fed, happy, and healthy—they are obviously well loved and cared for. They are also protected, by the gate, the guard, a shield or family crest, and the garden wall. While they seem too young for anything more than puppy love at this point, they might be a younger version of the couple who will grow up to become the Two of Cups. Waite called this card "Happiness."

In the Llewellyn Tarot, two equally well-kept children play together, along with an orange tabby cat—the family pet. There's a birdhouse in a nearby tree, a sign that all creatures are loved and cared for in this home. The card symbolizes friendship, play, and well-being.

In the Crowley deck, six golden chalices seem to dance in an elaborate arrangement of lotus stems, each one capped by a flower that streams water into the cups. They aren't yet full to overflowing. The card is designed to imply a pleasant sense of well-being, harmony, ease, and satisfaction. Three couples frolic in the background, protected by a goddess of the night. The astrological glyphs refer to the Sun—which symbolizes consciousness and enlightenment—in Scorpio. Crowley called this card "Pleasure."

What Does Your Future Hold?

- In a reading, the Six of Cups may describe your involvement with your brothers and sisters, or with friends you've known since childhood. You might want to organize a family get-together, or make plans to attend an upcoming class reunion—because you'll be pleasantly surprised by the happy fond memories that await you there. It could even portend a reunion with a childhood sweetheart.

- If the card shows up reversed, however, it could suggest that an encounter with someone from your past could be something of a disappointment. While you may have been in the same place at the same time, your experience—and your recollection—may be different, and you won't connect on quite the same level.

- When the card shows up in a spread, it might also be a good time to consider the gifts you have to offer the children in your life. Whether or not you are a parent yourself, there are undoubtedly children within your sphere of influence. They may be your children or grandchildren, your nieces and nephews, a godson or goddaughter, the children of friends, or neighbors. A kind word, a few minutes of friendly conversation, and a token of your time and energy could work wonders in a child's life. Offer them praise, just as you would offer them a flower of kindness and affection.

- One historic interpretation of the Six of Cups suggested that an inheritance was on the way.

For Future Reference

Keywords: Memories, nostalgia, reunions

Reversed: Homesickness, longing, excessive attachment to the past, false memories

By the numbers: Six is a number of peace and calm, particularly because it comes after the chaos and confusion that seems to mark most incidences of the number five in tarot.

Sixes historically symbolize the human being, because man was said to be created on the sixth day. Six also symbolizes the sixth sense—psychic ability—as well as the six directions of space: left, right, forward, backward, up, and down.

Timing and dates: In fortunetelling, the number six could refer to six hours, six days, six weeks, six months, or six years—or Friday, the sixth day of the week, or June, the sixth month. Astrologically, the Six of Cups is assigned to 10–20° Scorpio (November 2–12).

Seven of Cups

All is illusion

The Seven of Cups is a card of daydreams, illusions, options, and choices.

In the classic Waite design, a lone figure gazes wondrously at seven cups suspended in midair. The cups hold seven separate temptations. Are they vices, or virtues? Only the tarot reader knows for sure. Believe it or not, you've seen the contents of each cup before, in the cards of the major arcana. There's the head of the Empress, the veiled High Priestess, the Magician's serpent belt, the Tower, the jewels of the Wheel of Fortune, the wreath from the World card, and the fire dragon of the Sun. Waite called this card "Desire."

In the Llewellyn Tarot, a young woman looks up at seven similar cups. One holds a heart with wings, while a white dove perches on the rim of another. The card symbolizes dreams, imagination, and desire—and warns, in some cases, of the importance of good judgment and sound decision making.

In the Crowley deck, seven iridescent cups are precariously balanced in a teetering stack. By themselves, the cups would be beautiful. Unfortunately, their exterior beauty only hides the fact that they are empty vessels, with nothing to offer the world around them. The flowers aren't lotuses anymore; they're tiger lilies. They're dripping with green slime, too, which flows over and around the cups. The background imagery depicts the historic excesses of Christianity's darkest hours. The astrological glyphs refer to Venus in Scorpio, an uncomfortable match for the planet of attraction when it's forced to spend time in a sign that appreciates the dark side. Crowley called this card "Debauch."

What Does Your Future Hold?

- The Seven of Cups usually serves as a reminder that you must make choices in life. While daydreams have their place, the time comes when you need to face reality and set a course for the future. If you can't make a choice, time may make the decision for you, culling away opportunities lost through abandonment or neglect.

- The card doesn't mean it's impossible to set a new course for your future, though. The possibilities you have to choose from today might not look like the possibilities you had five years ago, or ten, or twenty. They may seem, at first glance, a little less glamorous: It's hard to backpack across Europe once you're married, working, and responsible for three kids and a dog. But now is the time to assess the possibilities that remain, and to prepare for the future you've always dreamed about.

- The Seven of Cups also symbolizes new possibilities that could surprise you, rising and materializing out of the mist of time. Don't make the mistake of thinking that they are merely illusions. If there's something you've always wanted to do—finish school, write a book, find a house in the country—get moving. Don't think it's simply too late, or that you're too old. If you don't start now, how much older will you be a year from now? Will there ever be a better time to reach out and grab your dream?

- Upright, the Seven of Cups promises possibility. Reversed, the card seems to suggest that the possibilities aren't nearly as tempting or close as they seem. It could even suggest that you might be a willing participant in your own self-deception. Be careful. If something seems too good to be true, it probably is.

For Future Reference

Keywords: Daydreams, fantasies, visions, illusions, imagination, meditation, contemplation, memories, dreams, reflections, ambivalence

Reversed: Action and forward motion: decisiveness, focus, determination, realism, and choices (In some cases, the card can also suggest failed promises, deception, error, drunkenness, wrath, violence, fornication, or deception.)

By the numbers: Seven is a mystical, magical number. Classically, there were seven days of creation. There are seven gifts of the Holy Spirit: wisdom, understanding, counsel, fortitude, knowledge, piety, and fear. There are seven deadly sins: envy, sloth, gluttony, wrath, pride, lust, and greed. There are seven virtues: faith, hope, charity, fortitude, justice, temperance, and prudence. (You can see most of them in the major arcana.) Alchemists had seven metals: gold, silver, iron, mercury, tin, copper, and lead. There are seven visible planets: the Sun, the Moon, Mars, Mercury, Jupiter, Venus, and Saturn. There are seven days of the week, seven notes in a musical scale, seven colors of the rainbow, and seven chakras. Because the seventh day is a day of rest, seven is the number of self-reflection and philosophy. To fully randomize your tarot deck before a reading, shuffle it seven times.

Timing and dates: In fortunetelling, the number seven could refer to seven hours, seven days, seven weeks, seven months, or seven years—or Saturday, the seventh day of the week, or July, the seventh month. Astrologically, the Seven of Cups is assigned to 20–30° Scorpio (November 13–22).

Eight of Cups

What's missing?

The Eight of Cups is a cautionary card, one that reminds us to make the best use of our limited resources.

In the classic Waite design, a solitary wanderer turns his back and walks away, leaving behind a carefully assembled collection of cups. They're perfectly balanced and lined up with precision, but there's clearly a void. Something is missing. When Waite described the card, he said the figure was abandoning all of his previous undertakings. The things that used to seem important no longer matter much to him. Waite called this card "Abandoned Success."

In the Llewellyn Tarot, a heavily gowned woman slowly moves away from eight golden cups, heading through a mountainous river valley where waves crash against a rocky shore. The shadow of a waning crescent moon seem to suggest that she is nearing the end of her journey, struggling toward a conclusion. The card symbolizes a sacrifice, a change in direction, and the end of a dream.

In the Crowley deck, the scene is bleak. The water is dark and muddy. The sky is filled with layers of black clouds. There's no sun, no rain, and no inspiration or incentive for growth. There are two flowers doing their best to fill the two cups in the middle of the card, but they're obviously only doing a partial job. Most of the cups are empty. All in all, the scene is lifeless and lackluster. Even the figures in the background seem resigned to a useless struggle against an unmoving force. The astrological glyphs refer to Saturn, the planet of limitations and restrictions, in Pisces, the sign of dreams. Crowley called this card "Indolence."

What Does Your Future Hold?

- Sometimes, no matter how much you have, it simply isn't enough—and you won't be satisfied until you find that missing piece. That could be a project you need to undertake, or to finish. It could even be a person.

- The Eight of Cups could suggest that you soon will find that missing piece … but then you'll be left to answer the question, "What next?"

- The Eight of Cups might also be telling you to think about the things you've been accumulating. Do your achievements and possessions make you happy, or do they weigh you down? If you don't like the answer you get, what might you need to leave behind in order to find satisfaction and fulfillment?

- Professional organizers—the ones who make a career out of telling the rest of us how to de-clutter our lives—have a saying: keep only what is beautiful, useful, or loved. It may be time to take a look around your home. Are the things you see around you beautiful, useful, or loved?

- One historic interpretation of the Eight of Cups said that it heralded marriage with a fair woman.

For Future Reference

Keywords: Temporary success, waning interest, troubled relationships, fear or lack of commitment, abandonment

Reversed: Finding that missing piece will be delayed, or come with strings attached that you didn't anticipate; refusal to move on

By the numbers: Eights represent infinity, because they resembles the lemniscate, the sideways symbol of infinity. There are also eight points on the Wheel of the Year. To Christians, eight is a symbol of baptism and spiritual rebirth; many baptisteries and baptismal fonts have eight sides. Eight also represents the eternal spiral of regeneration.

Timing and dates: In fortunetelling, the number eight could refer to eight hours, eight, weeks, eight months, eight years—or August, the eighth month. Astrologically, the Eight of Cups is assigned to 0–10° Pisces (February 19–28).

Nine of Cups
The party's here

Bartenders are uniquely archetypal figures. Blessed with the gift of gab, proficient in the language of small talk, and able to banter with anyone who might wander in, good bartenders are perpetually ready to set 'em up and hit 'em again. They're fully stocked with an array of cup-sized conversation-starters—sports, politics, books, movies, and news of the day—as well as the social skills they need to tailor every discussion to their customers, without alienating or antagonizing them.

In that way, bartenders are a lot like counselors and advisors. Bartenders hear a lot of confessions. Part of the job is offering advice and comfort in liquid form. They are the poor man's psychiatrists, after all.

For that matter, tarot readers have been called the same thing. You might even think of the bartender as a low-rent High Priestess, stationed before a curtain of drink that divides this world from the world of inebriation, where "spirits" trump material concerns.

In the classic Waite design, a grinning bartender sits comfortably in front of nine cups, all lined up on the curved bar behind him. He looks like he's already knocked back one or two drinks himself, and he's ready and willing to share the wealth. Waite called this card "Material Happiness."

In the Llewellyn Tarot, the woman in the center of the card is a vision—one who seems almost surreal. She is vaguely reminiscent of legendary fairies, who tempted passers-by with wishful magic elixirs. She symbolizes seduction, pleasures, relief, and inspiration. The bee in the foreground symbolizes energy, effort, and the sweet rewards of industry.

In the Crowley deck, nine emerald-colored cups are stacked in two vertical columns. They are all perfectly symmetrical, perfectly balanced, and filled to overflowing. The three cups at the top of the card symbolize the ideal blend of two extremes: like water from a tap, hot and cold combine in perfect measure. The astrological glyphs stand for Jupiter, the planet of luck and expansion, in Pisces, the sign of dreams and intuition. Crowley called this card "Happiness."

What Does Your Future Hold?

- It seems like everybody knows the figure in the Nine of Cups. He could be the bartender at your favorite bar. He could be your neighbor down the street, with a refrigerator full of beer out in the garage. And if you don't necessarily see him as a drinking buddy, the Nine of Cups could also represent the grandmother who always has cookies for the kids, or the co-worker who keeps a dish full of candy on her desk. In any case, the card depicts someone who has plenty of comfort to share.

- Of course, the smiling figure in the card might also be a facet of your own personality, always ready to entertain, and fully stocked with the tools and supplies you'll need to get the conversation flowing.

- In a reading, the Nine of Cups could foretell an evening of drinking and social pleasantries. It could describe parties and social events, either as a guest or a host.

- If the Nine of Cups shows up reversed, be careful with whom you confide your secrets. Don't let anything (like too much wine) lull you into letting your guard down and loosening your lips. The Nine of Cups reversed might also suggest that you could be too frank and open, and say things tonight that you'll regret in the morning.

- Historically, the Nine of Cups was said to bode well for military men, while its reversal was said to be good for business.

For Future Reference

Keywords: Social events, parties, gatherings, comfort, contentment, success, advantage, satisfaction regarding the question of the reading, a comfortable mix of business and pleasure

Reversed: Drunkenness, overindulgence, indiscretion, candor, faults, errors, mistakes, imperfections, deprivation

By the numbers: Because there are nine months of pregnancy, nines symbolize selflessness, compassion, universality, humanitarianism, and spirituality.

Timing and dates: In fortunetelling, the number nine could refer to nine hours, nine days, nine weeks, nine months, or nine years—or September, the ninth month. Astrologically, the Nine of Cups is assigned to 10–20° Pisces (March 1–10).

Ten of Cups
The happy family

The Ten of Cups bodes well for anyone who's concerned about family life. It's the card of happiness and lasting togetherness.

In the classic Waite design, a happy family—mother, father, son, and daughter—celebrate their life together under the protective arch of a colorful rainbow. The man has one arm wrapped around the woman's waist, and they both raise their arms in a gesture of wonder and salute. Meanwhile, the children hold hands and dance for joy. The family symbolizes a quaternary of four separate symbols and ideas that combine to form a whole, like the family groupings in the court cards. Waite called this card "Perfected Success."

In the Llewellyn Tarot, a happy couple embraces, while their children amuse themselves in the background. Their ten cups are positioned all around them, on either side of a swiftly flowing stream. The moving water is part of the river of life that runs from one card to another, connecting all of the cards in the tarot. It symbolizes the bond of energy and emotion that connects people in the real world, too. The card symbolizes the blessings of partnership, and the safety, security, and satisfaction of true love.

In the Crowley deck, ten cups are arranged in the shape of the Kabbalistic Tree of Life, superimposed over a background that looks like a giant lotus. However, the cups themselves are unstable. They are tilted. The design is meant to suggest completion, on one hand, as well as the new beginnings that follow. The figures in the background symbolize the principles of creation under the guardianship of a father god. The astrological glyphs symbolize Mars, the planet of energy and aggression, in Pisces, the sign of dreams and intuition. In other words, the dream is about to come to an end. This chapter will end, so that a new chapter can get underway. Crowley called this card "Satiety."

What Does Your Future Hold?

- Historically, in fact, the Ten of Cups represented a good marriage—one that turned out to be even better than expected.

- In a tarot reading, the Ten of Cups could represent quiet days, evenings, and weekends ahead, to be whiled away in the company of family members and close friends.

- The rainbow in the Waite version of the card is a sign of a covenant, a sacred obligation or agreement.

- Reversed, the Ten of Cups could indicate sorrow or a serious quarrel.

For Future Reference

Keywords: Peace, joy, happiness, contentment, love, family life, small-town life, a quiet, peaceful neighborhood, a good reputation, honor, virtue, complete good fortune

Reversed: Unhappiness, sorrow, arguments, disputes, betrayal, breakups of family members, wrath, anger, irritation, boredom, drug use

By the numbers: The number ten has primal, deep-seated significance for all of us. When babies are born, parents immediately do a quick count of fingers and toes. When we learn to count as children, we use our ten fingers as tools. Ten is the number of culmination, completion, and perfection. There are also ten spheres on the Kabbalistic Tree of Life, and ten numbered cards in each suit of the minor arcana.

Timing and dates: In fortunetelling, the number ten could refer to ten hours, ten days, ten weeks, ten months, ten years—or October, the tenth month. Astrologically, the Ten of Cups is assigned to 20–30° Pisces (March 11–20).

Page of Cups

If water could take human form, it would look like the Page of Cups—the physical embodiment of water.

In the classic Waite design, the Page of Cups stands on the shore of a rolling ocean. He holds a cup with a fish, which seems to be talking to him. Because the Page of Cups is the personification of water, he speaks the language of the seas. Waite described the Page of Cups as fair, pleasing, and somewhat effeminate—but one who could also be studious and intent.

In the Llewellyn Tarot, the Page of Cups carries two fish in his cup, reminiscent of the two fish that constitute the astrological symbol for Pisces. The card represents a cheerful young person with a trusting heart, and could portend good news or an invitation.

In the Crowley deck, the Page of Cups is called the Princess of Cups. In Crowley's version of the card, an Amazonian woman stands on the surface of the sea, surrounded by seafoam, watching a dolphin. She wears the crest of a swan with an open wing. In one hand, she holds a lotus. In the other, she holds a cup, from which a turtle is emerging. According to his description, the Princess of Cups is infinitely gracious. She is sweet, gentle, kind, and tender—a born romantic in a perpetual, rapturous dream. She might seem selfish and indolent, but she is not. She simply goes about her work, silently and effortlessly.

What Does Your Future Hold?

- Pages typically represent students and messengers. Cups correspond to emotional life. When you put them both together, and the Page of Cups falls in your reading, you can probably expect to learn a new lesson—or receive a clear message—about your emotional life.

- All of the cups cards are watery, which means that the court card personalities are emotional. The Page of Cups is still immature, so his emotions could swing wildly. If the Page of Cups represents you, be aware that you're going through an especially sensitive and vulnerable period, and try to keep your emotions under control.

- Waite said the Page of Cups was a fair young man, studious, and ready to serve.

- When the Page of Cups appears in a reading, it could also indicate that your imagination is about to be inspired. Now would be a good time to read poetry—or try your hand at writing a poem of your own.

- The Page of Cups is also associated with meditation and reflection.

For Future Reference

Keywords: Kind, sympathetic, romantic, tender, sweet, gentle, dreamy, and imaginative young person—also one who is sometimes unlucky in love

Reversed: An insincere person who tries to win support through flattery; jealousy, hypersensitivity, and melancholy

Astrological associations: Pages are purely elemental. In other words, the Page of Cups is the personification of water itself. The card isn't associated with any astrological sign, but it can be linked to the water signs of Cancer, Scorpio, and Pisces.

Knight of Cups

The four knights are all airy individuals who combine the element of air with the element of their suit. The knight of the watery suit of cups is a mixture of air and water—a combination that can express itself as humidity, fog, clouds, or even storms.

In the classic Waite design, the Knight of Cups is a warrior who doesn't seem particularly warlike. Instead, he is a dreamer and a visionary, who rides, gracefully and quietly, and his winged helmet symbolizes the misty clouds of his imagination.

In the Llewellyn Tarot, the Knight of Cups rides his steed through pounding surf, a symbol of his element. The card represents a romantic, creative, artistic man, like a musician, a poet, or a diplomat. The card often portends a promising proposal or collaboration, as well as an opportunity to learn from a friend or a lover.

In the Crowley deck, the Knight of Cups is called the Prince of Cups. He rides in a chariot drawn by an eagle, with the symbol of a scorpion on his wheel. He also wears the symbol of an eagle on his crown and his uniform. His armor looks like feathers, and he holds both a lotus and a cup. A serpent is crawling out of the cup, headed toward the lake beneath the chariot.

Crowley described the Prince of Cups as subtle, violent, crafty, and artistic, and said he had a fierce nature with a calm exterior. He could use his power for good or evil—and, Crowley said, evil had a tendency to attract him, particularly if it happened to come with power or wisdom. His calm, imperturbable exterior could hide his ruthless, crafty, and violent temperament. At his worst, the Prince of Cups could exist completely without a conscience, craving power and knowledge for his own designs, and feeling no sense of responsibility to others. The Prince of Cups could not be trusted.

What Does Your Future Hold?

- During medieval times, knights were adventurers and rescuers, sworn to defend the weak and helpless while they journeyed to fulfill a quest. When the Knight of Cups appears in a tarot reading, the card could signal an upcoming journey or quest of your own—or a rescue—in the cups' realm of emotions and relationships.

- When the Knight of Cups appears in a tarot reading, you might also be creatively or artistically inspired.

- You might be blessed with psychic visions or messages.

- The Knight of Cups is often thought of as a romantic figure.

- Historically, the Knight of Cups was said to herald a visit from a friend, who would bring unexpected money.

For Future Reference

Keywords: Romantic adventure, poetry, artistic creativity, a dreamer, a visionary

Reversed: An evil, merciless man; mischief, trickery, fraud, duplicity, swindle

Timing and dates: 20° Libra to 20° Scorpio (October 13–November 12)

REGINA DI COPPE   QUEEN OF CHALICES
REINE DE COUPES   REINA DE COPAS

KÖNIGIN DER KELCHE   BEKERS KONINGIN

Queen of Cups

QUEEN OF CUPS   REGINA DI COPPE
REINA DE COPAS   REINE DE COUPES

KÖNIGIN DER KELCHE   BEKERS KONINGIN

Queen of Cups

The four queens of the tarot are all watery individuals. Each one combines the element of water with the element of her suit. The queen of the watery suit of cups embodies the placid combination of water with even more water.

With all that water coursing through her veins, the Queen of Cups is the ideal woman—and for many, she represents the perfect wife and mother. She is kind and giving, a wellspring of love and devotion, and naturally sensitive to other people's feelings.

In the classic Waite design, the magnetic Queen of Cups sits on a seashell-shaped throne, and contemplates the depths of the golden chalice in her right hand. She is surrounded by water, which seems smooth and calm on the surface. Be aware, however, that still waters run deep.

In the Llewellyn Tarot, the Queen of Cups is indisputably regal. She wears a dress of seafoam green, and gazes calmly at the water and waves that surround her. She represents a romantic, compassionate woman—one with a powerful imagination, who encourages the dreams and talents of others. She sometimes represents true love for a man, but a romantic rival for a woman.

In the Crowley deck, the Queen of Cups is fair and lovely, seated on a throne that floats on water. Her crown and her gown are decorated with ibis birds—and a real-life ibis stands beside her. She holds a cup with a crayfish inside. Crowley described her as imaginative, poetic, kind, yet not willing to take much trouble for another.

What Does Your Future Hold?

- The Queen of Cups typically represents the perfect wife and mother—a woman who is caring, giving, nurturing, sensitive, protective, and kind.
- The Queen of Cups could suggest a period of creativity and inspiration, particularly in arts and crafts.
- Historically, the Queen of Cups was said to foretell a rich marriage for a man and a distinguished one for a woman. Reversed, she was said to represent a distinguished woman who couldn't be trusted.

For Future Reference

Keywords: A fair woman; good, honest, devoted, intelligent, warm, nurturing, healing, protective, sensitive, psychic, intuitive; a counselor or therapist; the perfect wife and mother

Reversed: A meddling woman, or a suffocating, overbearing woman

Timing and dates: 20° Gemini to 20° Cancer (June 11–July 11)

King of Cups

The four kings are all fiery individuals. They combine the element of fire with the element of their suit. The king of the watery suit of cups is a steamy mix of fire and water.

In the classic Waite design, the King of Cups holds a short scepter in his left hand and an oversized cup in his right. His throne seems to float on the sea. Waite described the King of Cups as a fair man, who was often associated with business, law, or the ministry. The King of Cups is also connected to art and science, too.

In the Llewellyn Tarot, the King of Cups seems lost in thought. Two life-size, realistically carved fish are mounted on the arms of his throne; they seem to leap from the surf that surrounds him. The King of Cups typically represents a strong, dignified man of vision. He is artistic and reflective, intuitive, and somewhat reclusive.

In the Crowley deck, the King of Cups is called the Knight of Cups. He's depicted as a winged warrior on a white horse, with a peacock helmet and a cup with a crab inside. (The crab is a symbol of the astrological sign Cancer.) Crowley described the Knight of Cups as a graceful, poetic man with a short attention span. While he could be enthusiastic, his attraction usually doesn't last long. Crowley also said that the Knight of Cups is innocent and pure, but also shallow and superficial.

What Does Your Future Hold?

- Kings are active rulers and protectors, willing to defend their realms and dispense justice on behalf of their countrymen. Cups cards all relate to emotional issues. When the King of Cups appears in a tarot reading, you can expect your emotions to be actively defended and protected.

- Traditionally, the King of Cups was said to be a fair-haired man, typically associated with business, law, or the ministry. The King of Cups is connected to art and science, too.

- Oddly enough, the King of Cups was also said to be a man in a powerful position who could be shifty in his business dealings. Historically, the King of Cups was a cautionary card, warning of ill-will on the part of a man of position; he could be a hypocrite, and only pretend to help.

- Many tarot readers today believe that the King of Cups represents a devoted husband and father, committed to his wife and family, and protective of their feelings.

For Future Reference

Keywords: A good, honest man; kind, generous, wise, compassionate, artistic, cultural, inspired, tolerant, intuitive, empathic, sensitive

Reversed: Idleness, untruthful, dishonest, shifty, double-dealing, two-timing, alcoholic

Timing and dates: 20° Aquarius to 20° Pisces (February 9–March 10)

Ace of Swords

Get to the point

All of the aces represent pure promise and possibility. They hold limitless potential: succeeding cards in each suit stem from this single starting point. All of the aces also represent new beginnings, and the Ace of Swords symbolizes a new beginning in intellectual life.

In the classic Waite design, all four aces share a similar design: a giant hand parts the swirling mists of a silver cloud, holding the emblem of the suit. In this case, that emblem is a gleaming silver sword, held aloft like Excalibur from the legends of King Arthur. Its steely blade glints in the sun, and its tip pierces a crown adorned with olive and palm branches.

Like the Ace of Wands, the Ace of Swords is held in the right hand, which symbolizes action. (The Ace of Cups and the Ace of Pentacles are both held in the left hand, which symbolizes receptivity.) Whoever holds the sword is invisible: the weapon seems to float on the air currents that correspond to the airy nature of this suit. Waite called this card the "Root of the Powers of Air."

In the Llewellyn Tarot, the Ace of Swords is a card of quick, confident decision making. It symbolizes action and determination, along with force and control. The Ace of

Swords also represents the powers of discrimination, and the ability to cut through excess and clear the air.

In the Crowley deck, the sword belongs to the magician, and it seems to part the dark clouds and clear a path for the sun, which represents the mind. There's a serpent wrapped around the hilt, which is engraved with the symbols of the waxing, full, and waning moon. The hilt of the sword pierces a crown of twenty-two rays of pure light, which symbolizes the twenty-two letters of the Hebrew alphabet and the twenty-two paths between the spheres on the Kabbalistic Tree of Life. The sword itself points down, channeling cosmic energy from above to the earthly world below. The blade is inscribed with the Greek word Thelema, which means will. Crowley said the Ace of Swords represented the primordial energy of air.

What Does Your Future Hold?

- Crowley said a raised sword symbolized divine spiritual power, but a sword with its tip pointed down represented a demonic force. That's one reason the Ace of Swords has historically been associated with great power—for good or evil.

- The Ace of Swords is a forceful card. It denotes triumph, conquest, victory, and success on the battlefield. That battlefield, of course, is metaphoric, and it could relate to any arena: work, home, love, money, or health. The crown symbolizes leadership and authority, but on a higher level it symbolizes the higher power that created the universe.

- The sword is a longstanding symbol of justice, liberation, and truth. The goddess of justice holds a sword. So did medieval knights, who were sworn to protect and defend those who couldn't fight for themselves. In a tarot reading, the Ace of Swords could represent an aggressive defense. It might even represent, in Crowley's words, "Justice upholding Divine Authority," or "the sword of wrath, punishment, and affliction." All told, the Ace of Swords may be telling you that it's time to take up arms and make your point.

- Many versions of the Ace of Swords clearly suggest impregnation, as the long sheath of the blade penetrates the circular opening of the crown. Even if a physical pregnancy isn't in your cards, the seeds of intellectual growth and expansion will soon be planted. You may find yourself engaged in a learning adventure—a new class, a new book, or a new hobby or interest to master.

- Historically, the Ace of Swords was said to portend either great prosperity or great misery. Reversed, the card was believed to symbolize a broken engagement for a woman, because of her own lack of prudence.

For Future Reference

Keywords: Triumph, fertility, intellectual ability

Reversed: Intellectual failure, impotence

By the numbers: All of the aces represent pure promise and possibility, because they hold limitless potential: succeeding cards in each suit stem from this single starting point. In fact, the Ace of Swords is said to be the root of the powers of fire.

Timing and dates: In fortunetelling, the ace could refer to one hour, one day, one week, one month, one year—or Sunday, the first day of the week, or January, the first month. Astrologically, the Ace of Swords is associated with all of the powers of air—the element associated with Gemini, Libra, and Aquarius.

Two of Swords
A balanced mind

In some secret societies, initiates are blindfolded to symbolize their spiritual and physical blindness. The Two of Swords illustrates the growth that can take place in darkness.

In the classic Waite design, a lone woman, dressed in a long gown, perches on a stone bench as regally as if she were sitting on a throne. She clasps two swords, which are practically as long as she is tall. The weight of their tempered steel blades must be overwhelming, but she is balanced, peaceful, and composed. She is also blindfolded. The sky above her is dark and cloudy, lit only by a sliver of the waning crescent moon. Waite called this card "Peace Restored."

In the Llewellyn Tarot, the blindfolded woman stands on a windswept shore. She seems to be keenly aware of the world around her, even though she can not see. She makes up for her loss of sight by engaging her other senses: the feel of the breeze in her hair, the sounds of the creatures of the night, and the scent of the water. She is in a protected bay, but she hardly seems protected from the damp, salty spray of the mist on a chilly seaside breeze. The card symbolizes an uncertain peace, a frail alliance, and impasse.

In the Crowley deck, two crossed swords are unified by a blue, five-petaled rose. The rose is emitting a geometric pattern of white rays, which symbolizes equilibrium, as well as four spiraling shapes that symbolize the swirling energy of the four elements. At the top and the bottom of the card, the astrological glyphs for the Moon and Libra are balanced on the tips of two small daggers. The glyphs are a symbol of the Moon, the planet of cycles and change, in Libra, the sign of balance. Crowley called this card "Peace."

What Does Your Future Hold?

- When the Two of Swords appears in a reading, it typically represents a difficult decision—a choice between two options, or conflicting thoughts, ideas, and emotions.

- You may find that you have to base your decision on instinct, because you can't see the whole picture. You might even feel as though you're being forced to choose between the lesser of two evils.

- If you can't see the correct decision, or if you can't visualize the route you should take, you may need to tune in to your other four senses—as well as your sense of intuition.

- The blindfold might also symbolize your unconscious or subconscious state. You might need to travel deep within yourself to get the information you need, and block out the distractions of the outside world so that you can hear your own inner voice more clearly.

- The swords in the image could represent a temporary truce or ceasefire.

- Historically, the Two of Swords was said to represent friendship and harmony, as well as gifts for a woman or influential protection for a man in search of help. Some also said that the Two of Swords symbolized interaction and dealings with rogues.

For Future Reference

Keywords: Decisions, choices, impasse, a lack of information

Reversed: False friends, disloyalty, treachery, lies, and delays in decision making.

By the numbers: Twos represent duality and choices. The number two suggests pairs and combinations, as well as relationships, partnerships, and the attraction between two people. Twos also represent conversation and debate—the point and counterpoint of two opposing ideas, or the antithesis that rises up in response to almost every thesis.

The very nature of the number two also signifies a wide range of concepts that come in pairs: heaven and earth, male and female, active and passive, conscious and unconscious, and day and night. Written as a Roman numeral II, the number suggests a gateway or a doorway, as well as female genitalia.

Timing and dates: In fortunetelling, the number two could refer to two hours, two days, two weeks, two months, two years—or Monday, the second day of the week, or February, the second month. Astrologically, the Two of Swords is assigned to 0-10° Libra (September 23-October 2).

Three of Swords
The broken heart

The classic card of broken hearts, the Three of Swords hardly needs to be interpreted or explained to most people. Even those who have never seen tarot cards before see it for what it is—often with a pained laugh of recognition. That's because most people have experienced a heartbreak at some point in their past, as well as the horrible realization that someone has stabbed them, metaphorically, in the heart.

In the classic Waite design, three stainless steel swords have pierced a red heart—but this is no Valentine, rosy and pink and trimmed with lace. Instead, it's a lifeless, disembodied heart which floats suspended in a cloudy, dark, and rain-filled sky. Underneath the heart, a grief-stricken man struggles to regain control of his emotions. Waite called this card "Sorrow."

In the Llewellyn Tarot, a bedraggled young woman sits on soggy ground with her arms wrapped around her knees. Three oversized swords, dark and gray like pewter, surround her on three sides. The sky is cloudy and full of rain. The card symbolizes heartache, pain, abandonment, and estrangement.

In the Crowley deck, we peer into what Crowley called the womb of chaos. "There is an intense lurking passion to create," he wrote, "but its children are monsters." It is dark and heavy, and storm clouds roil and turn in the background. A long sword has driven its point between two shorter, curved swords, and destroyed the white rose in the top half of the card. The astrological glyphs at the top and bottom of the card symbolize Saturn, the planet of limitations and restrictions, in Libra, the sign of balance. Like Waite, Crowley also called this card "Sorrow."

What Does Your Future Hold?

- The Three of Swords often suggests the bad breakup of a couple torn apart by bitterness and acrimony. It could refer to divorce—particularly a divorce caused by adultery or faithlessness, in which the sanctity of marriage has been destroyed by the introduction of a third person.

- Occasionally, the Three of Swords also symbolizes the grief and sorrow that follows a miscarriage or stillbirth.

- In rare cases, the Three of Swords could suggest anxiety or panic attacks, heart disease, or surgery.

- The Three of Swords could simply suggest that you're dealing with someone who has a bleeding heart—someone who sympathizes with anyone who has a sad story to tell. It could represent vulnerability.

- In the most positive interpretation of all, the card could even represent a heart pierced three times by Cupid's arrows, which means its owner will have at least three chances for lasting love and romance.

For Future Reference

Keywords: Sorrow, sadness, grief, loss, romantic breakups, divorce, affairs, infidelity, depression

Reversed: Healing and recovery

By the numbers: Threes symbolize creation—the result of two separate forces combining to create a third entity. A mother and a father produce a child together. A thesis and an antithesis combine to produce a synthesis. The number three can also represent body, mind, and spirit, or past, present, and future. Many religions believe in a holy trinity, such as Father, Son, and Holy Spirit, or Maiden, Mother, and Crone, or the triple goddess of the New, Full, and Old Moon.

Timing and dates: In fortunetelling, the number three could refer to three hours, three days, three weeks, three months, three years—or Tuesday, the third day of the week, or March, the third month. Astrologically, the Three of Swords is assigned to 10–20° Libra (October 3–12).

Four of Swords

Rest and recovery

In the classic Waite design, the effigy of a knight has been carved into the lid of a tomb. He's flat on his back, and his hands are clasped in perpetual prayer. One carved sword is laid across the crypt. Three more swords are suspended above the knight, either suspended in mid-air or mounted on the chapel wall. The stained-glass window in the background shows one person ministering to another. Waite called this card "Rest from Strife."

In the Llewellyn Tarot, a princess lies, a true sleeping beauty. Her faithful canine companion rests with her, and the outside world sleeps, too—including a nearby tree nymph, imprisoned in the body of a barren, snow-covered tree. The card symbolizes silence and withdrawal, isolation and asylum, and the surreal sensation that one is veiled and set apart from the real world. It sometimes represents a reprieve, a recovery, and a time to prepare for future work.

In the Crowley deck, four swords are displayed in the shape of a St. Andrew's Cross, fixed and rigid. Their points are sheathed in a rose with forty-nine petals that symbolize social harmony—or, at its worst, compromise and appeasement that bring only a temporary peace. In the background, a centaur flexes his bow, a goddess raises her glass, and an underworld god crosses his arms and raises his hands in a mixed gesture of blessing. Crowley called this card "Truce."

What Does Your Future Hold?

- The Four of Swords typically symbolizes a brief but welcome respite. In the classical religious sense of the image, the person in the image isn't dead—just sleeping. The card could represent a retreat, or a period of reflection and recuperation.

- It can even represent something of a warning: you might be trying to push yourself too hard. If you don't take a break, your body will find a way to force you to slow down. Eat well, exercise, and don't short yourself on sleep, or you could find yourself flat on your back for a virus-fueled, mandated retreat.

- The swords suspended in mid-air often symbolize the worries and fears and intellectual cares and concerns that may just now be coming to the fore of your consciousness. Hanging frozen in time, the three swords don't seem so threatening. But if—and when—you awaken to the dangers they pose, you be called upon to defend yourself before you even have a chance to take a full breath. It might be a good idea to deal with your problems now, before they multiply and grow.

- The Four of Swords can also represent dreams, mystic journeys, or out-of-body travel and experiences.

For Future Reference

Keywords: Rest, retreat, recuperation, recovery, relaxation

Reversed: A wake-up call

By the numbers: Fours symbolize structure, stability, and security, because four points come together to form a solid. There are four walls in a room, and four corners to a house. There are four dimensions: width, length, height, and time. There are four cardinal directions: north, south, east, and west. There are four seasons, four winds, and four phases of the moon. There are four elements, and four corresponding suits in the minor arcana.

Timing and dates: In fortunetelling, the number four could refer to four hours, four days, four weeks, four months, or four years—or Wednesday, the fourth day of the week, or April, the fourth month. Astrologically, the Four of Swords is assigned to 20–30° Libra (October 13–22).

Five of Swords
To the victor go the spoils

Back in the Five of Wands, we saw five young men engaged in a struggle. Here in the Five of Swords, we see what could be the aftermath of that event.

In the classic Waite design, a lone victor collects the spoils of war, while two others, their backs turned toward us, collect their thoughts. The winner seems to smirk, satisfied that he has gotten the better of his enemies. His apparent lack of sportsmanship, however, leads many to wonder whether he really is the champion. Waite called this card "Defeat."

In the Llewellyn Tarot, a young woman moves across a battlefield, gathering the weapons of the fallen while two knights patrol the land behind her. The blue standard that flutters over the field is tattered and worn, a sign of struggle and dissolution. The card symbolizes loss, sorrow, regret, and defeat. It represents a loss of confidence and a lack of strength and resources.

In the Crowley deck, five swords are arranged in the shape of an inverted pentagram, a symbol of the triumph of matter over mind. They lie in the shadow of a goddess of the night; one of the blades is bent and broken. Crowley said the Five of Swords illustrated the decline of virtue, as well as corruption that could disintegrate a civilization. Like Waite, Crowley also called this card "Defeat."

What Does Your Future Hold?

- The Five of Swords usually refers to the humiliation and defeat of adversaries and opponents. The swords in this card, however, are all double-edged. The card could illustrate the fact that you have been cheated and tormented—or that you've been the poor sport. The card could also suggest that you've been tempted to treat others as badly as you have been treated in the past.

- In the swords cards, the battle scenes usually represent intellectual battles. After all, you'll probably never find yourself actually engaged in a round of swordplay in real life. However, the card could illustrate that tensions around you have been building for some time, and now you must be on your guard.

- You might also want to make sure you develop a network of friends and alliances you can trust for support.

- Historically, the Five of Swords also warned of an attack on the querent's finances.

For Future Reference

Keywords: Defeat, humiliation, degradation, failure, loss, dishonor, disdain, poor sportsmanship, sadness, mourning, anxiety, trouble, malice, slander, lies, spite, gossip

Reversed: A short-lived victory

By the numbers: Fives are almost always trouble, indicating a crisis and the need for continuing resolve at the halfway mark. Fives represent a halfway point in the progression from one to ten. In the tarot, "five" cards often symbolize a crisis: they're the midway point, when events can either take a turn for the better or go horribly awry. Fives also symbolize the five senses, the five points on a star, and the five vowels in the English alphabet. Some metaphysicians suggest that five is important because it symbolizes a fifth element—Spirit.

Timing and dates: In fortunetelling, the number five could refer to five hours, five days, five weeks, five months, or five years—or Thursday, the fifth day of the week, or May, the fifth month. Astrologically, the Five of Swords is assigned to 0–10° Aquarius (January 20–29).

Six of Swords
A bridge over troubled water

In ancient myth, a lone ferryman—a psychopomp—would ferry the souls of the recently departed across a river to the underworld. In ancient Greek mythology, Charon was the ferryman who guided the souls of the newly dead across the river Acheron or the River Styx, if they could pay his fare. Those who could not pay were doomed to wander the banks of the river for a hundred years. Historically, people were often buried with gold coins over their eyes or under their tongues so they would have a source to pay their way.

In the classic Waite design, a ferryman steers his craft across a small body of water, from one shore to the other. The bottom of the boat has been pierced by six long swords, which stand upright like ghostly passengers. No one seems to notice them. The water in front of the ship is calm, but the water they have crossed is choppy. Waite was careful to point out that the freight was light, and that the ferryman didn't have a difficult task ahead of him. He called this card "Earned Success."

In the Llewellyn Tarot, two figures huddle; they may be sisters, friends, or mother and child. A winged angel carved into the bow of the ship seems to lead the way through mist and fog, to the shore just coming into view. The card symbolizes movement, safe passage, guidance and assistance from others, and travel over water.

In the Crowley deck, the six swords are arranged in the shape of a hexagram. Their tips all point to a red rose in the center of a golden, six-squared cross, embossed on the cover of an oversized book. An ancient wizard holds the book and cross-references it against the cosmic sphere in his outstretched hand. At his feet, four geometric figures represent the physical realities of earth, air, fire, and water. The astrological glyphs at the top and the bottom of the card symbolize Mercury, the planet of speed and communication, in Aquarius, the sign of futuristic thinking. Crowley called this card "Science."

What Does Your Future Hold?

- There is often a haunting, ghostly spectral quality to the Six of Swords. Sometimes the card connotes death, but just as the Death card itself rarely indicates a literal, physical death, the Six of Swords may refer to a smaller, less deadly assault on your soul or your spirit, such as a crudely hurled insult, the jab of a sharp word, or the humiliation of a public slight.

- When a ship's structure has been pierced by six swords, they can't be removed: the craft would be left full of holes, and it would sink. Symbolically, the swords in this image could represent old injuries, wounds, and assaults. While they probably have healed by now, they've left scars—and those scars are part of who you are today.

- While the Six of Swords often symbolizes a spiritual journey, it can also represent a literal journey—a short trip across water, and typically, a pleasant one. Keep your overnight bag packed.

- The Six of Swords might also represent an envoy or a messenger who will travel to see you.

- Historically, the Six of Swords was said to herald a public declaration of love or a proposal, or an unfavorable end to a lawsuit.

For Future Reference

Keywords: Journeys, voyages, travel by water

Reversed: Stasis, delay

By the numbers: Sixes historically symbolize the human being, because man was said to be created on the sixth day. Six also symbolizes the sixth sense—psychic ability—as well as the six directions of space: left, right, forward, backward, up, and down.

Timing and dates: In fortunetelling, the number six could refer to six hours, six days, six weeks, six months, or six years—or Friday, the sixth day of the week, or June, the sixth month. Astrologically, the Six of Swords is assigned to 10–20° Aquarius (January 30–February 8).

Seven of Swords

A thief in the night

Historically, the Seven of Swords was said to be a very good card. Fortunetellers in the past said it suggested a dark girl, and promised a peaceful life in the country. Reversed, it heralded a positive news release or public announcement.

In the classic Waite design, a thief in the night absconds with several swords left unguarded in an enemy camp. His opponents' flags and banners still fly above their tents; their campground seems to be completely intact. As the thief walks away, he hardly even tries to conceal his escape. Waite called this card "Unstable Effort."

In the Llewellyn Tarot, an old man moves past a darkened army camp. He carries a pack on his back, filled with swords. A young boy trails behind him, collecting swords that lie on the ground. The card symbolizes resignation and acceptance, the end of an ordeal, and release.

In the Crowley deck, one giant, upraised sword seems to take on six smaller swords; they stand little chance in the face of superior firepower. A hooded figure in the background holds the decapitated head of a toga-clad warrior, who stumbles and gropes for his missing visage. The astrological glyphs symbolize the Moon, the planet of emotion, in Aquarius, the sign of futuristic thinking. Crowley called this card "Futility."

What Does Your Future Hold?

- While old-fashioned fortune tellers welcomed the Seven of Swords, these days it usually serves as a warning: there may be a traitor in your camp. The invader could be a sworn enemy or a saboteur. He could be a spy. He could even be a simple opportunist. At any rate, keep your guard up.

- The Seven of Swords can also be a warning not to put your total faith in others—and not to fall asleep when you're supposed to be on watch. Stay vigilant and aware, and be prepared to defend yourself.

- At its worst, the Seven of Swords could indicate that it's already too late to ward off some treachery, damage, or loss, but that you still have a few swords left to defend.

For Future Reference

Keywords: Theft, sabotage, humiliation, defeat, sneak attack, spies, enemies, unreliable friends

Reversed: Neglected advice

By the numbers: Seven is a mystical, magical number. Classically, there were seven days of creation. There are seven gifts of the Holy Spirit: wisdom, understanding, counsel, fortitude, knowledge, piety, and fear. There are seven deadly sins: envy, sloth, gluttony, wrath, pride, lust, and greed. There are seven virtues: faith, hope, charity, fortitude, justice, temperance, and prudence. (You can see most of them in the major arcana.) Alchemists had seven metals: gold, silver, iron, mercury, tin, copper, and lead. There are seven visible planets: the Sun, the Moon, Mars, Mercury, Jupiter, Venus, and Saturn. There are seven days of the week, seven notes in a musical scale, seven colors of the rainbow, and seven chakras. Because the seventh day is a day of rest, seven is the number of self-reflection and philosophy. To fully randomize your tarot deck before a reading, shuffle it seven times.

Timing and dates: In fortunetelling, the number seven could refer to seven hours, seven days, seven weeks, seven months, or seven years—or Saturday, the seventh day of the week, or July, the seventh month. Astrologically, the Seven of Swords is assigned to 20–30° Aquarius (February 9–February 18).

Eight of Swords

Eight of Swords
The ties that bind

If this is the same blindfolded woman we first met in the Two of Swords, things haven't gotten any better for her. In fact, she's even more powerless now than she was before. She is, at least, standing under her own power, but she will have to work hard to free herself from her bonds.

In the classic Waite design, a young woman stands alone, bound, blindfolded, and surrounded by eight swords that encircle her like the bars of a cage. She's not completely bound, and she doesn't seem particularly uncomfortable; in fact, she seems healthy and strong, despite her unfortunate circumstances. Waite called this card "Shortened Force."

In the Llewellyn Tarot, the bound and blindfolded woman is staked to a watery coastline, where waves crash against her bare legs. The card symbolizes frustration, fear, and a sense of powerlessness. It represents mistreatment at the hands of others, controlling behavior, vulnerability, and deceit.

In the Crowley deck, two very long swords are positioned on top of six small swords—three pointing right, and three pointing left. Crowley identifies the six small swords as a kriss, a kukr, a scramasax, a dagger, a machete, and a yataghan. The astrological glyphs at the top and the bottom of the card symbolize Jupiter, the planet of luck and expansion, in Gemini, the sign of speed and communication. Crowley called this card "Interference."

What Does Your Future Hold?

- When the Eight of Swords shows up in a tarot reading, you may find that you, too, are bound and entrapped—and that you'll need to find a way to free yourself. If you can't get your blindfold off, you might need to feel your way out of your prison by stepping gingerly through the row of swords.

- Alternately, you could also shimmy up to one of the swords to cut the ties—and that could be a metaphor: it might be time to cut some ties in your own life. Of course, if you should stumble or fall in the process, any one of those razor-sharp blades could slice into you. That might be a risk you just have to take.

- If you prefer to wait for a while, just in case rescuers are on their way, now would be a good time to reflect on the circumstances that landed you in this prison.

- The Eight of Swords could also suggest that you will soon find yourself in a position to rescue a metaphorical damsel in distress. Do you recognize her—or him? What is it that draws you to this person? Do you attract people whose lives mirror your own? Or do you actively search for people you can help?

- Historically, the Eight of Swords suggested a scandal for a woman, spread by rumors and gossip. Reversed, it symbolized the departure of a relative.

For Future Reference

Keywords: Restriction, imprisonment, bondage, entrapment, victimization, crisis, criticism, blame, misfortunes, disgrace

Reversed: Treachery and unexpected occurrences

By the numbers: Eights represent infinity, because they resembles the lemniscate, the sideways symbol of infinity. There are also eight points on the Wheel of the Year. To Christians, eight is a symbol of baptism and spiritual rebirth; many baptisteries and baptismal fonts have eight sides. Eight also represents the eternal spiral of regeneration.

Timing and dates: In fortunetelling, the number eight could refer to eight hours, eight days, eight weeks, eight months, or eight years—or August, the eighth month. Astrologically, the Eight of Swords is assigned to 0–10° Gemini (May 21–31).

Nine of Swords
Nightmare on Elm Street

The Nine of Swords is one of the most disliked cards in the tarot deck, because it depicts the anxiety and distress of a sleepless night, and the overwhelming burden of worries and fear.

In the classic Waite design, a woman sits bolt upright in bed, her hands over her face in anguish. She seems haunted and overwhelmed, and her long, white nightgown seems to suggest that she is an innocent victim of a cruel fate. In the inky blackness of the night, the nine swords that hang on the wall behind her bed seem larger than life. They almost look like a curtain of fear and oppression. Waite called this card "Despair."

In the Llewellyn Tarot, a young woman holds her head, while the nine swords behind her seem to pose a series of sharp-edged steps that can never be climbed. She is haunted by an array of past hurts and injustices. The card symbolizes nightmares and suspicion, worry and depression, longing and misery.

In the Crowley deck, nine scarlet swords point down, as perfectly formed drops of blood fall from their tips. Above them, a black knight shouts, his arms raised in triumph. Crowley said the card represented intellectual consciousness, but not reason. He said it symbolized animal instincts, psychopathic impulses, and fanatical beliefs—like an inquisitor who poses as an intellectual only to hide his temper and rage. The astrological glyphs symbolize Mars, the planet of war, in Gemini, the airy sign of intellect, thought, and communication. Crowley called this card "Cruelty."

What Does Your Future Hold?

- In a tarot reading, the Nine of Swords often symbolizes nightmares, phobias, insomnia, and worry—particularly the type of worry that strikes at three in the morning, waking us up from a sound sleep, and keeping us awake while we ponder all the horrible fates that could befall us or the ones we love. Ultimately, however, the type of fear expressed by the Nine of Swords almost never seems as dire the next morning, when the sun comes up and we can see in the bright light of day.

- It's always darkest before the dawn. When you get the Nine of Swords in a reading, remember that your mind is simply not sharp during the wee hours of the morning. Don't dwell on your worst fears. If you can't sleep, get up and read a book, or clean the kitchen, or find a movie on TV. Don't just lay in bed and allow the shadows to consume your thoughts. Everything will look better and brighter in the morning. If it comes up as a future card, you could be in for a nightmare, unless you can take steps now to keep a situation from growing out of hand.

- In many renditions of the card, the woman in the image sleeps under the comfort of an astrological quilt. Like her, you can take comfort in the fact that the heavens above protect you, that the world will keep turning on its axis, and that the planets will continue in their orbit around the sun.

- The woman in the card could also take comfort from the fact that the bed she sleeps upon is carved with scenes of conquerors and heroes. She is literally resting on the bedrock of ancient myths and stories, and she can learn from their experience.

- Occasionally, the Nine of Swords refers to grief and mourning, after a death, a miscarriage, or a stillbirth.

- Historically, the Nine of Swords was said to refer to a minister, a priest, or some other member of the clergy, as well as a temple, church, monastery, or convent. It was also said to suggest that someone's suspicions or misgivings about a shady character were well founded.

For Future Reference

Keywords: Nightmares, obsession, despair, insomnia, mental cruelty, grief, sorrow, loss, lamentation, guilt, shame

Reversed: Doubt, suspicion, reasonable fear, shame, imprisonment

By the numbers: Because there are nine months of pregnancy, nines symbolize selflessness, compassion, universality, humanitarianism, and spirituality.

Timing and dates: In fortunetelling, the number nine could refer to nine hours, nine days, nine weeks, nine months, or nine years—or September, the ninth month. Astrologically, the Nine of Swords is assigned to 10–20° Gemini (June 1–10).

Ten of Swords
Overkill

After a long and bloody series of adventures, the ten swords finally come to a rest.

In the classic Waite design, the ten swords find an unfortunate final landing—right in someone's flattened form. It's a gruesome lineup: they run the full length of his body, ensuring a complete and utter ending. Heavy dark clouds hang low over the horizon, where only a sliver of light hints at a sunrise or a sunset on the horizon. Waite called this card "Ruin."

In the Llewellyn Tarot, the ten swords merely surround the corpse of a young woman, but the message is the same: she will not rise again. She lies face down in a bed of crashing waves, her body is sprawled across an algae-covered rock, and her long hair is tangled in the swords near her head. The card symbolizes destruction and loss, the breakdown of relationships, disillusion, and grief.

In the Crowley deck, ten swords battle it out against a blazing red and orange backdrop. The hilts of the swords are positioned like the ten spheres on the Kabbalistic Tree of Life, with the Fool embarking on his journey through the spheres. One of the swords, piercing a heart in the center of the design, has broken into three pieces. At the top of the array, the goddess of justice Maat tips the balance of the scales. The astrological glyphs at the top and the bottom of the card symbolize the Sun, the luminary of light and consciousness, in Gemini, the sign of speed and communication. Crowley said the card represented the logic of lunatics, and reason without reality. Like Waite, Crowley also called this card "Ruin."

What Does Your Future Hold?

- When the Ten of Swords appears in a reading, you might feel as though you've been stabbed in the back by a friend or someone you trusted. The Ten of Swords frequently refers to situations in which gossip is a factor.

- The good news—if there's any—is that the situation is over. In fact, when the Ten of Swords appears in a reading, a final conclusion is inarguable.

- What's more, if you're the person who's been victimized, you truly are free to go. Obviously, your ability to fight back on this plane is gone—but at the same time, your spirit has been released. You can leave the scene of the crime and move on to greener pastures.

- Historically, fortune tellers were careful to point out that the Ten of Swords was not a card of violent death. However, it sometimes did suggest imprisonment or treason—especially if it was followed by an ace and a king.

For Future Reference

Keywords: Ruin, defeat, grief, disruption, desolation, sadness, distress, gossip

Reversed: Temporary success, advantage, power, authority

By the numbers: The number ten has primal, deep-seated significance for all of us. When babies are born, parents immediately do a quick count of fingers and toes. When we learn to count as children, we use our ten fingers as tools. Ten is the number of culmination, completion, and perfection. There are also ten spheres on the Kabbalistic Tree of Life, and ten numbered cards in each suit of the minor arcana.

Timing and dates: In fortunetelling, the number ten could refer to ten hours, ten days, ten weeks, ten months, ten years—or October, the tenth month. Astrologically, the Ten of Swords is assigned to 20–30° Gemini (June 11–20).

Page of Swords

If air could take human form, it would look like the Page of Swords—the literal, physical embodiment of air.

In the classic Waite design, the Page of Swords is an active young man who holds a sword in both hands. He is designed to look as though he's walking across a rugged landscape, under a sky filled with billowing clouds. His hair is blowing in the wind, and he seems to pause, just for a moment, as though he's heard a sound carried on the breeze. Waite described the Page of Swords as idealistic, youthful, energetic, precocious, and imaginative. He even said the young man could be a prodigy.

In the Llewellyn Tarot, the Page of Swords has sheathed his sword, but he still has it at the ready. He stands next to his white horse, apparently thinking about the message he holds in his left hand. The card symbolizes secrets, plots, an undercurrent of danger, and a need for caution.

In the Crowley deck, the Page of Swords is called the Princess of Swords. Crowley described her as a mix of Minerva, the Roman goddess of wisdom, and Diana, the Roman goddess of the hunt. She is slim and light-footed, and she stands on a bank of clouds. She holds a sword in one hand, and rests her other hand on a small, silver altar.

What Does Your Future Hold?

- Pages typically represent students and messengers. Swords correspond to intellectual life. When you put them both together, and the Page of Swords falls in your reading, you can probably expect to learn a new lesson—or receive a clear message—about your intellectual life.

- All of the swords cards are airy, which means that the court card personalities are intellectual. The Page of Swords is still immature, so his intellect is not fully developed. If the Page of Swords represents you in a reading, you might want to apply yourself to a formal course of study.

- The Page of Swords is also connected to spies, surveillance, undercover operatives, and secret service employees.

- Historically, the Page of Swords was said to suggest that an indiscreet person would pry into your secrets.

For Future Reference

Keywords: Intelligence, keen powers of observation, vigilance

Reversed: Spies, revealed secrets

Astrological associations: Pages are purely elemental. In other words, the Page of Swords is the personification of air itself. The card isn't associated with any astrological sign, but it can be linked to the air signs of Gemini, Libra, and Aquarius.

Knight of Swords

The four knights are all airy individuals who combine the element of air with the element of their suit. The knight of the watery suit of swords is a uniform mixture of air and water—a combination that's so pure, it's rarified.

In the classic Waite design, the Knight of Swords stands at the ready, his sword raised, and one leg poised as if he's ready to charge into battle. Waite described the Knight of Swords as a prototypical hero of romantic chivalry, like Galahad, one of King Arthur's knights.

In the Llewellyn Tarot, the Knight of Swords is riding at full speed, as if he's scattering his enemies. The card symbolizes a daring and impressive man of action. While he's typically heroic, he can also be impulsive and rash.

In the Crowley deck, the Knight of Swords is called the Prince of Swords. He is seated in a chariot drawn by pentagram fairies. He wears a pentagram crown on his head, and he holds a sword in one hand and a sickle in the other. Crowley described the Prince of Swords as full of ideas and thoughts and designs. He could kill his ideas as fast as he created them, however, and his character was marked by suspicion, distrust, and caution. At his worst, the Prince of Swords could be harsh, malicious, plotting, obstinate, and unreliable.

What Does Your Future Hold?

- During medieval times, knights were adventurers and rescuers, sworn to defend the weak and helpless while they journeyed to fulfill a quest. When the Knight of Swords appears in a tarot reading, the card could signal an upcoming journey or quest of your own—or a rescue—in the swords' realm of intellect and communication.

- Because swords are associated with intellectual and verbal skills, the Knight of Swords often refers to someone who is intelligent, articulate, and analytical. If that's you, the card may be a sign that it's a good time to polish or put those skills to use.

- When the Knight of Swords appears in a reading, it often refers to someone who is quick thinking, enthusiastic, energetic, and brave. His courage sometimes borders on the foolhardy—almost as though he thinks he's immortal.

- The Knight of Swords is often a fighter, not a lover. If he shows up in your reading, he may not be the best choice for long-term romance.

- The Knight of Swords sometimes refers to a soldier or man of arms, and predicts that he will be involved in heroic action.

- Historically, the Knight of Swords reversed was said to foretell a dispute with an imbecile. If it fell in a spread for a woman, the card symbolized victory in a struggle with a rival.

For Future Reference

Keywords: Skill, bravery, battle, combat, defense, opposition, resistance

Reversed: Boredom, sarcasm, incompetence, ineptitude, foolishness, folly, stupidity, impertinence, extravagance, ridicule, fraud, mischief, cunning

Timing and dates: 20° Capricorn to 20° Aquarius (January 10–February 8)

Queen of Swords

The four queens are all watery individuals. Each one combines the element of water with the element of her suit. The queen of the watery suit of cups embodies the placid combination of water with even more water.

In the classic Waite design, the Queen of Swords raises her weapon in her right hand, resting the hilt on the arm of her throne. She extends her left hand out, with an expression that's meant to suggest firm, loving kindness—and a familiarity with sorrow.

In the Llewellyn Tarot, the Queen of Swords sits with an upraised sword in her right hand, and her left hand outstretched, as if she's trying to determine which way the wind is blowing. A hawk, a symbol of her airy suit, soars overhead. The card represents a confident, self-assured leader, with determination as steely as the blade of her sword. She is a trailblazer.

In the Crowley deck, the Queen of Swords is a graceful woman with wavy, curling hair. She is seated on a throne that seems to float on clouds. She holds a sword in one hand, and a severed head in the other. Crowley described the Queen of Swords as intensely perceptive, keenly observant, subtle, quick, and confident. He said she was also graceful and fond of dancing and balancing.

What Does Your Future Hold?

- When the Queen of Swords appears in a reading, you can expect to meet a woman who embodies all of the qualities of the airy swords cards—a quick thinker with a keen intelligence, heightened powers of observation, quick wit, and a sharp tongue.

- She didn't get to be the Queen of Swords by staying quiet, and you can count on her to make her observations and thoughts clear, in any company. She can be diplomatic, but just as often she can be autocratic and demanding.

- If she's on your side, the Queen of Swords can be the life of the party. If not, you might want to take cover if she decides to cut you down to size.

- Historically, the Queen of Swords was thought to represent a widow, but these days she can represent anyone who has suffered a devastating emotional loss, including the loss of a lover or a child. The Queen of Swords has also been associated with miscarriage and infertility.

- Some people compare the Queen of Swords to a misguided mother-in-law, determined to do battle with her son's wife.

For Future Reference

Keywords: Eloquence, grace, charm, logic, intelligence, power, discernment, analysis, science, professionalism, objectivity, self-reliance

Reversed: Angry willful, hateful, cruel, sly, sharp-tongued, bigoted, hypocritical, and deceitful

Timing and dates: 20° Virgo to 20° Libra (September 12–October 12)

King of Swords

The four kings are all fiery individuals. They combine the element of fire with the element of their suit. The king of the airy suit of swords is a smoky blend of fire and air.

In the classic Waite design, the King of Swords sits on his throne, holding his sword, and looking very much like the Judgment card. Waite said his pose was designed to demonstrate his power over life and death.

In the Llewellyn Tarot, the King of Swords rules his domain from a throne embossed with an eagle, while behind him, two real birds soar overhead. The card represents a powerful man with a quick temper—a daring, effective leader, whose presence is as commanding as his sword.

In the Crowley deck, the King of Swords is called the Knight of Swords. He's depicted as a winged warrior on a brown horse, riding through the clouds, with a winged, six-pointed star as his crest. The symbol is a nod to Castor and Pollux, the twin Greek gods who have been immortalized in the constellation Gemini.

Crowley described the Knight of Swords as active, clever, subtle, fierce, delicate, courageous, skillful, and inclined to domineer. He also said the Knight of Swords would tend to overvalue small things. At his worst, Crowley said, the Knight of Swords could be deceitful, tyrannical, and crafty.

What Does Your Future Hold?

- Kings are active rulers and protectors, willing to defend their realms and dispense justice on behalf of their countrymen. Swords cards all relate to intellectual issues. When the King of Swords appears in a tarot reading, you can expect swift, decisive action in the realm of the intellect.

- Traditionally, the King of Swords was said to represent lawyers, doctors, surgeons, and senators.

- When the King of Swords appears in a reading, it could also indicate that you'll be dealing with legal, financial, or medical advice.

- Historically, the King of Swords meant that it was time to put an end to a ruinous lawsuit.

- Today, the King of Swords often describes a man of action, with a keen intellect that generates a steady stream of ideas.

For Future Reference

Keywords: Judgment, power, command, authority, law

Reversed: Cruelty, perversity, barbarity, evil

Timing and dates: 20° Taurus to 20° Gemini (May 11–June 10)

Ace of Pentacles

Pennies from heaven

The Ace of Pentacles symbolizes a new beginning on the physical plane. It represents a metaphorical gift of health, wealth, or good fortune, yours simply for the taking.

In the classic Waite design, the right hand of God—or the Magician—emerges from a silver cloud. It holds a giant golden pentacle, a symbol of the physical world. Beneath the pentacle, off in the distance, a flowered arbor gate stands as an invitation to a garden of earthly delights. Waite called this card the "Root of the Powers of Earth."

In the Llewellyn Tarot, orange poppies bloom, wheat ripens in the sun, and two trees stand entwined, forming a natural gateway into a better world. The card symbolizes income and recognition—perhaps as the result of a new job or work-related project. The card also represents confidence, investment, and divine intervention.

In the Crowley deck, the disk is inscribed with Crowley's personal seal: the sun and the moon, three interlinked circles that symbolize creation, a heptagram, two interlaced pentagrams, a wheel with ten spokes, and the words "To Meta Ohpion," which means "The

Great Beast"—one of the titles Crowley had given himself. Like Waite, Crowley also called this card the "Root of the Powers of Earth."

What Does Your Future Hold?

- Waite said the Ace of Pentacles was the most favorable card in the deck, because it symbolizes wealth and abundance on many levels.

- The most precious gift, of course, is the gift of life, and the Ace of Pentacles sometimes heralds a new life—which could be the birth of a baby, or simply a new lease on life through better health and a more optimistic attitude.

- Because pentacles represent money, the Ace of Pentacles could also symbolize the start of a new career, a raise, a promotion, or a rewarding investment.

- And because pentacles correspond to the physical world, the ace could suggest the acquisition of land or a new home. There is nothing more tangible than real estate; it's an investment that's grounded in real property, as opposed to paper money, stock certificates, or bonds, which have no value in and of themselves.

- Of course, wherever your treasure is, your heart will be, too. The Ace of Pentacles could describe the ideals and values you treasure most, not just physically, but also spiritually. It's a reminder that you may be experiencing life on earth, but that doesn't separate you from a higher existence. You are a spirit in physical form.

For Future Reference

Keywords: Perfect happiness, contentment, physical comfort, ecstasy, joy, financial rewards, gold, money, treasure

Reversed: Love of money as the root of all evil, the misuse of resources, squandered wealth, the evil side of wealth, bad intelligence, great riches, prosperity, comfort

By the numbers: All of the aces represent pure promise and possibility, because they hold limitless potential: succeeding cards in each suit stem from this single starting point. In fact, the Ace of Pentacles is said to be the root of the powers of earth.

Timing and dates: In fortunetelling, the Ace of Pentacles could refer to one hour, one day, one week, one month, one year—or Sunday, the first day of the week, or January, the first month. Astrologically, the Ace of Pentacles is associated with all of the powers of earth—the element associated with Taurus, Virgo, and Capricorn.

Two of Pentacles

The song and dance man

In the classic Waite design, a juggler dances. He is part clown, part court jester, and part showman. He's only juggling two balls, but he's moving them in a complicated pattern, weaving them in and out of a ribbon in the figure-eight symbol of infinity, the lemniscate. (The lemniscate also figures prominently in the Magician and Strength cards.) Waite called this card "Change."

In the Llewellyn Tarot, a red-capped entertainer stands on one leg, spinning tales as effortlessly as he spins his golden spheres. Like Renaud, the legendary trickster fox, this juggler has a tail. Two ships in the distance rise and fall with the waves, symbolically depicting the rise and fall of fortune and economic well-being. The card symbolizes the balancing act of time and money, along with timing and dexterity.

In the Crowley deck, we see two spheres, black and white, linked by the serpent who has twisted himself into a lemniscate, the symbol of infinity. They are still revolving, still in constant motion, like the two opposing forces they represent. Both spheres contain yin and yang symbols, which symbolize the union of male and female. Behind them, a decapitated warrior approaches, his head in his hands, and his purse spilling coins upon the ground. The astrological glyphs in the background refer to Jupiter, the planet of luck and expansion, in Capricorn, the sign of career and public image. Like Waite, Crowley also called this card "Change."

What Does Your Future Hold?

- Life is a constant juggling act, and when the Two of Pentacles appears in a reading, your life may be in a steady state of flux. Because the suit of pentacles relates to money and material existence, you may be balancing two jobs, or trying to live in two worlds—work and home, for example.

- The balancing act might even be literal, as you try to make income and expenses balance out in your checkbook at the end of each month.

- The juggling also implies a perpetual ebb and flow of gain and loss, weakness and strength. There is a harmonizing effect, too, as you keep two opposing forces in balance.

- Because the juggler is a performer, you may be feeling as though you have been ordered into a command performance.

For Future Reference

Keywords: Harmony, balance, dexterity, juggling

Reversed: Agitation, trouble, embroilment, embarrassment, awkward positions, confusion, concern, worry, difficulties

By the numbers: Twos represent duality and choices. The number two suggests pairs and combinations, as well as relationships, partnerships, and the attraction between two people. Twos also represent conversation and debate—the point and counterpoint of two opposing ideas, or the antithesis that rises up in response to almost every thesis. The very nature of the number two also signifies a wide range of concepts that come in pairs: heaven and earth, male and female, active and passive, conscious and unconscious, and day and night. Written as a Roman numeral II, the number suggests a gateway or a doorway, as well as female genitalia.

Timing and dates: In fortunetelling, the number two could refer to two hours, two days, two weeks, two months, or two years—or Monday, the second day of the week, or February, the second month. Astrologically, the Two of Pentacles is assigned to 0–10° Capricorn (December 22–30).

Three of Pentacles
Creativity manifests

In the classic Waite design, a stonemason— a master of his art—stands on a bench in the nave of a church, carving out a creation of order and beauty. He follows the instructions—the divine guidance, if you will—of the clergymen nearby. Waite called this card "Material Works."

In the Llewellyn Tarot, a young woman creates a masterpiece of her own design, lovingly embroidered into a richly colored tapestry. In some ways, she's like the spider weaving the web above her head. Around her, red poppies blossom and wheat stands ready for the harvest. She is content to sit for now, however, sustained by the jug of water or wine at her feet. The card symbolizes talent, skill, comfort, and accomplishment.

In the Crowley deck, we have a bird's-eye view of a pyramid with three wheels at its base. According to Crowley's description, they're all floating on the sea of the great mother in the night of time. The wheels are inscribed with the alchemical symbols for Mercury, sulfur, and salt, which correspond to air, fire, and water, as well as the three letters Aleph, Shin, and Mem in the Hebrew alphabet. Hathor, the cow-headed goddess of fertility, dominates the background, where the baboon of Thoth takes aim at a vulture with a bow and arrow. The astrological glyphs at the top and the bottom of the card symbolize Mars, the planet of energy and aggression, in Capricorn, the sign of career and public image. Crowley called this card "Works."

What Does Your Future Hold?

- When the Three of Pentacles shows up in a reading, it is a reminder that all art is a form of creative expression. It might suggest that you have artistic gifts that you should develop. It could even be telling you to use it or lose it.

- If your creative drive is especially strong, the Three of Pentacles could be your signal to follow your destiny, and make it your *métier*—a French word for an occupation or profession for which you are especially well-suited. The word is derived from the Latin word *ministerium*, which means "ministry." In this case, the artist in the Three of Pentacles is performing a ministry through his work.

- Make no mistake about it: you will need to work to develop your creativity. While a lot of people dream about creating something, someday, the true mark of most artists is the simple fact that they not only pursue their dream, but they take concrete steps to manifest their vision. All artists go through a period of study. They practice. They experiment. They learn discipline. And over time, they become masters of their art. That mastery carries with it an inherent responsibility, both to share their gifts with society at large, and to teach, train, and pass along their knowledge to other fledgling artists.

- In the Waite version of the card, the stonemason's artistry elevates him: he stands higher than his observers. Those observers, however, symbolize divine guidance. The card seems to reinforce the belief that many artists have about their work: while they are fully engaged in the act of creating, they say, the work doesn't feel as though it's coming from inside them. Instead, they feel as though the work is coming through them, as if they're channeling a vision and a consciousness far greater than their own.

- You'll notice that the sculptor holds a hammer and a chisel. In the wrong hands, those tools could be used as weapons of destruction. In the artist's grip, however, they become instruments of creation. He chips away at the unforgiving matter of time and space, and carves out a new reality for himself.

- The best artists are also teachers, because they reveal, carving by carving, brush stroke by brush stroke, some truth about the human condition. They communicate on a primal level.

- Historically, if the card fell for a man, it was said to portend celebrity for his eldest son. Early tarot scholars also related the card, when it was reversed, to children, childhood, or childlike impulses.

For Future Reference

Keywords: Skill, creativity, talent, ability, renown, nobility, elevation, dignity, rank, aristocracy, power, fame and fortune

Reversed: Mediocrity, puerility, pettiness, weakness, humility (Your artistic goals may be frustrated, blocked, or thwarted.)

By the numbers: Threes symbolize creation—the result of two separate forces combining to create a third entity. A mother and a father produce a child together. A thesis and an antithesis combine to produce a synthesis. The number three can also represent body, mind, and spirit, or past, present, and future. Many religions believe in a holy trinity, such as Father, Son, and Holy Spirit, or Maiden, Mother, and Crone, or the triple goddess of the New, Full, and Old Moon.

By the numbers: Threes are the number of creation, as the product of the addition of one and two, a natural progression, the chorus that follows a call and repeat song, the response.

Timing and dates: In fortunetelling, the number three could refer to three hours, three days, three weeks, three months, three years—or Tuesday, the third day of the week, or March, the third month. Astrologically, the Three of Pentacles is assigned to 10–20° Capricorn (December 31–January 9).

Four of Pentacles
Compound interest

While a Midas touch might seem like a blessing, a single-minded obsession with money can soon become a curse.

In the classic Waite design, a stern-looking king glares at the world from his throne. Ensconced behind walls, he holds fast to a golden coin, clutching it possessively to his chest, and keeping a solid grasp of two other coins that he's planted firmly under his feet. A fourth coin is perched on top of his head. He is tenaciously guarding his mind, heart, soul, and physical position. Waite called this card "Earthly Power."

In the Llewellyn Tarot, a young king adopts a similar pose, guarding his earthly riches at the expense of his physical comfort. While he seems extremely wealthy, he is totally and completely alone. The card symbolizes the danger of overidentifying with one's material possessions, parading one's wealth, and ostentation.

In the Crowley deck, we see a four-sided fortress from above, with four watchtowers in the corners. The towers are topped with the symbols for the four elements: water in the top left corner, fire in the top right, earth in the bottom right, and air in the bottom left-hand corner. Behind them, a goddess and a bull-headed god both explore treasure troves of wisdom and riches. The astrological glyphs at the top and bottom of the card symbolize the Sun in Capricorn, the sign of career and social status. Crowley called this card "Power."

What Does Your Future Hold?

- When the Four of Pentacles appears in a reading, you might find yourself focused on your material and physical existence. You might even find that you're obsessed with making sure your money and property is all in order. The card could also refer to a concern about your physical health and well-being.

- The Four of Pentacles could be a cautionary card. Take steps to protect your health, your physical well-being, and your finances—but don't wall yourself off from family, friends, and the outside world.

- The Four of Pentacles often guarantees a certain measure of financial security and stability.

- Historically, the Four of Pentacles was said to herald pleasant news from a lady, for a bachelor. Reversed, it was believed to represent a cloister, a monastery, or a convent.

For Future Reference

Keywords: Material gain, possessiveness, asset management, determination, self-protection, borders, boundaries, limits, isolation

Reversed: Delay, opposition, hindrances, obstruction, obstacles, loss

By the numbers: Fours symbolize structure, stability, and security, because four points come together to form a solid. There are four walls in a room, and four corners to a house. There are four dimensions: width, length, height, and time. There are four cardinal directions: north, south, east, and west. There are four seasons, four winds, and four phases of the moon. There are four elements, and four corresponding suits in the minor arcana.

Timing and dates: In fortunetelling, the number four could refer to four hours, four days, four weeks, four months, or four years—or Wednesday, the fourth day of the week, or April, the fourth month. Astrologically, the Four of Pentacles is assigned to 20–30° Capricorn (January 10–19).

Five of Pentacles
Money trouble

When people see the Five of Pentacles in a reading, they often wonder if joblessness, poverty, and destitution are on the way. The card addresses a very real fear that many people harbor, in an age when some people threaten that we're all just a paycheck away from being homeless.

In the classic Waite design, two figures struggle through snow and freezing wind. In his Pictorial Key to the Tarot, Waite said the pair were mendicants—monks who lived a life of poverty and preaching. The mendicants were so committed to poverty that they didn't even have monasteries, like most other religious orders at the time. They lived and worked in the streets, depending solely on the charity of others. Eventually, the church recognized four mendicant orders: the Dominicans, the Franciscans, the Carmelites, and the Friars Hermits of St. Augustine.

The figures in the card are dirty, hungry, and handicapped by time and circumstances. One, on crutches, literally doesn't have a leg to stand on. Even so, they're making their way past the stained-glass window of a church, where a bright light glows from within. With any luck, they'll make their way to the entrance, where sanctuary and warmth await. Waite called this card "Material Trouble."

In the Llewellyn Tarot, a windswept woman and a small child make their way through a churchyard, past a tall, carved Celtic cross. The stained-glass window behind them gleams with a jewel-toned Tree of Life design. The card symbolizes loss, loneliness, exhaustion, and a struggle to stay afloat. Happily, it also suggests that the hardship is temporary.

In the Crowley deck, five disks are arranged in the shape of an inverted pentagram, a symbol of matter over spirit. It seems unstable, and yet it doesn't seem as though it's in danger of imminent collapse. The disks are inscribed with five Hindu tatwas—a triangle, square, moon, ellipse, and circle—to illustrate the qualities or principles that make up the human body. The astrological glyphs at the top and bottom of the card symbolize Mercury, the planet of speed and communication, in Taurus, the earthy sign of stability. Apis, an Egyptian bull god, stands guard over the tatwas; in the background, Isis reigns. Crowley called this card "Worry."

What Does Your Future Hold?

- For most people, however, the card addresses only the fear, not the reality. It may be a reminder to save for a rainy day—or in this case, a snowy one.

- On a more philosophical level, the card might also address a type of poverty that's not on the top of everyone's list: a poverty of spirit. Both of the figures in the card seem to have been wounded. By what, we don't know—it could be words, it could be actions, or it could be the happenstance of chance.

- There are also a lot of people in the world who have been grievously injured by the tenets of organized religion, by ministers and clerics who betrayed the very faith they claimed to represent. The Five of Pentacles could refer to people who feel they can never measure up spiritually, who feel guilt and shame, or who feel condemned to make their way through a cold world without the warmth and support of a spiritual group.

- Others see a suggestion that the devil is at work, corrupting men's souls as easily as their bodies can be destroyed. The tattered clothes could symbolize holes in the spirit—a holiness that doesn't normally come to mind when we think of spiritual affairs.

- One historic interpretation of the card connected it to love and lovers—wives and husbands, lovers, mistresses, and paramours. It even suggested a sweet, pure, and chaste relationship between a chivalrous man and a refined woman.

For Future Reference

Keywords: Poverty, material troubles, fear, anxiety, loss, destitution, bankruptcy, ruin, disorder, disgrace, chaos

Reversed: Troubles in love, debauchery, licentiousness, discord, conflict

By the numbers: Fives represent a halfway point in the progression from one to ten. In the tarot, "five" cards often symbolize a crisis: they're the midway point, when events can either take a turn for the better or go horribly awry. Fives also symbolize the five senses, the five points on a star, and the five vowels in the English alphabet. Some metaphysicians suggest that five is important because it symbolizes a fifth element—Spirit.

Timing and dates: In fortunetelling, the number five could refer to five hours, five days, five weeks, five months, or five years—or Thursday, the fifth day of the week, or May, the fifth month. Astrologically, the Five of Pentacles is assigned to 0–10° Taurus (April 21–30).

Six of Pentacles

Balancing the scales

The Six of Pentacles is the consummate card of good fortune, of sharing wealth, and investing in the future.

In the classic Waite design, a wealthy merchant drops a handful of change into a beggar's outstretched palm, weighs money in a pair of scales, and distributes it to the needy and distressed. The beggars are dressed a lot like the two figures pictured in the previous card, the Five of Pentacles. The merchant, on the other hand, is well dressed and well groomed. He's completely protected from the elements, and he's dressed in a stylish fur-trimmed cloak and hat, a clean tunic, and boots. He holds a merchant's scale, and he seems to be using it to find a balance between business and charity. Waite called this card "Material Success."

In the Llewellyn Tarot, a businesswoman is disbursing some change—but those on the receiving end don't necessarily look like beggars. In fact, they almost look as though they're selling flowers from the side of the road. The card symbolizes charity, exchange, reward, and support for a cause. It also represents relief, restitution, and the resolution to a problem.

In the Crowley deck, six disks are arranged in the shape of a hexagram. Each one is inscribed with a planetary glyph. Starting at the top and going clockwise, they are Saturn, Jupiter, Venus, the Moon, Mercury, and Mars. The Sun, in the center, surrounds a rosy cross—which in itself is a symbol of the Sun's illumination and enlightenment. The four figures standing around the hexagram represent the four elements, each in a ritual pose. The astrological glyphs at the top and the bottom of the card symbolize the changeable Moon in Taurus, a sign of stability. Crowley called this card "Success."

What Does Your Future Hold?

- The Six of Pentacles is closely connected to business and industry. Money doesn't grow on trees, as they say—it's earned, through business and investment. When those ventures pay off, some people think of charity and philanthropy as a means of giving back to society.

- The businessman in the Six of Pentacles is committed to fairness and ethical trading. His scale is legal for trade.

- The merchant in the card also seems to recognize that he has been more fortunate than most. He knows that all rights—and privileges—connote an equal measure of responsibility. He demonstrates the belief that gifts should be shared, not hoarded. All told, the image is a testimony to his own success in life, as well as to his goodness of heart.

- He also seems to be talking to the men he is benefiting, which is a reminder that a kind word can be worth its weight in gold.

- When the Six of Pentacles shows up in a reading, it may suggest that you have been on the receiving end of charity, or that you have been charitable yourself. In either case, it implies that you understand the value of giving to others. If it comes up as a card of the future, it might even mean that you will someday be in a position to help many others less fortunate and less experienced than yourself.

- On a purely predictive level, the Six of Pentacles might also suggest that you are going to be on the receiving end of gifts, presents, and favors from benefactors with riches to spare.

For Future Reference

Keywords: Business, commerce, trade, charity, presents, gifts, favors

Reversed: Envy, jealousy, unsatisfied ambition (Also, taxation without representation, and the forced redistribution of wealth through unfairly administered government programs.)

By the numbers: Sixes historically symbolize the human being, because man was said to be created on the sixth day. Six also symbolizes the sixth sense—psychic ability—as well as the six directions of space: left, right, forward, backward, up, and down.

Timing and dates: In fortunetelling, the number six could refer to six hours, six days, six weeks, six months, or six years—or Friday, the sixth day of the week, or June, the sixth month. Astrologically, the Six of Pentacles is assigned to 10–20° Taurus (May 1–10).

Seven of Pentacles

Watching, waiting, hoping

When the Seven of Pentacles appears in a reading, you can probably expect some down time—a brief pause, while you wait, reflect, and hope for the best as all of your endeavors come to fruition.

In the classic Waite design, a young field hand leans on a hoe and gazes at a crop of seven ripening pentacles. He may be taking a brief break before he gets back to work, or he might be thinking about quitting altogether. While harvest day is approaching, at this point he's still poised between failure and success. Waite called this card "Success Unfulfilled."

In the Llewellyn Tarot, the pentacles grow from a tree, already laden with red and ripening fruit. A robed and hooded figure looks up at the branches. The card symbolizes patience, ingenuity, and reward, along with growth in personal and business life.

In the Crowley deck, seven lead disks are arranged in the form of a Rubeus, a geomantic symbol that represented the dark side of Scorpio and Mars, such as aggression, destruction, and addiction. They're laid around a Christlike figure, who lies on the ground as though he's been laid out for burial. The astrological glyphs on the discs—and at the top and the bottom of the card—refer to Saturn, the planet of limitations and restrictions, in Taurus, an earthy sign of stability. Crowley called this card "Failure."

What Does Your Future Hold?

- While money itself doesn't grow on trees, the Seven of Pentacles does suggest that it's possible to grow your finances through careful planting and cultivation. It could even refer to seed money.

- The card could also refer to the brief period of stagnation and inertia that can sometimes overtake you after the initial excitement and enthusiasm of a new project—especially if you're exhausted from the planning, preparation, and planting process.

- Remember that you can't rush Mother Nature, and that patience is a virtue.

- While success seems imminent, the card might be a warning, of sorts: the young man could be thinking about the rich harvest he expects, but that thinking could be premature. Late summer storms occasionally rumble through, and they flatten even the hardiest of crops. All in all, the image could be reminiscent of the old adage, "Don't count your chickens before they hatch."

- Crowley offered a bleak interpretation for the card: he said the Seven of Pentacles meant that you would find yourself doing a lot of work for nothing.

- Historically, the Seven of Pentacles was believed to symbolize arguments, quarrels, and fights—or, alternately, the qualities of innocence and ingenuity. Alternately, the Seven of Pentacles also was believed to suggest a raise, promotion, or some other improvement in position for a lady's future husband.

For Future Reference

Keywords: Money, finance, business, barter, gain, profit, financial success

Reversed: Money worries, anxiety about a loan, impatience, apprehension, suspicion, disappointment, a failed harvest

By the numbers: Seven is a mystical, magical number. Classically, there were seven days of creation. There are seven gifts of the Holy Spirit: wisdom, understanding, counsel, fortitude, knowledge, piety, and fear. There are seven deadly sins: envy, sloth, gluttony, wrath, pride, lust, and greed. There are seven virtues: faith, hope, charity, fortitude, justice, temperance, and prudence. (You can see most of them in the major arcana.)

Alchemists had seven metals: gold, silver, iron, mercury, tin, copper, and lead. There are seven visible planets: the Sun, the Moon, Mars, Mercury, Jupiter, Venus, and Saturn. There are seven days of the week, seven notes in a musical scale, seven colors of the rainbow, and seven chakras. Because the seventh day is a day of rest, seven is the number of self-reflection and philosophy. To fully randomize your tarot deck before a reading, shuffle it seven times.

Timing and dates: In fortunetelling, the number seven could refer to seven hours, seven days, seven weeks, seven months, or seven years—or Saturday, the seventh day of the week, or July, the seventh month. Astrologically, the Seven of Pentacles is assigned to 20–30° Taurus (May 11–20).

Eight of Pentacles

Working for a living

Remember the artist in the Three of Pentacles? Here is his counterpart, the artisan who actually makes money with his work. Granted, the artisan's creations probably aren't as rarified as the artist's. They might even be categorized as crafts. But what the artisan lacks in quality, he makes up for in quantity. He might not be strictly spiritual, but he's definitely more practical. In fact, as a craftsman, he's probably more likely than a starving artist to generate income, put food on the table, and keep a roof over his head—all without sacrificing his creativity. Ultimately, he may even be *more* spiritual, because he's better suited to the task of keeping body and soul together.

In the classic Waite design, a stonemason carves a series of pentagrams on a series of golden disks. In the illustration, he is literally making money. He wears a heavy leather apron, to protect him from chips and shards of wood or stone. Waite called this card "Prudence."

In the Llewellyn Tarot, a younger, more colorful version of the stonemason is hard at work, under a blossoming spring tree. He's not alone: a hummingbird hovers overhead, a robin perches nearby, and a swallow rests on the rim of a wooden bucket. The mason's cat, apparently well fed, rests at his feet, content to simply watch the birds. The card symbolizes employment, achievement, commissions, schedules, and deadlines.

In the Crowley deck, the eight disks are arranged in the shape of a Populus, a geomantic figure that symbolized a group of people. It grows underground, where a winged green demon and a fertility goddess study its pomegranate fruits. Above ground, Mother Nature controls the seasons and the spinning Wheel of the Year. The astrological glyphs at the top of the card symbolize the Sun, a symbol of consciousness and enlightenment, in Virgo, the sign of health, cleanliness, and order. Like Waite, Crowley also called this card "Prudence."

What Does Your Future Hold?

- When the Eight of Pentacles appears in a reading, you can expect to develop your skills and talents—and market them, even while you're still learning all the tricks of your trade.

- The card could represent new opportunities in the development of your career, including rewarding new projects and assignments. It could even suggest the possibility of going into business for yourself.

- Crowley said the card symbolized intelligence, lovingly applied to material matters—like agriculture and engineering.

- Historically, the Eight of Pentacles was said to represent either a young businessman or a dark girl.

For Future Reference

Keywords: Art, craft, artistry, craftsmanship, workmanship, apprenticeship, tutelage, study, mastery, practicality, a money-making opportunity, practical use of a skill or a talent, artistic creations for sale or trade, work for hire

Reversed: Loss of ambition, cunning, intrigue, vanity, greed, troubles with a loan, pennywise and pound-foolish

By the numbers: Eights represent the cyclical nature of business, finance, and working for a living. Eights represent infinity, because they resemble the lemniscate, the sideways symbol of infinity. There are also eight points on the Wheel of the Year. To Christians, eight is a symbol of baptism and spiritual rebirth; many baptisteries and baptismal fonts have eight sides. Eight also represents the eternal spiral of regeneration.

Timing and dates: In fortunetelling, the number eight could refer to eight hours, eight days, eight weeks, eight months, eight years—or the eighth month (August). Astrologically, the Eight of Pentacles is assigned to 0–10° Virgo (August 23–September 1).

Nine of Pentacles
A woman of means

In the classic Waite design, a woman stands alone in an elegantly cultivated garden. She is surrounded by wealth, luxury, and the comforts of material security. The nine pentacles that give the card its name are growing on the grapevines that surround her. It's not hard to see that the coming harvest will help assure her continued comfort and prosperity. She will have wine in the winter, and fruit for her bread. She holds a trained falcon on her leather-gloved hand. Even though the falcon is a bird of prey—as well as a hunting weapon that's notoriously difficult to master—she handles the bird with a natural grace and ease. Waite called this card "Material Gain."

In the Llewellyn Tarot, a raven-haired woman assesses the state of her lands, along with an assistant who seems to be reading or taking notes. In addition to the falcon on her glove, a pair of geese accompanies them. The card symbolizes prudence, assessment, and the successful handling of a multi-faceted venture.

In the Crowley deck, the nine discs are arranged in three groups of three. Six of the disks are inscribed with planetary symbols. Clockwise from the top, they are Saturn, Jupiter, Venus, the Moon, Mercury, and Mars, the six ancient planets of astrology. The three discs in the middle are large, three-dimensional spheres, in the primary colors of red, yellow, and blue. Each one casts a colored ray out into the universe. The astrological glyphs at the top and the bottom of the card symbolize Venus, the planet of love and attraction, in Virgo, the sign of health, cleanliness, and order. Crowley said this card symbolized good luck and good management, and he called this card "Gain."

What Does Your Future Hold?

- The Nine of Pentacles often suggests both good luck and good management of one's resources. When it comes up in a reading, you probably have a history of putting yourself in the right place at the right time. You may even have a knack for making your own luck. When opportunity knocks, you answer the door. When you see the Nine of Pentacles, you might want to get ready, again, to take advantage of any opportunity that presents itself—especially if that opportunity comes from the business or financial realm of the pentacles.

- The Nine of Pentacles also suggests that you have mastered the art of being alone, without being lonely. You might want to set aside some time for quiet contemplation and meditation—in solitude, of course.

- You might also expect to spend some time in proximity to your extended family. That's because the woman in the Nine of Pentacles is enjoying her garden alone, but three generations of her relations are gathered and waiting for her in the next card.

For Future Reference

Keywords: Material well-being, riches, inheritance, pleasure, prudence, safety, success, accomplishment, certitude, discernment, solitude, peace

Reversed: Theft, deception, loneliness, restlessness

By the numbers: Because there are nine months of pregnancy, nines symbolize selflessness, compassion, universality, humanitarianism, and spirituality.

Timing and dates: In fortunetelling, the number nine could refer to nine hours, nine days, nine weeks, nine months, or nine years—or September, the ninth month. Astrologically, the Nine of Pentacles is assigned to 10–20° Virgo (September 2–11).

Ten of Pentacles
Family wealth

The wealth of detail in the Ten of Pentacles is as rich as you would expect in a card that suggests wealth and satisfaction—not only on the material level, but also spiritual, emotional, and intellectual.

In the classic Waite design, three generations of a family—a wizened old grandfather, a young married couple, and their child—sit comfortably together, along with their dogs. They're all positioned behind an emblem of ten pentacles shaped like the Kabbalistic Tree of Life. Their family crest is hanging on a back wall. The old man is wearing an elegant cloak, which implies wealth, social status, and security. The dogs also hint at the family's status: they are greyhounds, a breed that used to be reserved for noblemen and aristocrats. The young couple is standing under an arch, an ancient architectural construct that still stands as one of the strongest, longest-lasting designs for any building. The structure suggests a permanence and support for their relationship. Waite called this card "Wealth."

In the Llewellyn Tarot, a well-dressed young mother offers a piece of fruit to her daughter, who's sitting on the edge of a table. Nearby, a young man practices his riding skills by putting a show horse through his paces, while onlookers admire their abilities. The card symbolizes freedom from financial concerns, prosperity, and stability. It also suggests gifts, inheritance, and family reunions.

In the Crowley deck, ten pentacles take the shape of the Kabbalistic Tree of Life. One is inscribed with astrological glyphs for the seven ancient planets. Two of the discs feature six- and seven-pointed stars. Another boasts a checkerboard pattern, symbolizing the interplay of dark and light forces in the universe. Like Waite, Crowley also called this card "Wealth."

What Does Your Future Hold?

- In most readings, the Ten of Pentacles suggests the richness of family life. It symbolizes inheritance, not only of resources, but also of wisdom, experience, family values, and beliefs, all passed along from generation to generation.

- Ultimately, it also symbolizes the love and support of family, and it bodes well for future generations. As each generation grows older and makes room for the next, parents are usually delighted to see their children become healthy, happy adults, with husbands, wives, and children of their own.

- For someone whose children are young adults, the Ten of Pentacles could even serve as the "grandparent's card," suggesting that grandchildren are on the way. It also implies a happy retirement and old age.

- Crowley suggested that the Ten of Pentacles is a reminder to put your money to good use, rather than simply acquiring it.

- Historically, the Ten of Pentacles was said to symbolize gambling, games of chance, and loss.

For Future Reference

Keywords: Riches, family life, home, household, inheritance, pension, legacy

Reversed: Disharmony, discord, strife, arguments with family members

By the numbers: The Ten of Pentacles is the last numbered card in the minor arcana, which suggests the end of one phase of a journey, and preparation for the next chapter.

Timing and dates: In fortunetelling, the number ten could refer to ten hours, ten days, ten weeks, ten months, ten years—or October, the tenth month. Astrologically, the Ten of Pentacles is assigned to 20–30° Virgo (September 12–22).

Page of Pentacles

If earth could take human form, it would look like the Page of Pentacles—the literal, physical embodiment of earth.

In the classic Waite design, a young man stares intently at the pentacle he holds in both hands. His feet are both firmly planted on the ground; he's moving slowly, focused only on the treasure in his hands.

In the Llewellyn Tarot, the Page of Pentacles holds an oversized golden coin, while a soft breeze blows his red cape out behind him. He stands next to a sheaf of wheat, a symbol of prosperity, and two poppies. The page represents a young, hard-working achiever, and the card symbolizes business communications, proposals, and offers.

In the Crowley deck, the Page of Pentacles is called the Princess of Spheres. She stands near a grove of trees, in a pose that's meant to suggest Hebe, the Greek goddess of youth, Ceres, the Roman goddess of the harvest, and Persephone, Ceres' maiden daughter. She wears a ram's head as a crown, and holds both a scepter and a pentacle in her hands.

Crowley described her as generous, kind, diligent, benevolent, careful, courageous, and persevering.

What Does Your Future Hold?

- Pages typically represent students and messengers. Pentacles correspond to physical life. When you put them both together and the Page of Pentacles falls in your reading, you can probably expect to learn a new lesson—or receive a clear message—about your physical health and well-being, your tangible assets, or your material possessions.

- All of the pentacles cards are earthy, which means that the court card personalities are physical. The Page of Pentacles is still immature, so his physical ability is not fully developed. If the Page of Pentacles represents you in a reading, you might want to exercise and develop your physical abilities.

- When the Page of Pentacles appears in a reading, you can also expect a burst of physical strength, an improvement in your overall health and well-being, and renewed energy.

- Historically, the Page of Pentacles was said to refer to a dark youth, a young officer, a soldier, or a child.

For Future Reference

Keywords: Study, physical development, news about physical existence

Reversed: Delays in physical development and maturity

Astrological associations: Pages are purely elemental. In other words, the Page of Pentacles is the personification of earth itself. The card isn't associated with any astrological sign, but it can be linked to the earth signs of Taurus, Virgo, and Capricorn.

CAVALLO DI DENARI   KNIGHT OF PENTACLES
CHEVALIER DE DENIERS   CABALLO DE OROS

RITTER DER MÜNZEN   MÜNTEN RIDDER

Knight of Pentacles

PRINCE OF SPHERES   PRINCIPE DI SFERE
PRÍNCIPE DE PENTÁCULOS   PRINCE DE SPHÈRES

PRINZ DER KUGELN   HEMELLICHAMEN PRINS

Knight of Pentacles

The four knights are all airy individuals who combine the element of air with the element of their suit. The knight of the earthy suit of pentacles is a dry and windy mixture of air and earth.

In the classic Waite design, the Knight of Pentacles rides a slow, heavy horse—a workhorse, and a powerful creature in its own right. He seems to gaze at his golden pentacle almost as if it were a crystal ball, while he contemplates his next mission.

In the Llewellyn Tarot, the Knight of Pentacles represents a hardworking, responsible young man with a traditional worldview. He is honest, dependable, and perseverant. He might also be just a little dull.

In the Crowley deck, the Knight of Pentacles is called the Prince of Spheres. He wears wings and sits in a chariot drawn by a bull. He also wears bull's horns on his headdress. There's a golden orb under his left hand, and an orb-and-cross scepter in his right.

What Does Your Future Hold?

- During medieval times, knights were adventurers and rescuers, sworn to defend the weak and helpless while they journeyed to fulfill a quest. When the Knight of Pentacles appears in a tarot reading, the card could signal an upcoming journey or quest of your own—or a rescue—in the pentacles' realm of physical and material existence.

- Because pentacles are associated with earning ability, the Knight of Pentacles often refers to new developments in your work or career life.

- When the Knight of Pentacles appears in a reading, it often refers to someone who is earthy and grounded. Sometimes, they're so well grounded that it takes them a lot of time to get moving and pick up speed.

- The Knight of Pentacles sometimes to refer to people who are steady, reliable, practical, patient, slow moving, methodical—and, occasionally, a little dull. They are slow to anger, but furious when they're finally enraged.

- Historically, the Knight of Pentacles reversed was said to foretell a brief period of unemployment.

For Future Reference

Keywords: Solid, useful, responsible, practical, grounded

Reversed: Inertia, idleness, stagnation

Timing and dates: 20° Aries to 20° Taurus (April 11–May 10)

Queen of Pentacles

The four queens are all watery individuals. Each one combines the element of water with the element of her suit. The queen of the earthy suit of pentacles embodies a fertile mix of water and earth.

In the classic Waite design, the Queen of Pentacles is a dark woman who embodies the soul of greatness. Waite described her as keenly intelligent and able to see many worlds in the pentacle she holds.

In the Llewellyn Tarot, the Queen of Pentacles is dressed in a rich embroidered gown. Her throne has been in one place so long that a tree has grown around it, in an embracing, curving shape. The card represents a calm, capable businesswoman, and the steady progress that takes place under her leadership. She is a strong, protective role model, and a caring, fair employer.

In the Crowley deck, the Queen of Pentacles is a dark-haired woman, seated on a throne that rests solidly on the earth. One side of her face is light, the other dark. She has adopted a winged goat's head as her crest, and a real goat is by her side. She holds a cube-topped scepter in one hand, and a golden orb in the other. Crowley described her as impetuous, kind, timid, and charming, great-hearted, intelligent, and truthful. She could also be moody, he said, and at her worst she was indecisive, capricious, changeable, and foolish.

What Does Your Future Hold?

- When the Queen of Pentacles appears in a reading, you can expect practical help from a serious, well-rounded woman.
- The Queen of Pentacles is usually earthy, practical, sensible, and resourceful—but she has a sensual side, and an innate understanding and gift for practical magic.
- Because the suit of pentacles is associated with money and material possessions, the Queen of Pentacles is also connected to riches, wealth, and opulence.
- Historically, the Queen of Pentacles was said to refer to a dark woman.
- The Queen of Pentacles was also believed to foretell presents from a rich relative, and a rich and happy marriage for a young man.

For Future Reference

Keywords: A dark woman, wealth, security, generosity, magnificence, confidence, candor

Reversed: Evil, suspicion, suspense, fear, mistrust

Timing and dates: 20° Sagittarius to 20° Capricorn (December 13–January 9)

King of Pentacles

The four kings are all fiery individuals. They combine the element of fire with the element of their suit which means the King of Pentacles is a scorching blend of fire and earth.

In the classic Waite design, the King of Pentacles is a dark figure, designed to suggest a brave personality—along with just a hint of lethargy. The king's throne is embellished with bulls' heads, a symbol of earth and Taurus.

In the Llewellyn Tarot, the King of Pentacles meditates under an apple tree. Red poppies grow at his feet. He is contemplative and serene.

In the Crowley deck, the King of Pentacles is called the Knight of Spheres. He's depicted as a dark warrior, with wings on his helmet. He rides a light brown horse, and carries both a scepter and a huge shield. Crowley described the Knight of Pentacles as a hulk of a man: heavy, dull, material, laborious, clever, and patient. At his worst, he could be greedy, demanding, and jealous. Crowley said he wasn't particularly courageous.

What Does Your Future Hold?

- Kings are active rulers and protectors, willing to defend their realms and dispense justice on behalf of their countrymen. Pentacles cards all relate to material and physical concerns. When the King of Pentacles appears in a tarot reading, you can expect to be physically defended and protected.

- Traditionally, the King of Pentacles was said to represent dark men, along with merchants, employers, and professors of math, science, and physics.

- Historically, the King of Pentacles was tied to mathematical gifts, achievements, and success. Reversed, it symbolized a vicious old man, or a dangerous man.

For Future Reference

Keywords: A savvy, successful businessman, wealth, investment, business acumen, mathematical ability, and success

Reversed: Vice, weakness, ugliness, perversity, corruption, peril

Timing and dates: 20° Leo to 20° Virgo (August 12–September 11)

Sample Readings

Start Packing

Question

My lease will run out in a year and want to know if you see me moving. The area I live in is kind of pricey and I live in an old building where the rent isn't too much. I don't know if I will be able to afford to move. Thanks for the reading in advance.

Answer

There's one card in the tarot deck that almost always means a move is in the works: the Tower. Believe it or not, that's what came up when I asked if you would be moving when your lease is up.

Now, don't be alarmed by the drama of the image. In some cases, the Tower can symbolize a sudden and forceful change of residence—just like the picture shows.

In your case, however, the Tower is there simply to let us know that a move is the most likely outcome of your current situation. I really want to emphasize that your move won't be this dramatic. When it comes to questions about moving, the Tower is simply one of the cards you expect to see. It's like a shorthand.

Here is one other important thing to note: While it seems as though you are probably going to move, the future isn't written in stone. The card I drew for you today simply depicts the path that you're on right now, at the present moment. If you truly like where you're living, and you want to stay, you can take action now to change course. If you still have a year on your lease, you definitely have time to make arrangements to enter into a new lease ... or to find a new home that you like just as well.

I don't know if this is the answer you were hoping or expecting to hear, but it's definitely the clearest answer I could imagine to your question.

Response

That's the answer I wanted. Our building is old and the floors are warped. It's kind of annoying when you have to find the right spot for furniture as the floors are uneven. Thanks!

Someday, Your Prince Will Come

Question

There is a guy I'm interested in, and I want to know if you see anything in the cards about us getting together. If not, will there be someone else in the near future?

Answer

Oddly enough, the first card that comes up for you doesn't depict a man. Neither does the second, or the third. At first, the only cards that come up for you depict strong, beautiful, high-spirited females. First was a young woman dancing around the Wheel of Fortune, followed by the goddess of the Star card, and then the goddess of Justice.

In other words, the first cards that came up simply depicted you, alone. All three of those cards are from the major arcana portion of the deck, too—which tells me that you are a powerful force all on your own.

Since three single female cards came up first, I would be tempted to guess that a new romance is at least three months away ... and that if you're looking for a lifelong commitment, it could even be three years away.

But don't be disheartened or discouraged, because the man you should be looking for finally made himself known with the fourth card I pulled from the deck. He's the King of Pentacles.

I don't know if the man you currently have in mind is the King of Pentacles, so I'll describe him for you here.

The King of Pentacles is not the stereotypical knight in shining armor. Instead, he's a former knight—one who has already completed his initial forays into the world, and succeeded in his preliminary quest for adventure. As a result, he has graduated from knight to king. If he's not an older man, he certainly seems like an old soul. He's mature.

King of Pentacles

The King of Pentacles takes his responsibilities seriously. He might even be the most serious man in the tarot deck. He rules the realm of the physical and material world, which generally means that he moves a little slower than the other, lighter kings who rule air, fire, and water. The King of Pentacles literally has gravity on his side. He exemplifies the concept of "gravitas." And he may be a little heavier than some other men. That comes with the territory—but he's still physically fit. After all, he's the king of the physical world.

Because he rules the suit of pentacles, which symbolizes money, he also has some money of his own. He may even be wealthy. He is probably a businessman or an investor. He probably has some physical property of his own, too, in terms of real estate.

The King of Pentacles also has an appreciation for luxury and for beauty, both natural and man-made. You can expect him to surround himself—and the people he loves—with beautiful furnishings, in rich, luxurious colors and fabrics, as well as eye-appealing artwork and well-made clothing and accessories.

What's really nice about the King of Pentacles, however, is that he understands the spiritual worth of his material possessions. He recognizes that money and property are not an end, in and of themselves. He knows that money and property are valuable because they represent an investment of spiritual energy, and that they're a means to a much higher end. The treasures he acquires on the physical plane symbolize the things he treasures on a spiritual level.

He may not be the most eloquent or emotional man in the tarot deck, but his actions speak louder than words. He is honest, faithful, and above all, steadfast.

All told, the King of Pentacles makes an excellent partner, and he's well worth the wait. If you don't already know him, I hope you meet him soon.

Making Money the Old-Fashioned Way

Question

Can you tell me what I need to know now about a new business I'm starting?

Answer

The card that comes up for you is the Six of Cups. It's a lovely card that can only mean good things.

The Six of Cups depicts a young boy giving a little girl a bouquet of flowers. They're both sweet, angelic little children—well dressed, well fed, and apparently well cared-for, in a protected courtyard surrounded by gardens.

I usually read the Six of Cups as a card of nostalgia. It suggests a return to happier, simpler times, as well as fond memories of youth and childhood days. It can symbolize close connections with brothers and sisters, as well as reunions with long-lost friends and family members.

If you happen to be going into the antiques business, I'd say this card would promise you unqualified success!

You will also do well if your business relates to nostalgia, gifts, gardening, children, safety, security, or emotional and physical well-being.

If I didn't hit the mark with any of those categories, don't worry. All of the "six" cards in the tarot deck tend to indicate success, so this is a good card no matter what type of business you're starting.

I also think the Six of Cups offers a bit of practical advice for a new business owner. I think it suggests that your best success in business will come by focusing on the emotional concerns of your customers.

Put your customers' feelings first, even above their "wants" or "needs." Emphasize the emotional satisfaction they'll get from doing business with you. Appeal to their hearts, not their minds. If you can give your customers the sense that they're doing business with a trusted, lifelong friend, then you'll come out ahead.

Response

This is a terrific reading. My new business venture is intuitive energy healing. I am so glad the card indicates it will be successful. I really want to help others and believe my words and healings will give them the comfort and relief they seek. I feel your reading has given me another confirm-ation and boost of confidence that I am on the right path for me. Many thanks...I found your reading very insightful and right on target.

Bibliography

Akron and Hajo Banzhaf. *The Crowley Tarot*. Stamford, Connecticut: U.S. Games Systems, Inc., 1995.

The Applied History Research Group. *The End of Europe's Middle Ages*. Alberta: University of Calgary, 1997.

Banzhaf, Hajo, and Brigitte Theler. *Keywords for the Crowley Tarot*. York Beach, Maine: Samuel Weiser, Inc., 2001.

Butler, Bill. *Dictionary of the Tarot*. New York: Schocken Books, 1975.

Carr-Gomm, Philip, and Stephanie. *The DruidCraft Tarot*. New York: St. Martin's Press, 2004.

Cotterell, Arthur, and Rachel Storm. *The Ultimate Encyclopedia of Mythology*. London: Lorenz Books, 1999.

Crowley, Aleister. *The Book of Thoth*. Stamford, Connecticut: U.S. Games Systems, Inc., 1996.

Crowley, Aleister. *Tarot Divination*. York Beach, Maine: Samuel Weiser, Inc., 1998.

DuQuette, Lon Milo. *The Magick of Aleister Crowley*. San Francisco: Red Wheel/Weiser, Inc., 2003.

_____. *Tarot of Ceremonial Magick*. York Beach, Maine: Samuel Weiser, Inc., 1995.

Ferguson, Anna-Marie. *The Llewellyn Tarot Companion*. Woodbury, Minnesota: Llewellyn Publications, 2006.

Kaplan, Stuart R. *The Encyclopedia of Tarot, Volumes I and II*. Stamford, Connecticut: U.S. Games Systems, Inc., 1978 and 1986.

Negrini, Roberto. *Liber T: Tarot of Stars Eternal*. Torino, Italy: Lo Scarabeo, 2004.

Ozaniec, Naomi. *The Elements of Egyptian Wisdom*. Rockport, Massachusetts: Element, 1994.

Papus. *Tarot of the Bohemians*. Chatsworth, California: Wilshire Book Company, 1982.

Place, Robert M. *The Tarot: History, Symbolism, and Divination*. New York: Jeremy P. Tarcher/Penguin, 2005.

Riley, Jana. *Tarot Dictionary and Compendium*. York Beach, Maine: Samuel Weiser, Inc., 1995.

Revak, James W. "The Influence of Etteilla & His School on Mathers & Waite." *Villa Revak*. www.villarevak.org, 2000.

Revak, James W. "Tarot Divination: Three Parallel Traditions." *Villa Revak*. www.villarevak.org, 2000.

Storm, Rachel. *Egyptian Mythology*. London: Lorenz Books, 2000.

Waite, Arthur Edward. *The Pictorial Key to the Tarot*. Stamford, Connecticut: U.S. Games Systems, Inc., 1975.

Wanless, James. *New Age Tarot: Guide to the Thoth Deck*. Carmel, California: Merrill-West Publishing, 1986.

Webster, Richard. *Playing Card Divination for Beginners*. St. Paul, Minnesota: Llewellyn Publications, 2002.

Index

C

Cadair Idris, 157

Caer Arianhod, 120

Cancer, 29, 37–38, 60, 71–73, 91, 107–110, 170, 189, 193, 196, 198–199, 201–202, 204, 224, 228–229

Capricorn, 29, 37–38, 59–60, 71–72, 74, 139, 158, 241, 259, 265, 267–268, 270–271, 273, 291, 295

Capuchin, 115, 117

cardinal virtues, 111, 136

Jung, Carl, 7, 14

cartomancy, 3

Celtic Cross, 12, 35, 38, 275

Cerberos, 116

Ceres, 290

Ceridwen, 89

Cernnunos, 139

channeling, 7, 65, 84–85, 232, 270

clairaudience, 65

clairsentience, 64–65

clairvoyance, xiv, 65

clarification card, 40, 64

collective unconscious, 7, 14

combinations, 3, 18, 21, 43–44, 107, 136, 163, 199, 235, 267

Cronos, 117, 125, 132–133

crux ansata, 95

Cupid, 103, 105, 179, 238

D

Daniel, 10, 114

decantes, 73

Demeter, 91–92, 94, 201

Deuteronomy, 11

Diana, 148, 152, 256

Diogenes, 117

Dis Pater, 141

divination, xiii, 2–4, 8, 10–12, 50, 311–312

Dyfed, 127, 131

E

earth signs, 291

elements, 3, 16–17, 21–22, 43, 76, 85, 91, 97, 99, 101, 106–107, 116, 128, 135, 161, 169, 172, 174, 187–188, 190, 192, 196, 201, 205, 208, 224–225, 227, 229, 233, 235, 241, 243, 245, 257–258, 260, 262, 265, 272–273, 276–278, 291–292, 294, 296, 312

Eleusinian Mysteries, 91, 101

Elijah, 10, 109

empathy, 19, 65, 149, 151, 230

ephemeris, 72

Eros, 103, 105

ethics, x, 56, 278

Etteilla, 3–4, 312

Eurynome, 157

Eye of Shiva, 120, 141

F

Father Time, 117

fire signs, 152, 187

fixed signs, 99, 119, 157

Fool's Journey, 78, 80, 156

Freya, 94

future card, 252

fylfot cross, 127

G

Gabriel, 105, 134, 153, 155

Gaia, 94

Gemini, 29, 37–38, 60, 71–73, 87, 104–105, 222, 228, 233, 250, 252–253, 255, 257, 262–263

geomancy, 2

About the Author

Corrine Kenner is a certified tarot master and the award-winning author of the *Epicurean Tarot*, *The Ma'at Tarot Workbook*, *Tarot Journaling*, *Tall Dark Stranger: Tarot for Love and Romance*, *Crystals for Beginners*, and *Strange But True*.

Corrine has lived in Brazil and Los Angeles, where she earned a bachelor's degree in philosophy from California State University. She now lives in Minneapolis, Minnesota, with her husband Dan and daughters Katherine, Emily, and Julia. She teaches tarot classes and workshops on a regular basis, and she offers readings by appointment in her office near the Mall of America.

Visit her website at www.corrinekenner.com.

Free Catalog

Get the latest information on our body, mind, and spirit products! To receive a **free** copy of Llewellyn's consumer catalog, *New Worlds of Mind & Spirit,* simply call 1-877-NEW-WRLD or visit our website at www.llewellyn.com and click on *New Worlds.*

☽ LLEWELLYN ORDERING INFORMATION

Order Online:
Visit our website at www.llewellyn.com, select your books, and order them on our secure server.

Order by Phone:
- Call toll-free within the U.S. at 1-877-NEW-WRLD (1-877-639-9753). Call toll-free within Canada at 1-866-NEW-WRLD (1-866-639-9753)
- We accept VISA, MasterCard, and American Express

Order by Mail:
Send the full price of your order (MN residents add 6.5% sales tax) in U.S. funds, plus postage & handling to:

Llewellyn Worldwide
2143 Wooddale Drive, Dept. 978-0-7387-0964-2
Woodbury, MN 55125-2989

Postage & Handling:

Standard (U.S., Mexico, & Canada). If your order is:
$24.99 and under, add $3.00
$25.00 and over, FREE STANDARD SHIPPING

AK, HI, PR: $15.00 for one book plus $1.00 for each additional book.

International Orders (airmail only):
$16.00 for one book plus $3.00 for each additional book

Orders are processed within 2 business days.
Please allow for normal shipping time. Postage and handling rates subject to change.

Tarot Journaling
Using the Celtic Cross to Unveil Your Hidden Story

CORRINE KENNER

A tarot journal can help you learn more about the cards, but it can also teach you a great deal about yourself. Beginning tarot students are advised to keep a tarot journal, and many experienced tarot readers are devoted to the practice. The only book of its kind, *Tarot Journaling* covers everything needed to create, keep, and preserve a personal tarot journal.

Readers will discover hundreds of ideas to inspire and enliven their tarot journals, including considerations when choosing journaling materials, how to save time when recording readings, techniques for getting past writer's block, tips for turning negative energy into a positive brainstorming tool, and innovative ideas for protecting privacy. *Tarot Journaling* offers readers the tools to record and reflect upon the stories told by the cards—the stories of our lives.

978-0-7387-0643-6
6 x 9
216 pp. $12.95
appendices, bibliog.

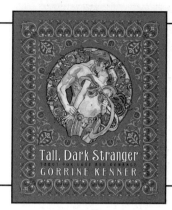

Tall Dark Stranger

Tarot for Love & Romance

CORRINE KENNER

For centuries, the love-struck, lovesick, and lovelorn have consulted the tarot—a tradition still thriving today. *Tall Dark Stranger* makes it easy for anyone to explore matters of the heart through tarot. There is even a guide to tarot terms and symbols.

Corrine Kenner's tour of the tarot begins with its colorful, romantic history. She goes on to describe the deck itself—explaining its structure, suits, symbolism, archetypes, and astrological associations—while relating its special significance in love and relationships. The second part of the book is devoted to the nitty-gritty of tarot readings: choosing a deck, preparing for a reading, asking appropriate questions, timing events, and interpreting cards and spreads. By the end of the book, readers will have a powerful edge in conquering the ever-mysterious ways of love.

978-0-7387-0548-4
7 ½ x 9 ⅛
312 pp. $15.95
illus.

Tarot for Beginners

An Easy Guide to Understanding & Interpreting the Tarot

P. Scott Hollander

The tarot is much more than a simple divining tool. While it can—and does—give you accurate and detailed answers to your questions when used for fortunetelling, it can also lead you down the road to self-discovery in a way that few other meditation tools can do. *Tarot for Beginners* will tell you how to use the cards for meditation and self-enlightenment as well as for divination.

If you're just beginning a study of the tarot, this book gives you a basic, straightforward definition of the meaning of each card that can be easily applied to any system of interpretation, with any tarot deck, using any card layout. The main difference between this book and other books on the tarot is that it's written in plain English—you need no prior knowledge of the tarot or other arcane subjects to understand its mysteries, because this no-nonsense guide will make the symbolism of the tarot completely accessible to you. You will receive an overview of the cards of the major and minor arcana in terms of their origin, purpose, and interpretive uses as well as clear, in-depth descriptions and interpretations of each card.

978-1-5671-8363-4
5 ¼ x 8. $12.95
384 pp.
illus
Spanish Edition Available

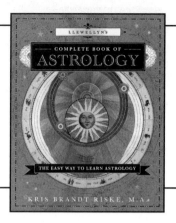

Llewellyn's Complete Book of Astrology
The Easy Way to Learn Astrology

Kris Brandt Riske, M.A.

The horoscope is filled with insights into personal traits, talents, and life possibilities. With *Llewellyn's Complete Book of Astrology*, you can learn to read and understand this amazing cosmic road map for yourself and others.

Professional astrologer Kris Brandt Riske introduces the many mysterious parts that make up the horoscope, devoting special attention to three popular areas of interest: relationships, career, and money. Friendly and easy to follow, this comprehensive book guides you to explore the zodiac signs, planets, houses, and aspects, and teaches how to synthesize this valuable information. Riske also explores the history of astrology going back to the ancient Babylonians, in addition to the different branches of contemporary astrology.

Once you learn the language of astrology, you'll be able to read birth charts of yourself and others, determine compatibility between two people, track your earning potential, uncover areas of opportunity or challenge, and analyze your career path.

978-0-7387-1071-6
8 x 10 $18.95
360 pp.
appendices

To order, call 1-877-NEW-WRLD

Prices subject to change without notice

Mystic Faerie Tarot

ARTWORK BY LINDA RAVENSCROFT
BOOK BY BARBARA MOORE

Step inside the enchanting world of the fey. Rich watercolor images by renowned artist Linda Ravenscroft capture the vibrancy and grace of faeries, sprites, elves, and nymphs in their lush gardens.

Each suit tells a "faerie tale" as the nature spirits embark on magical adventures. A water nymph and wood elf learn that love is a gift not to be taken lightly, while a foolish faerie queen and her kingdom are nearly overtaken by a magical blue rose. These stories offer lessons and fresh insights in all matters of life, while remaining true to tarot archetypes.

The Mystic Faerie Tarot kit includes a 288-page book that introduces tarot and describes the major and minor arcana in detail. Perfect for beginners, you'll also find faerie-themed spreads to use, along with sample readings and a quick reference guide to the cards.

978-0-7387-0921-5
Boxed kit (5 ³⁄₁₆ x 8 ¼) includes an 78-card deck,
288-page book, and an organdy bag with a satin cord $24.95

The Llewellyn Tarot

Anna-Marie Ferguson

Over a century ago, a young boy left Wales and journeyed to America, where he started a small press, now known as Llewellyn Publications. Llewellyn George's adventurous spirit and Welsh heritage embodies The Llewellyn Tarot, which also celebrates the publisher's enduring legacy.

From the creator of the popular Legend: The Authurian Tarot Kit, this lavishly illustrated deck offers universal appeal (based on Rider-Waite) with a Welsh twist. A compelling story unfolds starring Rhiannon as The Empress, Bran the Blessed as The Emperor, The Wild Herdsman as The Horned God (the Devil), Gwydion as The Magician, Llew Llaw Gyffes as the Bringer of Light, and other figures from Welsh mythology. Watercolor imagery beckons us forth into a mystic world of ancient forests, sensuous seascapes, and wondrous waterfalls—gorgeous landscapes brimming with mystery, meaning, and magic. Also included is The Llewellyn Tarot Companion, which features an introduction to the craft and history of tarot, along with Welsh legends infused in this deck.

Anna-Marie Ferguson (Alberta, Canada) was born in Hampshire, England, where she became fascinated with the tarot and Celtic legends. She strives to keep this bygone age alive through her art.

978-0-7387-0299-5
Boxed kit (5½ x 8½) includes 78-card deck, 288-pp. book,
and a sheer golden brocade pouch with beads and tassels $24.95